DISCIPLES HIGHER EDUCATION SERIES

General Editor
D. DUANE CUMMINS

Manuscript Editor
LAWRENCE S. STEINMETZ

CAMPUS MINISTRY IN THE COMING AGE

by

Thomas R. McCormick

CBP Press
St. Louis, Missouri

Library of Congress Cataloging-in-Publication Data

McCormick, Thomas R. (Thomas Richard)
  Campus ministry in the coming age.

  Bibliography: p. 176.
  Includes index.
  1. Church work with students—Christian Church (Disciples of Christ.   2. Christian
Church (Disciples of Christ)—Education.   I. Title.
BV1610.M29   1987   259'.24   87-13834
ISBN 0-8272-0452-3

Printed in the United States of America

To KAREN

*Grateful and abiding appreciation
is expressed
to the following contributors
whose generous gifts
made possible the publication
of this volume*

CLIFF AND DONNA ALBRIGHT

OREON E. SCOTT FOUNDATION

ROBERT AND MARILYN MICKEY

Table of Contents

FOREWORD

How can the church most effectively engage in ministry to the campus in the coming age? The purpose of this book is to face the problems and challenges of the new age with this question foremost in mind. This study begins with a review of the initial involvement of the Christian Church (Disciples of Christ) in ministry on the tax-supported campuses through the Bible Chairs, traces developments in campus ministry through the years, and suggests ways in which the church's ministry to the campus can be done more effectively in the future.

Although various individuals have written about parts of this history, to the best of my knowledge, this is the first attempt at a more comprehensive history of the Disciples in campus ministry. While tracing the continuous thread of Disciples involvement in public higher education since 1893, I have attempted to couch this history in the broader context of significant changes which were occurring within higher education, the church, and the society.

This book is addressed both to persons in the church and in higher education who share a common concern for seeking the leadership of God's Spirit in discovering new paths of ministry for the future. It addresses a theological rationale in support of the continuing engagement of the church with the community of higher education. It offers a description of some of the most perplexing problems in higher education and in the church's attempts to minister on the campus. Some practical advice is offered for the local churches, the regions, and the general manifestations of the Christian Church (Disciples of Christ). It is my hope that the style of the book will stimulate the thinking of interested parties in such a way that new and creative responses will be generated by the readers in approaching this vital ministry of the church for the coming age.

This book has drawn from twenty years experience in campus ministry. Like most other Disciples campus ministers, I had no special preparation for such a ministry. In my senior year in college (1955-1956) I served on weekends as the director of young people's programs at Englewood Christian Church, Portland, Oregon. While attending seminary at Drake University from 1956-1960, I was a student pastor for four years to two small rural congregations in the communities of Diagonal and Benton, in southwest Iowa. Following graduation from Drake Divinity School, I served five years (1960-1965) as pastor of a small, racially integrated, inner-city congregation bordering on a large government supported housing project in Seattle, Washington. I entered the campus ministry on January 1, 1966, accepting a call at the Koinonia Center, a campus ministry of the American Baptists, the Disciples, and the United Church of Christ at the University of Washington.

Although these experiences did not prepare me specifically for ministry on the campus, these ministries did confirm my calling as a minister, or my choice of vocation. They confirmed my sense of satisfaction in working with people in a broad variety of settings and taught me the power of loving relationships which work both ways. My real preparation for campus ministry might best be called "on the job training" or even "life-long learning." Over the past twenty years I have learned much from my colleagues in campus ministry, from the students, faculty and staff on the campus, and from colleagues in ministry in local congregations and in extension ministries of various kinds. I have learned from my participation with the Pacific Northwest Commission on Ministries in Higher Education, from serving on the board of directors of United Ministries in Higher Education, and later United Ministries in Education, that the issues and concerns do indeed transcend denominational lines. My colleagues in campus ministry from the other denominations have been supportive and caring allies in our common mission. Likewise, my years on the board of directors for the Division of Higher Education of the Christian Church (Disciples of Christ) and on the Council on Ministry in Higher Education gave me particular opportunities for insight into the broad concerns of my own denomination regarding ministry in higher education.

In 1974 I accepted a one-third time faculty appointment at the School of Medicine in the Department of Biomedical History as lecturer in bioethics, while continuing to serve as a campus minister in the ecumenical partnership. This dual role has provided an interesting opportunity to have one foot in the university and one foot in the church for over a decade, and contributes in part to my perspective. I am especially grateful to my colleagues at the Campus Christian Ministry, University of Washington for their support during the writing of this book: Rev. David Royer, Rev. Susan Yarrow Morris, Pastor Jon Nelson, Rev. Tom Forster/Smith, Rev. Lucy Forster/Smith, Fr. Richard Younge, Fr. Robert Christian, Fr. Raymond Finnerty, Sister Joan Unger, and our secretaries, Barbara Ledger and Mary Tyson.

This book is supported by a grant from the Division of Higher Education of the Christian Church (Disciples of Christ) through the generosity of Cliff and Donna Albright, Robert and Marilyn Mickey, and the Oreon E. Scott Foundation. Dr. Lawrence S. Steinmetz has been of extraordinary help in the writing of this volume and in providing insightful critique. The cooperation and collaboration of the authors of the companion volumes has been deeply appreciated, Dr. D. Duane Cummins, President of the Division of Higher Education, and Dr. Ronald Osborne, former Distinguished Professor of Church History at the School of Theology at Claremont.

I greatly appreciate the cooperation of all of those campus ministers and regional ministers who took the time to fill out the survey instruments which were distributed as part of this study. I am especially grateful for the contributions my colleagues in campus ministry which are found in the case studies of campus ministry at Disciples-related colleges in chapter four and in the case studies of Disciples campus ministers serving in an ecumenical setting on the state supported campuses in chapter five.

A special note of thanks is in order for the patience and support of my family and friends who have found me largely inaccessible and socially unresponsive during the seasons of research and writing. It has been hard to convince my nine year old grandson, Ricky, that working on the book could be more important than "going fishin," a question which I leave for the reader to decide.

Finally, a word of deep appreciation for Karen, my spouse, who patiently and uncomplainingly endured considerable solitude on many evenings, weekends, and holidays while I closed the door to my study, turned on our Texas Instruments computer, booted up my word processor, and worked on "the book."

Chapter **1**

CAMPUS MINISTRY:
A HISTORICAL PERSPECTIVE

The Christian Church (Disciples of Christ) was the first church body to enter campus ministry in the state supported universities by means of a Bible Chair concept. The Disciples launched this movement in the 1890s, at Ann Arbor, Michigan. Its origins were surrounded with controversy. The orthodoxy of its early leaders was questioned. Criticisms were leveled at the small number of students who responded to this special ministry. The problem of financing ministry on the state supported campuses seemed to some to be in direct competition with other traditional ministries of the church. Some feared this new ministry would detract from the strength and influence of Disciples colleges. Others criticized the early leaders for failing to teach the Bible, or for not teaching it properly.

On the other hand, this early campus ministry had many strong advocates. Some claimed it was ". . . a type of enterprise which is the Disciples' most distinctive contribution to American education."[1] Others set pen to paper in defending this fledgling ministry through the religious journals of that era. The Dean of Lubbock Christian College, Dr. Jack Bates, affirmed the importance of this new ministry coexisting along with the Christian Colleges. He believed that it was important to "utilize every opportunity in modern life to preserve faith, to build character, and to develop happy, useful Christian personalities. To that end, I heartily commend the work of the Bible chair [sic] in its unique contributions to our youth"[2]

Increasingly, church-going families recognized that the majority of their sons and daughters were attending the state universities and faced the responsibility for working out a plan to meet their religious needs on the state campuses.

Contemporary church folk and educators who wrestle with the current issues in campus ministry and seek to define the mission of the church in higher education for the future may find it ironic or humorous to discover these issues in the very origins of campus ministry. The early controversies are not unlike the conversations surrounding campus ministries in some regions today. Remembering our history helps us place the issues of the present in clear perspective.

1

The Disciples created their first institution of higher education, Bacon College, at Georgetown, Kentucky. This was in 1836, near the beginning of a period of prolific college building by the churches. Before the close of the century, Disciples had initiated a new and unique form of ministry, the Bible Chair, at the state university campus. It was within the Bible Chair movement that campus ministry had its origins. The birth of campus ministry occurred in a context of change and ferment in higher education. It was a time of divided opinions. Was higher education to remain a prerogative of the elite, or was it to become available for the common person? Was the highest goal of education the cultivation of the mind or the development of the soul? Would the establishment of colleges be left to the denominations or to the state?

At an earlier age in America, higher education was considered the prerogative of the elite, those of social and economic standing. It was for the clergy, but not for the common man. In former times the purpose of higher education had clearly been: "to advance learning and promote piety, and to supply a ministry which would be instrumental for both, under an Anglican establishment."[3] However, by the middle of the nineteenth century, there was a growing demand for access to education for the common person, and the forces of Industrialization and Urbanization led to the democratization of education. Providing broader access to higher education inevitably meant that the state would have to invest in the building and developing of colleges and universities. For Alexander Campbell, there was no question about the proper goals of higher education:

> I give my vote for learning and science and for high attainment in all branches of useful knowledge, but I would not give morality for them all; and therefore I have resolved never to speak in favor of any literary institution, from a common school to a university, however superior their literary eminence, that does not first of all, and above all, exercise a sovereign and supreme guardianship over the morals of its students and wards, and endeavor to make good rather than great men.[4]

He was not alone in such a position, for his attitude reflects the general feeling of church and denominational leaders of that period. This conviction provided a strong motivation for the founding of so many denominational colleges and, later, shaped the attitude of church leaders toward the secular state university.

The rise of the state supported colleges and universities

The passage of the Morrill Land Grant Act in 1862 was the most significant single factor in spurring the growth of state supported universities. This positive involvement of the federal government in higher education marked a turning point. This bill, and the Morrill Act of 1890, provided both land and money from the federal government to the states to enable the construction of universities designed to provide education for the servants of society, farmers, teachers, engineers, lawyers and physicians.

In 1890, the actual number of state supported universities was small, only thirty of the 415 colleges and universities in the country. However, they wielded a considerable influence, they were a new phenomenon and they were very much in the public eye. By this time, many of the church colleges were viewed as sectarian. The public was placing an increasing value on nonsectarian public education, and the effectiveness of elementary and high schools had helped prepare a larger cohort of students who were now ready to work competitively in public higher education. Speaking of this changing tide toward public higher education, a committee of the North American Baptist Church Convention meeting in 1910 reported:

> The growth of the state universities is one of the most striking educational phenomena of the day. Twenty-five years ago hardly one of the state institutions was regarded with general seriousness as an important factor in the educational world. Today, of the first six universities in America numerically, four are state schools . . . of the twelve largest universities in America only two are classed as other than state or nonsectarian.[5]

As the state became involved in public higher education, the doctrine of separation of church and state came into play. Citizens of the nineteenth century were of the opinion that there must be a radical separation of state and church in the universities which were supported by the public. There were both legal and philosophical reasons to support such an opinion. The American legal system had, by this time, clarified the notion that all public schools should remain free from religious control. This was a provision of the Bill of Rights which set a precedent at the federal level. State governments had clearly prohibited the use of tax money to benefit any religious group. Since religion at that time was virtually synonymous with "sectarianism" it became commonly understood that religion could not be taught at these new state universities which were attracting so many of the nation's young people.[6]

This prohibition was understood, not just by the secular public, but by proponents of what was to become known as the Bible Chair movement as well:

> Whatever may be true of schools under private management, the public school cannot make religion its end, or religious instruction and worship its necessary function. It must leave to other agencies that religious instruction and training that looks to the salvation of the soul . . . we can take to them (the great state universities) the mighty dynamic of religious faith and morals. Public education, as such, in America, does not generate and foster these. This is our inevitable inheritance from our political institutions.[7]

In addition to the legal reasons for the exclusion of religion from the public universities, there were philosophical reasons going back to the Enlightenment. This was the idea that education must be free from the control of the religious sects. It seemed impossible to consider religion as a true academic discipline which could be studied along with other disciplines. It seemed impossible to separate the idea of religion from religious sects. The result was that religion was not going to be taught at the state universities.

Each year an increasing number of young people flocked into these universities. The churches quickly realized that by far the majority of their own young people were now choosing to be educated in the state universities rather than the church-related private colleges. A new day was dawning. The church was awakening to the realization that if any effort was going to be made to continue the spiritual growth and religious education of their students on the state campuses—new plans must be forged.[8]

The Disciples of Christ were quick to see the problem. They recognized the separation of church and state, and the problems of sectarianism as well. Disciple leaders were also convinced that they had a special contribution to offer to this unique situation:

> True, we are thoroughly committed to the separation of church and state; it is also true that we cannot use state funds for religious instruction, but the law of our land is not opposed to the teachings of the Bible from the standpoint of history and literature, if Christian people are generous enough to endow Bible lectureships and Bible chairs for the benefit of University students . . . To refuse to recognize the authority of the Bible in the development of the students of our State universities would be contrary to the genius of our institutions and even to the spirit of our laws."[9]

Even though the Disciples were both willing and eager to explore the possibility of providing for the teaching of nonsectarian religion, this period was a time of considerable conflict between the church and the university. There was mistrust on both sides. Many of the church leaders described the state institutions as "godless universities." This claim was based not only on the fact that religion was not taught, but because the classical form of education was now being replaced by a practical, vocational, and technical style of education. It was difficult for church leaders to conceive of how this idea of education could nurture the moral character and spiritual nature of students.

Many university leaders, on the other hand, were mistrustful of the church. They had witnessed the rise of the church colleges. Many of these colleges suffered in the quality of education which they offered due to problems of funding and the inability to attract competent faculties. There was also ample evidence to justify the attack that the denominations had created many of these colleges primarily to promote and defend their own denominational tenets. Believing that church colleges were established to compete with other denominations for new territories and for new converts, the leaders of the new universities were determined to keep this kind of narrow, competitive, sectarian religion out of their institutions.

In actuality, the pagan nature of the universities was exaggerated by critics. Many of the faculty were churchmen, and many of the students were church members as well. Many within the church placed high value on the quality and diversity of the university. But the question remained, how could the church provide for the continuing religious education and spiritual nurturance of the young people whom they sent off to the state schools?

It was in this context that the Disciples of Christ founded the Bible Chair movement, "apparently the first systematic attempt in the country to deal with the problem of teaching religion in the state universities."[10]

Disciples commitment to the unity of the church

The Disciples believed they were uniquely suited to approach this issue in a nonsectarian manner. Early Disciples leaders had cherished a vision of a church "united." The Springfield Presbytery in Kentucky had been formed in 1803 when members withdrew from the former presbytery in order to witness for the unity of the church based solely upon the pattern of the church in the New Testament. On June 28, 1804, with Barton W. Stone as their leader, the Springfield Presbytery dissolved and members called themselves "Christian" only, as a witness to the unity of the church.

In Pennsylvania, during September 1809, Thomas Campbell and a like-minded group formed the Christian Association of Washington when they left their own presbytery. They believed that church unity could be restored if Christian people would return to the essential faith and practice of the New Testament. Thomas Campbell claimed:

> . . . The New Testament is as perfect a constitution for the worship, discipline, and government of the New Testament Church, and as perfect a rule for the particular duties of its members, as the Old Testament was for the worship, discipline, and government of the Old Testament Church, and the particular duties of its members.[11]

In 1832 the movement led by Stone and the movement led by Campbell united and became an independent religious body, dedicated to the proposition of the unity of the church. They were confident that restoration of the New Testament pattern of worship would lead to a basis for unity in Christendom which could appeal to all believers. Campbell came to believe that in matters where the Scriptures were silent, modern Christians are left on their own to determine efficient and practical ways of resolving issues and problems facing the church.

The Disciples, from their origins, were interested in education. The major leaders of the movement were well educated, and shortly following the merger in 1832, began to establish private church-related colleges, and to teach in them. As the movement matured it advocated for both an educated clergy and an educated laity. Alexander Campbell passionately held a vision of education which was Bible-oriented and non-sectarian. Such an education provided the only hope of developing sincere and moral citizens who would be ethically fit to provide leadership for the church and community. Furthermore, if young people were to be leaders in the Restoration Movement which was based upon a textual understanding of the New Testament, then the Bible was a crucial text. Barton W. Stone, the other founding father of the Disciples, believed in the perfectibility of individuals as the foremost mission of the church and looked upon education as a powerful tool in the pruning and shaping of individual character. It was natural that the Disciples should turn their attention to the problem of the lack of religious instruction in the state colleges and universities.

The Bible Chair Movement

In the autumn of 1893, the first Bible Chair in the nation was opened by the Disciples at the University of Michigan. The first courses were offered in October by the founding faculty. Interestingly, it was the women of the church who were mid-wives to the birthing of this exciting and innovative venture in public higher education.

In 1888 a committee of Disciples in Missouri explored the possibilities of creating a Bible Chair at the University of Missouri. Before these plans were accomplished, however, it was the Christian Woman's Board of Missions who established the first Bible Chair in Ann Arbor, at the University of Michigan. In 1891 the Christian Woman's Board of Missions had established a Disciples church in Ann Arbor. The first minister, C. A. Young, had apparently caught the vision of the Bible Chair idea from Thomas Jefferson. Jefferson had proposed that the differing sects should be allowed to establish schools around the University of Virginia. However, his original idea appears to be the reverse of Young's, as Jefferson believed the Divinity Schools rimming the university would benefit from their students taking science courses from the state schools, and that such contact might minimize sectarian divisiveness.[12]

Young envisioned the University of Michigan as an appropriate place to begin such an effort, except that his goal was clearly to provide religious instruction to students attending the state university. He wrote, "it remained for Christian women to realize what Mr. Jefferson, once President of the United States, and Dr. Laws, once President of the University of Missouri, hoped, but failed to accomplish."[13] Young is referring to the fact that Dr. Laws had for a long time kept a ten acre tract of land at the University of Missouri on which he hoped various denominations might establish centers for the teaching of religion.

The concept of the Bible Chair was imaginative. It was an arrangement in which a "chair," or teaching position, at a state university was either endowed or funded on an annual basis by a religious group. The instructor was usually chosen by the church, and was recognized by the university. The arrangement allowed students to take courses in religion at the Bible Chair, for which they might (or might not) be granted credit on their degree program.

Rev. C. A. Young appealed to the Christian Woman's Board of Missions for assistance in establishing a Bible Chair at Ann Arbor through the Michigan Christian Missionary Association, in 1892. In October of that year, the C.W.B.M. held their annual convention in Nashville, Tennessee. The national president, Mrs. O. A. Burgess, proposed to the assembly that this recommendation be supported. The following lines from her speech at the assembly capture the spirit, intent, and enthusiasm for this new project:

> We can see that it is the place and time for sowing the seed of the kingdom and instilling into the lives of young men and women the teaching of Jesus. This faithfully done will bear much fruit even to the ends of the earth. To say that here is the most promising opening, for taking hold of the young men and preparing them for usefulness in the mission field, or any in our land, is no reflection on our own schools. The way is open, if we have the courage to undertake it, for the establishing of an English Bible Chair. It is such an opening that does not often come to us nor to anybody. The great University is already established there and the courtesies of the institution are offered us. The demand for Bible study can be met by endowing a chair and putting a competent teacher in charge.[14]

A committee was appointed to study the possibility of endowing a Bible Chair at Ann Arbor. The committee enthusiastically endorsed the idea. The following excerpt from the committee's report is valuable in establishing the original philosophy and rationale behind the founding of this movement:

> 1. At Ann Arbor is situated the State University of Michigan, a purely non-sectarian institution supported by State funds, and one that of late years has shown itself to be the largest and most popular university in this country. It represents an educational plant of over three millions of dollars and is fully equipped to give instruction in all that goes to make up a liberal education, excepting in those branches pertaining specifically to Biblical study and the preparation for the ministry. Nearly three thousand students are enrolled annually and the great variety of people of all nationalities, colors and stations in life to be met with, give to the place a cosmopolitan character that is of much value to all students . . . The matter of economy, then, as well as the superior advantages in an educational point of view, would seem to offer the strongest kind of inducement toward the founding of a Biblical seminary at that place.
>
> 2. To secure these manifest advantages, it will be necessary to establish only one or more lectureships, and this can be done without any additional expense for buildings; as, for a number of years, the church parlors would be amply sufficient.
>
> 3. By endowing the undertaking you would secure for it the respect and recognition due from the University officials and the community at large.
>
> 4. You would make it possible to raise and receive the necessary funds for the endowment of one or more chairs.
>
> 5. Should the Christian Woman's Board of Missions authorize the work and permit it to be carried on under its auspices, it will have the satisfaction of

knowing that it has encouraged an enterprise in the field of ministerial education the results of which will be far reaching and incalculable. You can feel that
you have been instrumental in founding an institution that in time may realize
for the Disciples of Christ what Union does for the Presbyterians . . .[15]

Undergirded with such enthusiasm, high hopes for the future, and the
support of kindred spirits on the Christian Woman's Board, the work of the
Bible Chair was begun the following year, 1893. In keeping with their concern that the Bible be taught in a scholarly fashion to college students, Herbert
L. Willett and Clinton Lockhart, the founding faculty offered biblical studies
such as: "The History of Israel, Prophecy, The Life of Christ, Paul and the
Epistles, and a class in New Testament Greek."[16]

Since the Bible Chair movement is a precursor to the Disciples' engagement
in campus ministry, it is important to examine and analyze the rationale
which led them in this direction.

Although the church had played an instrumental role in the establishment
of higher education in America, the secular culture was at that time becoming
a dominant force in contemporary higher education. By the usual standards
of measurement, competence of faculty, size of library, tuition rates, physical
plant and educational resources—the markedly religious colleges tended to
be measurably weaker than the state supported institutions. The state universities were getting most of the students, while the church-related colleges were
showing a decline in enrollment.

Disciples viewed this situation with alarm, for due to the strictly enforced
doctrine of separation of church and state, it appeared that increasing
numbers of their young people would be attending state colleges and universities without benefit of religious instruction. There was a deep sense of
responsibility held by these early Disciples, to provide an opportunity for the
continuing spiritual growth and moral development of their college age
young people.

A second important feature of the Bible Chair was the fact that it was
founded by a group of visionary women whose principal reason for existence
was to support the mission outreach of the church. It was the Christian
Woman's Board of Mission which provided the money to begin the Bible
Chair at Ann Arbor. They were concerned that the younger generation "keep
the faith" through their educational years, so that they would perpetuate the
church in their older, productive working years.

The goal of the founders of this movement was not to proselytize on the
campus, but to provide for the moral and religious life of all students:

The Chairs were missionary in the sense that their purpose was to turn out
doctors, lawyers, and merchants with a fully developed religious sense, conse-
crated to take their places in life and in the work of the church. Sometimes the
zeal reached such a pitch that those involved in the project could say that their

purpose was to win people to Christ and to do the work that Christ would have them do.[17]

Others among the founders held a very optimistic notion that the Bible Chairs could provide a source of ministerial education. They held that individuals educated in a state university would possess an educational experience much like their peers in other professions. If courses in religion and biblical studies could be added to their curriculum through the Bible Chairs, it would provide a good background from which to enter the ministry.

Many Disciples ministers of that period were not well educated. This was due in part to a concept of ministry in which the minister was simply one of the elders who was apt to preach and carry out the ministerial functions, but who possessed no greater authority than any other layperson. This was a reaction to the perceived abuses of the position which, in the minds of early Disciples, led to the "disunity" of the church by emphasizing divisive doctrines which were not essential to the New Testament Church. With the changing times, it became apparent that ministers would need to be better educated if the church were to minister effectively to an increasingly educated laity. Many of the advocates of the movement saw a promising possibility that the Bible Chairs could provide a combination of biblical and religious studies with a university education for ministerial candidates, and an opportunity for practicing ministers living within reach of the state university to improve their education.

Still another reason for supporting the Bible Chair concept was economic. It was now clear that the state supported universities had a more secure financial base, and correspondingly, better buildings and faculties than many of the church colleges spawned in the early years of the nineteenth century. Disciples were quick to see that their students could have all the advantages of public higher education, and in addition, religious and biblical studies through the Bible Chair. This arrangement was far less costly than building, maintaining, and staffing a college of their own.

Some, albeit a minority opinion in the Disciples, saw the university as a place to be feared and the purpose of the Bible Chair as a means of protecting the faith of the students. These seemed to believe that not only did the university *not* teach religion nor the Bible, but that the forces of secularism and skepticism would pervert the faith of their children:

> It was the call of duty, and not mere expediency, which led our Sisters to undertake the most difficult problem which confronts the Christian church today—that of *snatching our youth from skepticism and training them for Christ*, at the most strategic State University in America.[18]

It appeared, however, that most Disciples were generally friendly toward the state universities. They did not consider the universities as evil or "godless" institutions. On the contrary, the leaders of the Bible Chair usually considered themselves friends of the university, with a primary responsibility to complement the educational enterprise with their own teaching. There was a strong belief at the time that no liberal education is complete without some knowledge and understanding of the Bible. Thus the larger purpose of the Bible Chair was to adequately equip the leaders of the future:

> If we long to see those who minister to the body all men and women whose hearts are aglow with love for Him who heals both body and soul; if we desire our laws to be more in harmony with God's will, that we may hope for prosperity and permanency for our government, what more need than to offer to those in our State Universities, while prosecuting other lines of study, an opportunity of becoming proficient in a knowledge of God's word and of having implanted in them a desire to incarnate its truths in their own lives.[19]

Still another rationale behind the Bible Chair movement was a theme which was central to the very origins of the Disciples—unity. It was clear by the last decade of the nineteenth century that sectarianism within the church was debilitating. From the very outset, Bible Chairs were to provide teaching and instruction for all students, not just Disciples students. Likewise, the course content was not to be sectarian. Again, the Disciples felt themselves to be uniquely prepared to teach in this manner. The Disciples' plea for unity had been founded on an appeal to the Scriptures. They felt a primary loyalty to Christ, not to denomination or sect:

> It is a high compliment to our brotherhood that we are loyal enough to our convictions that the Bible alone is all that is necessary to reveal the way of salvation and guide man in his efforts to walk in that way, to support this work. What other religious body is there that maintains an educational work of a purely religious character that has no denominational bias, and seeks to impart a knowledge of Scriptures to all who will receive instruction?[20]

This ecumenical emphasis was an essential world view of the Disciples. This plea for the unity of the church was the organizing principle behind their reason for existence as a body. This ecumenical and nonsectarian approach to the teaching of religion was a critical element in the founding of their original work on the campuses of the state universities.

The first Bible Chair is established at the University of Michigan

The first year at Ann Arbor went about as planned. Although the President of the University had written to the Christian Woman's Board of Missions to express his appreciation for the work of the Bible Chair, the original faculty members Willett and Lockhart resigned at the end of the first year.[21]

Although the records are not clear, it is most likely that C. A. Young, the first minister at the Disciples church in Ann Arbor provided teaching during the fall semester. Interim leadership kept the operation alive until G. P. Coler assumed the reins of leadership on February 1, 1895. He continued as faculty of the Bible Chair at Ann Arbor until 1913. Within a year the Bible Chair was affirmed by the enthusiastic report that its work had secured two medical missionaries for foreign service in India as well as a number of young men who had chosen to become preachers.[22]

As one might imagine, the establishment of this new work created a number of problems which demanded immediate attention. How would the work be funded? Given the separation of church and state, what building could appropriately serve as a home for the Bible Chair? A library was needed to provide access to religious and biblical scholarship for the students, since the university did not provide books on religion. In what cooperative efforts with other Christian organizations could the Bible Chair provide leadership? How might one best define the nature and scope of leadership that was to be provided by the faculty of the Bible Chair?

The need for a dependable and adequate method of funding was apparent. The first Bible Chair, at Ann Arbor, as a project of the Christian Woman's Board of Missions, received funds from special offerings and pledge drives. Attempts were made at Michigan, and most Bible Chairs which followed, to establish an endowment fund which would provide consistent interest income. Also, in most instances, congregations and individuals were solicited for support.

It was first thought that the Ann Arbor Bible Chair would be housed in the local Disciples of Christ Church which had also been initiated and funded by the Christian Woman's Board of Missions. However, through a fortuitous agreement, the first classes were held in Newberry Hall. This was the building in which the Students' Christian Association met. The agreement called for the instructors to provide leadership for the Student Christian Association by conducting lectureships, study groups, etc., as well as contributing to the utilities. The fact that the Bible Chair was housed in Newberry Hall, rather than in the local church, gave it a more ecumenical or nondenominational character and enhanced its popularity with students.[23]

In each Bible Chair which was subsequently established, the building of an adequate library was considered an essential corner stone of the program. The Michigan program appealed to Disciples throughout the nation to contribute to its library. As other Bible Chairs were founded, they made more limited regional appeals. While most housed the library within their own facilities, the University of Virginia provided space within its own library for the volumes which were owned by the Bible Chair.

In every case, the nature of teaching was nonsectarian. Usually, a pattern developed in which an agreement was reached between the Bible Chair and the university that the teaching be scholarly, in keeping with the requirements of other university courses, and that the course material be nondogmatic. Such requirements were enthusiastically received by Disciples leaders who believed that the very nature of the Disciples movement and its plea for unity created leaders ideally suited for such work.

Within a few years, other religious groups and denominations were co-operating at the Bible Chair in Ann Arbor by offering a variety of courses in religion. Instructors from the Y.M.C.A. and Y.W.C.A., the Baptist Guild, other university faculty and instructors from several other denominations offered courses to as many as 600 students by the 1909-1910 academic year:

> All the religious forces in and around the university have come together on a mutual plan and concerted program to offer at least twenty-five or thirty courses covering pretty largely the entire religious field in standard courses. The Guild workers, Bible Chair instructors, student pastors and members of the faculty co-operate harmoniously in offering a substantial opportunity to the students to do religious study in a worthy manner.[24]

In spite of the enthusiasm of the Disciples for a high degree of cooperation between the religious groups, enduring cooperation was elusive. It appears that the distinctions remained and each group eventually went its separate way in providing student programs.

The second dimension: Pastoral Care

In addition to their regular work of teaching courses, the Bible Chair instructors carried out a variety of other activities. Many of them advertised a willingness to counsel students concerning their search for vocation, religious questions, moral issues, or personal problems. "Coler often said that he felt that this was his most important and satisfying task outside the classroom teaching itself."[25] Instructors often taught Sunday School classes and preached frequently in local churches surrounding the campus. Lectures were held on the university campus for all members of the student body. Summer institutes were held in other communities with the dual aim of teaching the Bible, and raising funds to support the Bible Chair.

Changes in leadership shifted priorities in the work which was undertaken. At the University of Michigan, students never received credit toward their degrees for courses taken in religion or biblical studies. This, no doubt, influenced the approach of Thomas Iden, who inaugurated a Bible study program which he called the "Upper Room Class" in 1914. His approach was a mixture which was part-academic and part-evangelistic. The "Upper Room Class" was composed of university men, and developed a fraternity like atmosphere in their regular meetings each Saturday evening from seven to eight o'clock during the academic year.

In 1925, the University of Michigan opened a School of Religion, offering credit for academic courses in religion. Iden's work continued at Ann Arbor until the difficulties of the Depression. The United Christian Missionary Society had administered the Bible Chairs after 1919, and contributed to their funding. In 1930 decreasing revenues necessitated radical cut-backs to the Bible Chairs, and in 1932 all funding was discontinued. At the close of the school year in 1932 the doors of the Bible Chair at the University of Michigan closed for the last time.

Other Bible Chairs, established after the chair at Ann Arbor, created their own distinctive approach. At the University of Virginia, the Disciples' Bible Chair was the first to be granted credit for course work applied toward the student's degree program. This policy was initiated on a trial basis in 1906, and formalized in 1908, with the stipulation that it would never proclaim sectarian or denominational teaching. In agreeing to this provision, early Disciples leaders realized that the day might come when the instructor in the Bible Chair might be other than a Disciples. This idea was quite acceptable, as it fit well with the Disciples commitment to the unity of the church.

Following the work at Michigan and Virginia, Bible Chairs were established by the Disciples at the University of Georgia, University of Kansas, University of Texas, University of Missouri, Indiana University, and a number of other universities over the next few years. (See Appendix, Table 10)

Each of these had common elements, but unique characteristics as well. The major common element was the commitment to teach biblical studies for students on state supported campuses, with or without academic credit. Many of the unique differences centered around the concept of leadership held by individual Bible Chair faculty about the importance of their non-teaching functions and responsibilities. These differences were also shaped in part by the varying opportunities which arose on the different campuses.

At the University of Texas, for example, the local Disciples church was located about a mile from the campus. This made church attendance somewhat inconvenient. In 1905, the Bible Chair instructor, Frank Jewett, saw his role as inclusive of concern for the social and personal lives of the students. Together, they established a student church in the Bible Chair building:

> The Bible Chair is not a church; but, inasmuch as it is a mile from a Christian church, it serves as a sort of student church for Sunday meetings. Dr. Jewett is the student pastor. There is Sunday morning Bible school and also communion services in the Bible Chair auditorium. The students perform the duties of deacons and serve on the various committees, and the affairs of the student church are administered by a board of 30 students.[26]

In the disclaimer that the Bible Chair "is not a church . . . but serves as a sort of student church," there is revealed an ambiguity about the proper definition of the nature and scope of the Bible Chair, in its work beyond the class room. There is a parallel here between the development of campus ministry on the state supported campus and the development of the campus ministry, sometimes referred to as "chaplaincy" on the church supported campus, for neither does a chapel claim to be a church, though it may function "as a sort of student church."

Donald G. Shockley, Chaplain at Emory University, Atlanta, Georgia describes the development of the concepts of chapel and chaplain:

From a place where holy relics were venerated or merely stored, a chapel came to be understood as a place set apart for worship, i.e. private meditation, but which was not in fact a church. "Cappellani" or "chaplains," originally the custodians of such holy relics, began to preside over certain rites conducted in the places where they were stored. Eventually, there were chapels in castles, forts, embassies and all sorts of institutions, and there were clergy who served, essentially, as chaplains to royalty and other prominent families and individuals who, by virtue or wealth, status, or—perhaps—piety had their own chapels.[27]

The existence of a chapel, or a religious center, which is not itself a church has often provided a place not only for individual meditation, but a platform for prophetic critique. Unlike the role of the parish minister who is clearly called primarily to serve the members of his/her parish, the person in ministry to either the state supported university or to the church supported campus is called with an extraordinary assumption: "that a minister may serve in a meaningful way persons who do not share his or her religious affirmations and who are often total strangers."[28] This idea had in its roots radical implications for a ministry of servanthood to the campus community which ought not to be limited to members of one's own religious group or denomination. To a degree which is uncommon in other types of ministry, the campus minister serves a population which has been drawn together for reasons mostly unrelated to religion—the pursuit of higher education.

With this in mind, it is interesting to note the activities of the Bible Chair instructors outside the class room. Many of them, like William Forrest at the University of Virginia, did considerable preaching and teaching in surrounding cities and states. He often went to the churches of the state to appeal for funds to support his work. He taught extension courses in religion for the university. An innovative aspect of his outside work was the creation of an extension course in religion for high school students, with credit for graduation. This plan was approved by Virginia's State Board of Education.

It was not infrequent that the wives of the instructors were also involved in outside activities of a supportive nature. Some made themselves available, particularly for counseling women students. Others were active speakers and lecturers. Mrs. Payne, at the University of Kansas for example, was an active speaker at the sororities and fraternities. She also worked with her husband in providing instruction for the Haskell Institute, a school for Native Americans which was not far from the campus.

In the early days of the Bible Chairs, the outside activities of the instructors were important aspects of their mission to the campus. With the passing of time, it became important to make distinctions concerning the primary task of the instructors. This became especially important as courses were accepted for credit, and the instructors were expected by the university to carry out their scholarly function in a rigorous manner. One of the clarifications, or distinctions, was between such scholarly functions and the more pastoral functions which so often complemented the instructor's work with students. Wallace Payne, at Kansas, in 1928 promoted the idea that "the social-inspirational-pastoral approach to students should be by and through the church at Lawrence."[29]

This distinction is important, yet it was not shared by all of the leaders of the Bible Chair movement. The pastoral and evangelical mission remained a priority for some. This is reflected in the proud report which grew out of the Bible Chair at the Tri-State College, Angola, Indiana, that "over 200 young people went into full-time Christian service as a result of the Angola project."[30]

At Indiana University in Bloomington, a Bible Chair project was initiated by the Disciples students attending the university. The Christian Woman's Board of Missions turned down the request for support when it appeared that an instructor could not be found for the position. By 1910 an organization was formed to begin a Bible Chair. The plan called for course work to be delayed while the pastoral or student work aspects of the position were put into place. Joseph C. Todd, formerly the minister of the Christian Church in Bloomington, became an instructor for the Bible Chair during its first year. He remained in that position for over twenty-five years.[31]

The announcement that student pastoral work would precede the development of academic courses was the first occasion in which this distinction concerning a two-fold mission had been made quite so clearly. Although the two functions were being carried out in the other Bible Chairs also, there was usually some confusion about which was the prior mission. In Bloomington, leaders contacted students whose church preference was known when they arrived on the campus. They offered their hospitality to new students, and often kept in touch with the home church from which the student had come. Some aspects of their work was very much like that of some campus ministers today: helping students become related to the campus church, encouraging their social life, providing counseling for their problems, stimulating those with a "bent" toward the ministry, and consulting about vocations.[32]

Increasingly, it was expected that the leadership of the Bible Chairs would provide this dual focus, teaching religion and providing pastoral care for students in the university. These early beginnings of involvement in higher education were of considerable importance to the Disciples, but they found it difficult to provide planning and organization which kept pace with the rapidly changing scene. Joseph C. Todd, part-time secretary of University Work Department for the Board of Education since 1919, commented on this situation in his 1921 report through the *Year Book*:

> The Disciples were the first religious body in America to enter the state university field. Furthermore our approach has always been from the educational point of view. It is at least gratifying to see other bodies gradually adopting this point of view. . . . Although we were the first to enter, we have by no means kept pace. This has been due to a number of conditions, chief among which has

been our divided and sometimes divisive efforts in this direction. We have at present no unified or consistent method of attacking this problem.[33]

A variety of issues were emerging from the church's attempts to minister to the campus population. In addition to the question as to whether the primary aim should be the teaching of religion and biblical studies or the provision of pastoral care, other questions persisted. Was responsibility for organizing and funding work at the tax-supported universities the task of the local congregation in that city, of the state missionary society in the region served by the university, or of a larger body such as the United Christian Missionary Society or the Board of Higher Education? How could the organizing principles of ministry to the tax-supported institutions be developed in such a way as to strengthen the work with a consistent and unified approach? How could the Disciples foster the cooperation and interdependence of their work with that of other denominations in this specialized ministry on the campus?

There gradually developed a clearer distinction between concern for the student's religious life, worship and discipline—and concern for the scholarly teaching of religion and biblical studies. Gradually, the teaching function became more clearly distinguished as scholarly academic work. Over a period of time, and with increasing frequency the state universities began to develop departments of religion, while others allowed credit for Bible Chair courses, and still others like the University of Virginia allowed biblical studies to be taught in regular university class rooms. This trend led eventually, in the twentieth century, to the acceptance of courses in religion, religious studies, and biblical studies as a proper subject of study in state supported colleges and universities.

The role of the campus pastor, or student worker likewise began to emerge as a distinct function. It was this bifurcation of functions which led inevitably to the role and function which today we call "campus ministry," referring to the church's broader ministry in higher education.

Precursors to modern campus ministry

With no overall coordination, and depending upon the unique factors in the context of individual universities, campus ministry took a variety of expressions. Local congregations near the state colleges and universities began to employ either part-time or full-time staff to work with students. There were volunteers from the laity that developed program for students. The United Society, the Board of Education, State Societies, local churches, and independent workers were all working in the field of campus ministry, but as Joseph Todd complained, without much consultation or reference, when ". . . Nothing but a unified, persistent and enlightened attack will ever make any appreciable impress upon this colossal task."[34]

Todd noted in 1921 that there were 7,512 Disciple students attending 80 state universities, comprising 5 percent of the total enrollment in these schools.

(See Table 1) He argued for strong support for the care of students at these state universities, and reported that other denominations were outstripping the Disciples in this field which they had pioneered.

> Other churches such as the Methodist, Congregational, Presbyterian, Baptist and Episcopalian are spending large sums annually for the care of their students at tax-supported institutions. The Presbyterian church in the United States, for example, is supporting workers at forty-five state and independent universities through its Board of Education.[35]

Table 1. Religious Affiliation of Students in State Universities
From the Sixth Annual Report of the Board of Education *1921 Year Book* Christian Church (Disciples of Christ) p. 214.

In order to give an idea of the size of this job, we set forth the following tables, prepared from a survey recently made by the Council of Church Boards of Education, of which our Board of Education is a member. Dr. O. D. Foster, the University Secretary of the Council, made this survey and furnished the figures.

RELIGIOUS AFFILIATION OF STUDENTS IN STATE UNIVERSITIES

Communion	Total	Average	Percent	Percentage of Population	Student Percent. of Communions.
Baptist	14,516	181	9	7	.2
Congregational	9,476	118	6	.8—	1.2
Disciples	7,512	94	5	1.2	.6
Friends	261	3	.15	.1	.24
Hebrew	3,127	39	2	..	..
Lutheran	6,859	86	5—	2	.3
Methodist	36,605	457	24	7	.5
Presbyterian	23,181	290	15	2+	1.03
Protestant Episcopal	10,038	125	7—	1	.9
Roman Catholic	10,533	132	7	16	.065
Unitarian	930	12	.6	.08	1.
United Brethren	660	83	.4	.35	.2
Others	6,788	846	4.5	..	..
Total Reporting	130,486	1,631	85.5		
Members of Churches	65,232	815	43—		
Expressing Preference	17,847	223	12—		
Both	47,407	593	31		
Total Reporting	130,486	1,631	85.5		
No Information	21,975	275	14.5		
Total Enrollment	152,461	1,906	100		

NOTE—The above figures are for the eighty State Universities furnishing data.

According to the above figures the various communions have in the State Universities for each 100,000 of their membership, students as follows: Congregationalists, 1,200; Presbyterians, 1,030; Unitarians, 1,000; Episcopalians, 900; Disciples, 600; Methodists, 500; Lutherans, 300; Baptists, 200; United Brethren, 200; Roman Catholics, 65.

*NOTE—In this list are enumerated over fifty different religious bodies, with Christian Scientists heading the list and Mormons coming second.

By contrast, in the 1924 Annual Report of the United Christian Missionary Society, Department of Religious Education, for the Disciples, it was reported that:

> The department has for some years participated in the maintenance of student pastors for work among the students at several tax-supported institutions of learning—namely, at Purdue (Ind.) University, and the State Universities of Washington, Oregon, California and Oklahoma. The past year work was done at only two of these centers—Purdue and California. The student problem is approached from the standpoint of the local church.[36]

In 1925, Joseph Todd was able to spend more time in his capacity as secretary to the University Department and in the tenth annual report to the Board of Education he disclosed a careful analysis of the issues related to the Disciples work in public higher education. In that year, the Commission on State Universities, a committee of the Board of Education, recommended the following measures, which were accepted and approved by the Board:

> I. We desire to approve the basic principles of approach to the state university as laid down in the report of the state university secretary. They are three:
>
> 1. That the religious, pastoral, church and social activities of students should be centered around a well conducted church, provided with an adequate plant, capable leadership and an efficient staff to compass both its local and student program. It is our conviction that it is not wise to build up two separate centers about a campus for providing for the preaching, pastoral and social needs of the students.
>
> 2. That in student religious activities on the campus co-operative programs should be stressed and denominational emphasis, so far as possible, be confined to local church centered activities.
>
> 3. That the educational approach, which has been the distinctive emphasis and contribution of the Disciples in this field, should maintain our policy of giving Biblical and religious instruction on academic standard meriting credit alongside other curriculum courses. The educational approach should not be confused with the pastoral, social, or all-campus co-operative programs and the teachers of Biblical and religious courses should not be so supported, controlled or given other responsibilities as to prevent or interfere with their academic efficiency or standing on the campus as doing educational work on a par with other departments of the university.[37]

This action was a watershed decision, which followed the insight and vision of Joseph Todd, who no doubt possessed the most comprehensive picture of the state university situation at that time.

In the same meeting, other implementing actions were taken which are reflective of the vision of Todd and the Commission on State Universities. These actions called for: 1) the work of Disciples at state universities to be organized under the Board of Education, 2) further development of means to meet the needs of the church, pastoral, and social programs at university centers, 3) opening doors for interdenominational cooperation in both the educational and pastoral aspects of university ministry, 4) contacting students at the various campus centers—possibly through the employment of a team of traveling secretaries, 5) the development of state foundations which could create and support ministries to the state campuses, and 6) the provision of a full time secretary to oversee and coordinate university work.[38]

Encouraged by the assurance that the Board of Education would soon hire a full-time secretary, Joseph C. Todd resigned in 1926. In his last report he stressed the need for the Disciples to take an active leadership role in fostering interdenominational cooperation in university work. He poignantly emphasized the necessity of Disciples resolving their own internal problems in order to provide a united approach to university ministries, citing the difficulty of conflicting approaches by the Board of Education and the United Christian Missionary Society in the same field, and sometimes upon the same campus.[39]

Unfortunately, the optimistic plans to hire a full-time secretary to replace Todd were sidetracked when his replacement's services were needed in Texas. Todd was asked to return to part-time service as secretary to the University Department, to which he agreed. In 1928 he described the field of public higher education as both "alluring and perplexing." Todd counted increasingly upon the local church to carry a large responsibility for ministry to students where the church was situated next to a public campus. He recognized that the priority for including the university work depended greatly upon the pastor, the perceived mission of the congregation, and the resources available to the local church. He also emphasized the importance of interdenominational cooperation in all other aspects of ministry in higher education, recognizing the principle that "when agencies and institutions under the auspices of the Disciples became interdenominational and cooperative we would consider them no less our own.[40]

In that same year, the Department of Religious Education of the United Christian Missionary Society officially noted that their work at state universities was divided into two distinct groups, the Bible Chairs and the Student Pastors. At that time there were four Disciple Bible Chairs: 1) The Ann Arbor Bible Chair—Thomas Iden, 2) The John B. Cary Memorial Chair at the University of Virginia—W. M. Forrest, 3) The Kansas Bible Chair—S. B. Braden, and the Texas Bible Chair—F. L. Jewett, Instructor. Student work of a pastoral nature was being supported by the Society at 1) Purdue Christian Foundation—Robert Knight, Student Pastor, 2) University of Washington—Miss Edith McGinnis and Victor Wellman, 3) University of Missouri—Miss Grace Goslin, and 4) University of California—W. C. Parry, Director of Religious Education.[41]

Throughout the late 1920s and the early 1930s Joseph C. Todd's work was like a beacon for higher education. His far reaching view saw the importance of an education in which religious values were taught in the home, in the church, and in the college and university, preparing young people for the fullest expression of a faithful life. He feared that anything less than our best efforts in this field would allow the forces of secularism, particularly in the impressionable college years, to devalue the importance of the Christian faith in the college-age generation. His vision for the church's ministry in higher education held the work of the church-related college and the work on state supported campuses as of equal importance, and dedicated toward a common goal—the education and development of young people both intellectually and spiritually prepared for life and leadership in the world. He believed that through both of these avenues students could learn to integrate Christian values into profession, family life, and individual growth.

Todd was at once challenged by the immense opportunities for the church's mission in higher education, and appalled by the paucity of financial support which the Disciples were able to commit to such an enterprise. He was a loyal Disciple, yet committed to work cooperatively with other denominations in the field of higher education. He recognized that this was both a practical necessity, but even more, it was a basic tenet of Disciples theology. His travels to the campuses and the great centers of higher education across the nation reinforced his conviction that the local churches, the campus Christian Foundations, the State Missionary Societies, the Board of Education, and the United Christian Missionary Society must work in a cooperative and coordinated fashion to attain any degree of effectiveness. Yet the structures were not in place, nor was there sufficient funding, to provide such oversight. The Great Depression was taking its toll on church finances, and Todd cautiously advised that new work should not be initiated unless there was adequate funding to guarantee its continuing success. A barometer of the financial climate of that time is seen in Todd's decision in 1932 to continue his work, but without compensation.[42]

For a time it appeared that the work of Bible Chairs, Schools of Religion and campus pastors on tax-supported campuses would all be coordinated by the Board of Education, through the University Department. The United Christian Missionary Society began to divest its leadership in this area. However, in 1934 this plan was reconsidered. A Joint Committee on Student Work, representing the University Department of the Board of Education and the Religious Education Department of the United Christian Missionary Society was formed. Roy G. Ross, of the Religious Education Department served as the director of this committee. This step was made in an effort to provide more effective coordination and leadership in the church's ministry in higher education.

The cooperative effort began in a practical sense in 1934, although the legal transfer was not worked out until 1935. On September 1, 1934, Miss Lura Aspinwall, the first full-time Disciple to serve in this capacity, was called to become Director of Student Work. (Her beginning is usually reported as 1935 since this action was reported in the 1935 Annual Report to the International Convention.) At this time, Joseph Todd resigned, and the University

Department was discontinued. Harry O. Pritchard resigned as Secretary of the Board of Education, and on July 1, 1935 became the Secretary of the Department of Higher Education, within the United Christian Missionary Society. The Board of Education became the College Association. The Depression had taken its toll.[43]

The events of 1935 were a major turning point in the evolution of the Disciples approach to ministry in higher education. The Depression had eroded the financial base of the Disciples work in church-related colleges, Bible Chairs, and in ministry to the tax-supported universities. The transition in which the leadership and responsibility for ministry in higher education was transferred from the Board of Education to the United Christian Missionary Society was more than symbolic. Under the leadership of Lura Aspinwall as Director of Student Work the emphasis moved away from Todd's strong stand on the imperative of interdenominational cooperation toward a more denominationally oriented approach. This was reflected in both her stated goals and the nature of her activities. In 1937 she envisioned the purpose of her mision as follows:

> Student work as a function of higher education and religious education is responsible for developing and deepening the religious life of Disciple students wherever they may be and conserving them as churchmen and as intelligent participants in the building of a more Christian civilization.[44]

Much of her work centered around visitations to the various campus centers and developing training sessions for student workers and local pastors interested in student work, such as the National Disciple Student Work Seminar. She served as guest speaker to student conferences, published a monthly *Student Work Bulletin*, developed materials to promote Go to College Day in the churches, and arranged for Disciples missionaries and prominent pastors to speak at the various campuses. When Miss Aspinwall resigned in September 1938, there were continuing financial problems resulting in the appointment of her successor on a part-time basis.[45]

George Oliver Taylor was called to be National Director of Young People's and Student Work on April 1, 1939.[46] During his tenure the United States became involved in World War II and the all-out war effort brought changes to the college campuses as many entered military service and domestic programs took a second place. He continued in this position until the end of January 1944. During his tenure he continued the circulation of the Disciples *Student Work Bulletin*, and generally encouraged those engaged in student work with Disciples students. By 1943 he reported that there were two hundred fifty giving full or part-time to student work and three Bible Chairs which remained active in Michigan, Texas and Virginia. From his office he provided information and counsel to the campus workers on how they might better serve the service men and women on campus.[47]

Student Religious Societies

Although this author has claimed that the Disciples of Christ were the first religious body to begin campus ministry on the state supported campuses through the Bible Chairs, it is important to recognize the fact that student religious societies had a very early beginning. Clarence Shedd reports that one of the earliest references to student religious societies in colonial American Colleges is found in a funeral sermon preached by Cotton Mather for a young schoolmaster named Recompense Wadsworth. Mather mentioned in the funeral sermon that in 1706, Wadsworth made a covenant with God and with a handful of other students to form a student society.[48] Through the years to follow, when Mather dispaired over the "hopeless moral and religious condition" at Harvard, he found some solace in the piety of the student societies.[49]

These student societies grew up on many campuses in the succeeding years. In the winter of 1839 a Student Christian Association was founded at the University of Michigan. By 1865 they considered themselves a part of the Young Men's Christian Association. Although women were not admitted to the university until 1870, in the early years many women students belonged to the YMCAs.[50]

Virginia organized a chapter of the YMCA in October 1858, shortly after Michigan's informal beginning. Hence, Virginia receives credit for the first Student YMCA in the world, dating back to October 12, 1858.[51] (The city-YMCA began even earlier; it was first formed June 6, 1844 when twelve clerks at Hitchcock and Company formed a Christian Association and called it by that name.)

The International Convention in Indianapolis in 1870 urged development of Student YMCAs on college campuses across the nation. By June 6, 1877, thirty-three years after its founding, "25 delegates from 21 colleges in 12 states and the District of Columbia, met at a designated point in the Convention Hall in Louisville and then and there the Intercollegiate Y.M.C.A. Movement was born . . ."[52]

In summary, Christian Student Societies existed in the earliest colonial colleges. The Intercollegiate YMCA groups were active from 1877 on. They were interdenominational in character. The early student associations with Cotton Mather were devotional and attended to the personal religious life of its members. Later, the academic study of religion was initiated, as well as debate on religious topics. In the early nineteenth century there was a strong missionary fervor. Later, there was movement to relate one's religion to urgent problems in the community, the nation, and the world. Students in these associations had a clear sense of the ethical issues of the day, including problems of racial prejudice, war, and the social-economic order.[53]

John R. Mott, general secretary of the World Student Christian Federation, suggested that programs of a denominational nature ought to be carried out through the local church or parish, but that the cause demanded unity of purpose and effort in addressing the issues arising on the state campuses:

> Because of the greatness of our task, because of the forces that oppose, more especially the inertia, because of the advantages of unity in the way of comprehensiveness, in the way of continuity, in the way of power and in the way of speed—for these reasons we must have unity among all those who have at heart this great work. I go further, and say that not to have it is nothing less than sinful.[54]

In spite of the eloquent pleas for unity of effort among the denominations in relating to the opportunities for ministry on the state supported campuses, there was much "disunity" as denominations each sought to establish their own program of campus and student work.

The growth of public higher education and the spread of campus ministries

In the first twenty years of the twentieth century, campus ministry work was predominantly a Protestant enterprise, with only small numbers of Roman Catholic and Jewish campus workers. The call for unity in that time was an appeal primarily to the various Protestant groups. As Joseph Todd had noted in his annual reports on several occasion, the Presbyterians and Methodists in particular became much more vigorous and prolific than the Disciples in the spawning of campus ministries at the state supported colleges.

The enrollment in state colleges and universities had grown considerably in the period from 1900-1920; from 90,000 in 1900 to over 300,000 in 1920. In the next decade, there was another major increase as enrollment in 1930 numbered over 500,000 in the state universities.[55]

Along with this expanding enrollment, there was a greater proportionate increase in the enrollment of Jewish and Catholic students between 1920 and 1930. Gradually, the growth of Hillel Foundations and Newman Centers increased as Jewish and Catholic leaders sought ways to follow their students to campus and minister to their spiritual needs. While cooperation between Protestant groups had become standard practice by the 1920s, the theme of interreligious cooperation among Protestants, Jews, and Catholics became a new issue both locally and nationally.

At the University of Missouri, an interesting experiment in interreligious cooperation was led by the students. They created a council which provided for four categories of participants: 1) all Protestant groups; 2) all Catholic groups; 3) all Jewish organizations; and 4) "all religious organizations of undenominational interests or leanings." Parker Rossman describes the work which the Council outlined for itself:

> In 1927 the objectives of the S.R.C. were listed as follows: 1) welcoming new students to Columbia; 2) all-University religious meetings; 3) conferences of religious leaders; 4) union meeting during holidays; 5) co-operation with the Columbia churches; 6) encouragement of Bible College enrollment (a Protestant

and Jewish financed school of religion offering courses for university credit); 7) promotion of fellowship banquet, and 8) joint social events. In this council students and adults sat down together on an equal basis to plan a joint strategy for the religious forces on the campus . . . Adults and students took turns being president of the Board of Control which also had in its membership responsible administrative officers from the university.

On this basis the Council continued to operate smoothly and satisfactorily during the next ten to fifteen year period.[56]

One of the significant developments in religious cooperation was the work of the National Conference of Christians and Jews. This organization contributed greatly to the mutual understanding of its participating religious groups, and to the reduction of prejudice.

The NCCJ came into separate existence in 1928. Its work in the 1930s centered on providing a concerted effort of the Protestants, Catholics and Jews in combatting hateful and disruptive prejudices against minority groups which seemed to have blossomed in the aftermath of World War I.

The first director of the Conference was Everett R. Clinchy, a college chaplain at Wesleyan University in Connecticut. During the 1930s both private colleges and state universities followed the leadership of the Conference by conducting lectureships and roundtable discussions on ways in which prejudice might be overcome and religious people might work together for the fostering of good will. Events such as these continued the awareness and interest in religious cooperation.

The 1930s saw a flowering of religious liberalism in Protestantism. Devisive lines created by dogmatism were slowly vanishing. Some were bold enough to envision a future in which a new fellowship might emerge which would embrace all religiously minded persons. Disciples might especially relish the summary comments of Harry Emerson Fosdick when he described the tolerance and inclusiveness characteristic of liberalism:

> We were disgusted with dogmatic claims to orthodox finality . . . We were pioneers of the inclusive spirit which has created our inter-denominational churches and our national and world councils. Within the Christian fellowship we wanted unity, with tolerance of differences.[57]

Within the universities, there was a growing recognition that religious work, usually involving full-time professional ministers, was on the campus to stay. It was further recognized by most that the goals and objectives of the campus ministers in work with individuals and student groups was consistent with the aims of the universities for the students' growth and development. One of the problems the academic institutions faced was how to relate to the many groups, to enlist cooperation and order. In some cases the student affairs office was designated for this function. In private colleges, increasingly, full-time college chaplains were appointed to coordinate all religious activities on the campus.

Disciples colleges have had mixed patterns of practice regarding the employment of a campus minister, but for the most part such work has been seen as an integral part of campus life. From the beginning, Disciples colleges have served non-Disciples students, and the work of the chaplain or campus minister on the church-related college campus is much like that of colleagues on the state campus in that he or she is called to serve the needs of all students, without regard to denominational affiliation. The work of the chaplain on the church-related campus has unique aspects, however, in that such a person is an employee of the college and works within the lines of accountability of that system. Often, the college chaplain has played a major role in fashioning and implementing a pattern of cooperative ministry among the ministers from other denominations striving to minister to the varied needs of students.

The need for cooperation has often led to the formation of Religious Councils which provided both organization, representation of all interested parties, and a structure through which cooperative work in campus ministry could best be undertaken. Through the Councils, programs such as "religious emphasis week," religious census cards, and special day religious services of an inclusive nature were conceived and implemented. In less structured situations, interreligious committees were formed to work cooperatively on a specific project, but not on a regular basis. On some campuses there was no official structure for cooperation, but in an informal way, those who were paid to work with students full-time found ways to support and encourage one another.

During the years of World War II, a radically different situation existed on the campuses. Religious activity was reduced on some campuses, while on others new programs developed to meet the special needs of war time. The military assigned some units to selected campuses for special study programs, and campus ministry units developed programs to include the men and women in uniform in order that these "special" students might also have their religious needs met. The principle decided upon by the military officials was to rely upon existing campus religious organizations and staff, without attempting to assign military chaplains to the campus. In general, the prevailing mood of cooperation and "pulling together" toward a common goal encouraged religious cooperation on the campus during this period.

A number of factors made religious work on the campus difficult both before and during the war years. There seemed to be an overall decline in student interest in religion. Many who were religious were preoccupied with their own denominational group interests and community life, resulting in apathy toward any ecumenical approach. Furthermore, in both students and the professional campus ministers, there was often a prevailing ignorance about the values and traditions of other religious groups outside their own. This led to misconceptions about the limits of cooperation which could be expected from others.

Summary

In summary, the end of the nineteenth century witnessed the dramatic rise of public higher education and the containment of the private church college movement. The new phenomenon of the state university provided both a challenge and an opportunity to the churches. The doctrine of church-state separation which obviated the teaching of religion and Bible in most state institutions was seen as a challenge by the Disciples and led to the establishment of the Bible Chair movement. Through the Bible Chairs the church could offer such teaching as elements in a complete education, as had been the pattern in the liberal arts education of the church colleges in former times.

Early Disciples leaders had a mixture of theological presuppositions concerning the meaning of the church's mission on the campus. For some, the mission priority was teaching the Bible and religion in a scholarly fashion to young people who would soon assume places of leadership in the professions of society. They envisioned the professionals and leaders of tomorrow moving toward excellence of service through their recognition of the "*vocatio Dei*" (the call of God) to fulfill their vocation in the service of society. For others, the presence of the church on the state university was primarily for the sake of young Christians in attendance. The church followed its young to continue their religious instruction, to reinforce their moral convictions, to provide support and counsel. Still others fostered hopes that the provision of religious education and the building of moral character in the formative years of college might lead the best and brightest into the Christian ministry, or at least into leadership roles in the churches of their communities.

Disciples leaders who began work on the state university campuses were faithful to Stone and Campbell's plea for unity and carried out their teaching in a nonsectarian fashion while encouraging interdenominational cooperation. With the passing of time there evolved a distinction between the role of the scholarly teacher in the Bible Chair and the role of the pastor who nurtured the social and spiritual life of the students. The bifurcation became more pronounced as the roles were distinguished. In time, the role of the teacher diminished and the role of the campus pastor flourished. This was largely due to circumstances in which the universities gradually began to offer courses in religious studies as a legitimate part of the curriculum. Furthermore, students became more particular and were less inclined to subscribe to noncredit courses in religion.

Joseph C. Todd, secretary of the University Department of the Disciples Board of Education from its inception in 1919 until its demise in 1935 was one who had a broad vision of the church's role in public higher education. In the early 1930s he described the task as he envisioned it:

> ... what is our task as a people in the American student world? In a word, it is to keep constantly and accurately recorded on our brotherhood balance sheets our most valuable assets—our capable and amibitious youth in the processes

of idealization and purpose preparation. Work with them first of all in our church colleges then in the great state universities, state colleges, and teachers colleges, with the smaller and scattered groups attending other church colleges, and finally that selective leadership preparing for larger usefulness in the graduate schools—and also those already at work as professors and executives in colleges and universities. By every means at our command we need to express our interest in these, our hope for the future—make them aware of our need for them, and obligation to the Church of Christ and the Kingdom of God, and enable them to be truly educated by giving adequate attention to the richest heritage of the world—our religion—the leaders and institutions of spiritual life—the Bible—Jesus of Nazareth—and God.[58]

From 1935-1944 the emphasis of Disciples work shifted from Todd's comprehensive and ecumenical vision to a more narrow focus on student work. Following the difficult Depression years there was something of a survival mentality in the church which in part led to a strong denominational approach to campus ministry. The stressful years of the world at war contributed as well to this conserving philosophy as the church "followed its students" to the campus.

References

1. Garrison, W. E., and DeGroot, A. T., *The Disciples of Christ: A History* (St. Louis: The Bethany Press, 1958) p. 416.
2. Flowers, R. B. *The Bible Chair Movement in the Disciples of Christ Tradition: Attempts to Teach Religion in State Universities*, a Ph.D. Dissertation, School of Religion, University of Iowa. (Ann Arbor: University Microfilms, Inc. 1967) p. 296.
3. Westerhoff, John H., editor, *The Church's Ministry in Higher Education* (New York: UMHE Communication Office, Publisher, 1978) James H. Smylie, "Hope, History and Higher Education" p. 6.
4. Campbell, Alexander, *Millenial Harbinger*, 1837, "Bacon College" pp. 570-1
5. Shedd, Clarence P., *The Church Follows Its Students* (New Haven: Yale University Press, 1938) p. 6.
6. Flowers, R. B. *Op. cit.* p. 10.
7. *Ibid.* p. 11.
8. Shedd, C. P. *Op. cit.* p. 8.
9. Young, C. A., "Bible Teaching at the University of Virginia," *The Christian Evangelist* Dec. 14, 1899, p. 1575.
10. Flowers, R. B., *Op. cit.* p. 22.
11. Smith, S., Handy, R., and Leotscher, L., *American Christianity* (New York: Charles Scribner's Sons, 1960) Vol. I., Thomas Campbell, "Declaration and Address" p. 584.
12. Healey, Robert M., *Jefferson on Religion in Public Education* (New Haven: Yale University Press, 1962) pp. 219-226.
13. Flowers, R. B., *Op. cit.* p. 61
14. "History of the Bible Chair Movement." *Missionary Tidings*, January, 1894. p. 20.
15. "Report of the Permanent Committee Appointed to Make Arrangements for the Endowment of an English Bible Chair at Ann Arbor, Michigan," *Missionary Tidings*, December, 1892, p. 25.
16. Flowers, R. B. *Op. cit.* p. 79.
17. Colyer, G. P., "The Possibilities of Bible Work" *Missionary Tidings*, July, 1901, p. 70.

18. Young, C. A., "The Work of the Bible Chairs" *Missionary Tidings*, December, 1895, p. 198.
19. Campbell, Minnie M., "The State Universities as well as our Colleges Need the Bible," *Missionary Tidings*, April, 1984, p. 17.
20. Forrest, W. M., *Sowing the Seed of the Kingdom*, (Indianapolis: Christian Woman's Board of Missions, 1900) p. 1.
21. Flowers, R. B., *Op. cit.* p. 79.
22. *Ibid.* p. 80.
23. *Ibid.* pp. 84-85.
24. Jewett, F. L., "Religious Activities in State Universities," *Missionary Tidings*, November, 1910, p. 297.
25. Flowers, *Op. cit.* p. 96.
26. Jewett, F. L., "The Texas Bible Chair Report for 1910-11," *Missionary Tidings*, November, 1911. p. 243.
27. Shockley, Donald G., "The College and University Chaplaincy: A Theological Perspective," in *Invitation to Dialogue: The Theology of College Chaplaincy and Campus Ministry* (New York: Education in the Society, National Council of Churches of Christ, 1986), p. 40.
28. Shockley, Donald G., *Ibid.* p. 7.
29. Flowers, R. B., *Op. cit.* p. 141.
30. *Ibid.* p. 156.
31. "Indiana School of Religion Celebrates 25th Anniversary," *Christian Evangelist*, October 21, 1935. p. 1431.
32. Todd, Joseph C., "Indiana Preachers" *Christian Evangelist*, September 14, 1911. p. 1318.
33. Todd, Joseph C., "Annual Report" Board of Education *1921 Year Book*, Christian Church (Disciples of Christ) p. 213.
34. *Ibid.* p. 214.
35. *Ibid.* p. 213.
36. "Annual Report," United Christian Missionary Society, Department of Religious Education, *1921 Year Book*, Christian Church (Disciples of Christ) p. 142.
37. Todd, Joseph C., "Annual Report," Board of Education, *1925 Year Book* Christian Church (Disciples of Christ) p. 240.
38. *Ibid.* p. 241
39. Todd, Joseph C., "Annual Report" Board of Education, *1926 Year Book* Christian Church (Disciples of Christ) p. 224.
40. Todd, Joseph C., "Annual Report" Board of Education, *1928* Year Book Christian Church (Disciples of Christ) p. 36.
41. "Annual Report" United Christian Missionary Society, Department of Religious Education, *1928 Year Book*. Christian Church (Disciples of Christ) p. 94.
42. "Annual Report" Board of Education, *1932 Year Book* Christian Church (Disciples of Christ) p. 124.
43. "Annual Report" Board of Education, *1935 Year Book* Christian Church (Disciples of Christ) p. 70.
44. Aspinwall, Lura, "Student Work Report" Annual Report, U.C.M.S. *1937 Year Book* Christian Church (Disciples of Christ) p. 36.
45. *Ibid.* p. 36.
46. "Annual Report" United Christian Missionary Society, *1939 Year Book* Christian Church (Disciples of Christ) p. 39.
47. "Annual Report" United Christian Missionary Society, *1943 Year Book* Christian Church (Disciples of Christ) p. 20.
48. Shedd, C. P., *Two Centuries of Student Christian Movements* (New York: Association Press, 1934) p. 2.
49. *Ibid.* p. 5.
50. *Ibid.* pp. 96-97.
51. *Ibid.* p. 100.
52. *Ibid.* pp. 143-44.
53. *Ibid.* p. xviii.
54. Galpin, C. J., and Edwards, R. H. eds. "Church Work in Speech to the 3rd Annual Conference of Church Workers in State Universities" p. 29.

55. From the United States' Office of Education, Higher Education in American Democracy: Report of the President's Commission on Higher Education, Vol. VI, (Washington: U.S. Government Printing Office, 1957.)
56. Rossman, G. Parker, "Protestant Cooperation on State University Campuses" A Ph.D. dissertation, Graduate School, Yale University, May 1953, pp. 99-100.
57. Fosdick, H. E., *The Living of These Days* (New York: Harper and Brothers, 1956) pp. 259-60.
58. Todd, Joseph C., "The 17th Annual Report to the Board," Board of Education, *1932 Year Book*, Christian Church (Disciples of Christ) p. 127.

Chapter 2

ENCHANTMENT: THE GOLDEN AGE OF CAMPUS MINISTRY

Post World War II Changes in Public Higher Education

Following WWII there were notable changes in public higher education. As the returning veterans entered the colleges and universities throughout the country, undergraduate enrollment soared to new heights. The GI Bill of Rights enabled these young people to obtain the best possible education. They were older and more mature than college students of former generations. Many had traveled widely during the war years. Others had received excellent education from top universities to prepare them for military service. Some had developed language skills, particularly in German or Japanese. For the most part, this older cohort of students were serious about the task of pursuing their education and preparing for a life in the world of work which had been delayed by the war. They came from diverse backgrounds, and in distinction from earlier generations of students, many of these were married.[1]

Government leaders had grossly underestimated the number of GIs who would choose some form of higher education under the veterans educational assistance acts. It was thought that about 700,000 in all might attend college, with no more than 150,000 attending in any academic year.[2]

In actuality, 7,800,000 received training, with 2,200,000 of these attending college or university. They chose to return to the campus as a transition between military and civilian life. There existed in those years a threat of high unemployment and many anticipated that higher education could help them into a civilian career.[3]

By the fall of 1946 a million veterans swelled the ranks of students in colleges and universities as returning service men and women rushed to the campuses. These institutions of higher education proved remarkably responsive to the sudden influx of new students. In a cooperative spirit unique to those years, faculty willingly added additional courses to help share the load and students cheerfully endured crowded housing conditions on and about the campus.

Educators praised the veteran-students for their maturity and seriousness in the pursuit of learning, and a national survey described the class of 1949, 70 percent of which were veterans, in glowing terms for their self-discipline and excellence in achievement.[4]

The impact of this new constituency upon collegiate life was considerable, and occurred in a variety of ways. In former years there had existed a long tradition of *in loco parentis*. That is, the university took upon itself some of the gate-keeping and boundary setting functions for students which their parents had formerly done. Many college students were living away from home for the first time, and most parents found comfort in the paternalistic rules of the campus which distinguished separate dormitories for males and females, and imposed a curfew by which all co-eds were expected back in the dormitory or sorority house each evening. These old traditions which seemed to fit for a younger and less experienced student constituency seemed increasingly out of place for this more traveled and mature population. Furthermore, this older cohort of students was less subordinate to the hegemony of the faculty, another break with tradition, which may well have laid the groundwork for the coming academic revolution.[5]

In an analysis of this period, David D. Henry suggested that the influx of the veterans into college brought a number of significant changes:

1) Higher education clearly became a significant means to a national end for the policymakers—even for those whose interest was limited to veteran's readjustment and for those who were primarily concerned about preventing or alleviating unemployment and other negative economic conditions.

2) The nonveteran youth of the nation were quick to note the new priority for higher education.

3) Those who were concerned with the enlargement of educational opportunity, particularly for the economically deprived and young people disadvantaged in other ways, were given a national precedent for the value and feasibility of federal assistance.

4) Aid to students generally emerged, as it had in the Depression, as an appropriate way for the federal government to be involved in higher education with a minimum of federal control.

5) The public image of the veteran as a good student, reliable, mature, and well motivated, carried over into the public evaluation of college students generally.

6) The new status of higher education broadened the appeal of academic careers for increasing numbers of highly qualified young people.

7) The temporary acquisition of off-campus sites for "surplus" enrollments at a number of institutions served as beginnings for permanent new campuses in state systems, as foundations for new community colleges, and as later authorized permanent branches.

8) The tone of campus life was changed. Undergraduate discipline systems were altered. The married student came to stay. *In loco parentis* did not disappear for another decade, but a break-through was made that kept widening with succeeding years. Student personnel work grew in importance.

9) Many other internal practices, policies, and services were initiated that
would become permanent. . . . The new public esteem for higher education
would be a continuing asset of unmeasured value, psychologically and
pragmatically.[6]

Increasingly in the post war years, larger numbers of students began to
think of attending colleges of their choice, outside their own geographical
area. David Riesman estimated that roughly 10-20 percent of high school
graduates were prepared to be recruited nationally.[7] Black and other minority
students began to enter higher education in greater numbers. A significant
number of Jewish students were among those who were willing to go any-
where in the nation in search of a quality education.[8]

President Truman appointed a Commission on Higher Education which
published its report in the form of six small volumes between the end of 1947
and early 1948. The major importance of the report was its surprising
emphasis on the need to remove all barriers to educational opportunity. The
Commission believed that at least half of the college age population were
mentally prepared to complete two years of college and about 32 percent had
the ability to complete an advanced degree. With this in mind, the Commission
recommended doubling college enrollments by 1960, and addressing the
economic, racial, religious, and geographical restrains to education.[9] Such
concern for social justice in opening access to all capable students to the
powers and privileges of higher education had an important beginning which
would develop in the forth coming years.

The Commission was also conscious of social needs which went beyond
the needs of individuals, for which higher education had a responsibility. It
stressed the need to transcend the narrow nationalism of the past and to
develop knowledge of all the world and its citizens and cultures. It held a
keen awareness of the astonishing new power of atomic energy and recognized that the values being assimilated by the current generation of students
would have a tremendous impact upon the future development of atomic
power for positive uses or destructive possibilities. It conceived of a future in
which higher education would be available for all, appropriate to their own
capacities to use it.[10]

The Cold War

The 1950s brought further changes in the climate of higher education. The
United States was engaged in a "Cold War" with the Soviet Union. The
possibility of an armed confrontation with Russia seemed real, and was
described as "inevitable" by Stalin. The Berlin Blockade and the Korean War
served as grim reminders that a lasting peace had not been achieved, and this
country increased its spending for defense and continued the mobilization of
servicemen. Debate was rampant on the best means for the provision of a
standing army, and the two year mandatory draft was eventually approved.

Educators were faced with concern over the size of expected student enrollments. The World War II veterans were near completing their education and their numbers were in decline. Faculty morale was undermined by low salaries in the face of rising inflation in the cost of living.

The President's Commission on Higher Education was gravely concerned that by comparison with other professions the decade of the 1940's had been unkind to college professors. The Commission reported that:

> . . . after 14 years of experience, physicians had an average net income twice as high as that of the college teacher. The average real estate salesman would have 50 percent more net income. From 1940-47, the cost of living had increased about 57 percent while faculty salaries were raised 32 percent.[11]

It appeared that while working harder, teaching more students, and creatively resolving the problems of the postwar enrollment surge faculty were less well off than they had been in 1940.

The Cold War years of the 1950s were also the years of Senator Joseph McCarthy. His preoccupation with battling communism was unbounded and overflowed onto the campus:

> For most people in the academic community and for many other thoughtful people, the term "McCarthyism" has come to mean the exploitation of a complex public issue for politican gain by means of unproved allegations, name calling and innuendo, character assassination, institutional slander, guilt by association, and manipulation of publicity to smother opposition. Initially, the avowed issue was the extent of communist involvement in the affairs of the nation; later, the issue became the threat posed to the integrity of the legislative process by McCarthy's unscrupulous, demagogic drive for political power.[12]

The fear that McCarthy's investigations and allegations would strike the college or university, which at times it certainly did, was a debilitating factor, contrary to the spirit of free academic inquiry into any subject or situation. This was a time when civil liberties were abridged, and most felt intimidated against speaking out for fear of reprisal and retribution. The prevailing political atmosphere contributed in part to what has since been termed "the silent generation." Leaders in higher education experienced a sense of discouragement and malaise. The light-heartedness and buoyancy of the late 1940s had definitely cooled.

Preparing for the Tidal Wave

In the mid 1950s new population data gave rise to predictions that following a brief dip in enrollment between 1950-1954, there would be a significant increase in enrollment in the coming years. The President's Committee on Education Beyond the High School provided an interim report in the fall of 1956 which predicted that by 1970, enrollment would double or triple in colleges and universities. These predictions referred to a "tidal wave" of students seeking entry to higher education, not just college degree programs, but technical training, occupational training, apprenticeships, correspondence courses, and extension courses. These predictions turned out to be quite accurate as shown by David D. Henry's enrollment figures in the following Table:

. . . Opening fall enrollments, all institutions of higher education:

Degree credit enrollment		Percentage increase each half-decade
1955	2,678,623	
1960	3,610,007	35
1965	5,570,271	108
1970	7,920,149	196

13

Sputnik

When the Soviet Union launched Sputnik in 1957, it made a dramatic impact upon American higher education. The system was criticized as inadequate and behind the times. Faculty in the sciences, mathematics and physics stepped forward to help reshape the curriculum, not only in college and university, but in secondary schools as well.[14] The growing use of the Scholastic Aptitude Test (SAT) helped free high school students from the biases of their teachers or counselors, enabling them to seek higher education in the college of their choice if they were suitably qualified. The early use of the SAT had a liberating effect on education. Students began traveling further from home in pursuit of the kind of school and type of education which they deemed most desirable.

As Sputnik circled the earth, the questions concerning the quality of education in the United States found their orbit around the institutions of higher education. How did the Soviets achieve scientific superiority? How did the Soviet Union achieve such notoriety and noteworthy success in launching the first satellite into outer space? Competition with the Soviet Union may have succeeded where reason had failed, and the National Defense Education Act of 1958 was passed to provide aid to educational institutions.[15] Emphasis on excellence in education, particularly in the sciences, became the theme of the day.

Legislators and laypersons alike came increasingly to the opinion that the improvement of education was in the best national interest. Legislation was passed which provided funds to enhance the expansion of the universities, the development of scientific research, and to improve access for students to higher education. Such shifts in the national priorities in the United States paved the way for the beginning of a new wave of prosperity for higher education.

Growth of the Church's Presence on Campus

During this period of rapid expansion and increasing enrollment the churches increased their activities on the campus as well. Seymour A. Smith reported the number of full-time professional workers employed by the churches for campus work at about 200 in 1938, whereas, by 1953 the number had reached about 1,000, with 825 of these in the Protestant Churches, 100 Catholics and 75 Jewish.[16] In addition to these full-time professionals, there was a substantial number of local pastors and volunteers giving part of their time to campus ministry.

Dr. Kenneth Underwood reported that in the period from 1953-1963 the total growth in ordained clergy from eight reporting denominations was 15 percent, whereas, during that same period the number of campus clergy doubled. Dr. Underwood reported that in 1963 there were about 3,000 persons involved full-time in campus ministry.[17] In addition to full-time campus ministers, Underwood's figures included about 350 YMCA and YWCA secretaries, approximately 450 college chaplains and deans of the chapel, and a variety of others who could be identified as campus workers.[18]

An analysis of Dr. Underwood's research points to a figure of about 1,500 professional campus clergy in 1963—up from about 1,000 in 1953. This was a period of growth and expansion. Considerably more money flowed into this specialized ministry of the church than in former times to keep pace with the increased numbers of campus ministers and to meet the needs of the growing numbers of denominational centers. New foundation houses were built or acquired near the campus to facilitate these developing ministries. The major denominations each sought to acquire a center adjacent to the state university and state college campuses. The Methodist Church had its Wesley Foundation, the Presbyterian Church had its Westminster Foundation, the Episcopal Church had its Canterbury Club, the Lutheran Church had its Luther House, the Roman Catholic Church called its the Newman Center. There was the Baptist Student Union, the Disciple Student Foundation, the Congregational Church had its Pilgrim Club, and those of the Jewish faith built Hillel Foundations.

During this same period, literally millions of students had swelled the ranks of those enrolled in higher education, hundreds of new community colleges had been added, and hundreds more programs in professional and technical teaching had been added to the list of educational opportunities. Taken together, these factors created a situation which began to force the leaders of the church to rethink their goals and objectives in campus ministry. How would the personnel be distributed between the campuses? Toward which students should the ministry be directed? Should each denomination continue to carry out its own ministry—for its own students? What about the larger issues of higher education—and what could the church learn from the university which might help the church be the church? Could interdenominational cooperation in ministry to those on the campus provide a more effective means of meeting the needs? Could the churches actually afford to hire a campus minister and acquire a foundation at every institution of higher education?

Disciples work on the campus in the post war era

In the general cultural milieu described above, the Disciples continued their work in higher education. On January 1, 1945 John E. McCaw was called to serve as National Director of Student Work, under the Department of Religious Education of the United Christian Missionary Society. Prior to this, Dr. McCaw had served at Southern Illinois University where he had helped to found the first interdenominational and interracial student foundation, a work supported by the major Protestant denominations.[19]

John McCaw began his work as Student Director at a time when the most immediate concern was the return of the veteran to the campus and how best to minister to the changing student constituency. The international student movement had been ruptured by the war both in the European and Pacific arena. There was intense concern for the reconstruction of the World Student Christian Federation. It was a "hatching time" for the seeds of the ecumenical movement which would grow to fledgling status in the years to come.

Students on campuses in the United States and Canada rallied to the cause of reconciliation and the rebuilding of relationships with student groups in other countries. Money was raised to send abroad to provide relief for student groups who were impoverished and displaced by the war. American students went abroad to form work camps designed to help rebuild the war-torn cities of Europe. Student exchanges sponsored foreign students whose presence in colleges and universities in the United States could foster the rebuilding of collegial ties.

During his first months in office, John McCaw visited more than fifty college campuses and conferred with representatives of forty others. In the summer of 1946, for the first time in seven years, a conference for university pastors and student workers was held in Crystal Beach, Michigan. A Disciples student, Adelle Ringstorm, freshman at the University of Washington, was chosen as one of fifteen delegates from the United States to attend the meeting of the General Committee of the World Student Christian Federation in Geneva, Switzerland.[20]

The Student Workers Conference became an annual event and added to its objectives the training of new student workers who, in addition to attending the conference, were expected to participate in an intensive training program in the Missions Building in Indianapolis which was sponsored by Student Work, and to spend some time observing in one or more of the existing student centers.[21]

In 1946 there was a distinct split between the Christian Youth Fellowship (CYF), which continued as the organization for high school youth, and the

Disciples Student Fellowship (DSF), which became the college age organization. In December of that year, a national Disciples Student Fellowship Conference was held with Disciples students from sixty campuses participating. Russell Fuller was elected president and became a delegate to the Oslo World Youth Conference. This organization (DSF) provided a positive influence for many Disciples students, a significant number of whom have become leaders in the Christian Church (Disciples of Christ) at every level. The National Disciples Student Fellowship Conference or Ecclesia was held annually for several years, in the summer.[22]

When the Annual Student Workers Conference was held at Eureka College, July 1948, there were eighty-six college pastors and student workers from thirty-eight colleges in the United States attending. Also in that year the second Disciples Student Fellowship conference was held at Lawrence, Kansas and this body of student representatives from the various colleges was given the name, "The Disciples Student Fellowship Ecclesia." Something of the flavor of the activities of this group is captured in this report:

> The past president, Russell Fuller, Springfield, Ohio, spent a portion of the summer of 1947 attending the World Conference of Christian Youth at Oslo, Norway, and taking part in reconstruction projects in France. He spent 3 months in the fall of 1947 visiting some 50 student centers across the nation. Rhodes Thompson, Jr., the new president, spent several weeks of 1948 in summer student conferences in Europe. He will also spend 3 months visiting college campuses in the fall.
>
> Disciple students have been active in the ecumenical aspects of student work, including the Student Volunteer Movement, the United Student Christian Council and the World Student Christian Federation. Our students publish several issues a year of the *DSF Journal*, a magazine of news, religious articles and program interests.[23]

John McCaw resigned his post as National Student Director on September 1, 1950 to become Dean of the Divinity School, Drake University. By this time he had initiated a plan to assist the university pastors and student workers in contacting the Disciples students on their particular campus. The name of a contact person at each campus in the United States and Canada was printed under the student work report in the annual report in the *Year Book*, Christian Church (Disciples of Christ.) In some cases the contact person was the local pastor, in others it was a faculty member, a campus minister, or interdenominational worker. Hometown pastors were encouraged to send a list of students from their congregations who planned to attend these institutions.

Dr. McCaw became convinced during his tenure in office that the needs of students in the state supported colleges could not reasonably be met by the local Disciples congregation in the campus town. In the *World Call*, in 1946, he appealed for the development of student centers and foundations:

> No longer can the whole task of student work be left to the earnest efforts of local churches and devoted individuals. The church in the university or college

town, no matter how strong it is, can hardly absorb the responsibility of ministering to a concentrated and specialized university constituency which ebbs and flows with each academic year. Nor can such a church undergird with its local resources a ministry to several hundred—sometimes a thousand—new members to the congregation. In reality these student members are charges from congregations all over the brotherhood. Well-trained and full-time staff members are desperately needed for the important task of serving students.

In short, the day has come when the Disciples' churches, state missionary societies, national resources and ministerial training centers should undergird a brotherhood-wide student program with financial resources, leadership training, and program aids.[24]

The growing popularity of the Disciples Student Fellowship groups is reflected in the first Quadrennial Conference of Disciples of Christ Student Fellowship which was held December 27, 1949—January 1, 1950 at Drake University, Des Moines, Iowa:

Delegates from 26 states represented 84 colleges including 18 Disciple schools. Registration numbered 316 students, but there were more than 500 in attendance. The theme of the Conference was "The Student and His Faith." The difficult problems of faith and action were presented in the worship services, Bible study groups, discussion and fireside groups, and in the platform addresses given by Disciple leaders. Methods of evangelism, planning programs and worship, stewardship, recreation enlistment were studied in the workshops. The conference was a serious expression of student concern for their own lives, the life of their campuses and the life of the church. Its effects will be long felt in the churchmanship of today's students.[25]

The Board of Higher Education, reporting in 1950, could identify the following numbers of Disciples students enrolled in institutions of higher education: 1947—22,510; 1948—26,925; 1949—30,056; 1950—28,986. Harlie L. Smith, President of the Board of Higher Education predicted that the next few years would bring declining enrollment due to the low birth rate during the Depression years, and due to the increasing number of high school graduates involved in military service, due to the international situation.[26]

G. Parker Rossman was called to become Student Work Executive, a position in which he served from 1950-1958. Under his leadership, the first summer meeting of the Ecclesia (National Council) of the Disciples of Christ Student Fellowship was held at Camp Hollister, Missouri in June 1951. A year later there were 124 Disciples Student Fellowship groups reporting.

Ten were at Disciples-related schools, nine at independent colleges and the balance at state-supported schools. Reports from 50 of these groups showed 3,586 Disciple members. Four hundred six students attended 14 state DSF conferences; 762 attended week-end retreats. There was $2,230.00 given to the national DSF Fund. Four issues of the *DSF Journal* were published during the school year, and mailings averaged about 1,000 copies each issue.[27]

At the DSF Ecclesia Conference at Estes Park, Colorado in August 1952 there were 308 students and adult leaders from 66 campuses attending. This meeting was noteworthy as the national society for Disciples university women, the Kappa Beta, became integrated with the national DSF.[28]

States and regions were also becoming more organized in their approach to student work by this time, and many of the state organizations held two annual retreat weekends during the academic year for Disciples students in the state. On the local level "Disciples Student Fellowship" (DSF) groups were organized for Disciples students and working young people of college age. In the local churches, the long range goal was identified in 1952 as follows: "Each church maintaining an active contact with its college students to encourage their growth in the Christian life."[29]

In 1952, the *Christian Education Magazine* (Sept-Oct) reported the objectives of the Department of College and University Religious Life:

1. To lead all members of the college and university community to accept the Christian faith in God—Father, Son and Holy Spirit—according to the Scriptures, and to live as true disciples of Jesus Christ.

2. To deepen among students and faculty an understanding, a knowledge, and a love of the Bible as the Christian's guidebook of faith.

3. To deepen the Christian faith of college and university men and women.

4. To interpret to the campus community the mission and message of the Christian Church.

5. To develop local campus fellowships which are warm, loving, forgiving, and deeply committed to Christ, and in which students and faculty can mutually strengthen one another in Christian thinking and living.

6. To develop ecumenical understanding among students and faculty, individually and in campus Christian groups.

7. To foster a plan of Christian education aimed at producing a Christlike character.

8. To offer projects of practical Christian service.

9. To interpret Christian vocation as the individual's total response to the will and purpose of God.

10. To interpret the religious life of the college and university as an integral part of the program of higher education.

11. To be more than a student movement and to become in truth a University Christian Movement.

12. To promote on the campus a concern for the world Christian community.[30]

It is clear that by this time, the work of the Bible Chairs was overshadowed by the student work movement. The United Christian Missionary Society had related to four Bible Chairs, at the Universities of Virginia, Kansas, Texas, and Michigan. In 1946 the Bible Chair at Austin had organized the University Christian Church and throughout its existence, the congregation had met on the Bible Chair property. In May 1953 construction was begun on a new sanctuary for University Christian Church which had grown to some 350 members. The church and the Bible Chair saw themselves as partners in ministry to the University of Texas.[31]

Reports from the *Student Work Bulletins* of this period document current concerns. There was a growing dissatisfaction with the name "student worker" and it was proposed at the business meeting of the Student Workers Association Conference in 1952 that such terminology should be changed. Men and women who enter the campus ministry were to be recognized as equal in every way to those who enter the parish ministry. Therefore, ordained persons who have completed their theological degree should be known as "Campus Ministers." Furthermore, the Student Work Office should become known as the Office of Campus Ministry of the Department of Religious Education of the United Christian Missionary Society.[32]

The authors of this recommendation were ahead of their time, the motion failed to pass and the official terminology remained the same.

A related issue of that year was the recruitment of highly qualified and thoroughly educated young persons for campus ministry. A variety of strategies were offered including vocational conferences for high school students, summer internships for college students, and year-long internships for seminary students. It was recognized that on some campuses the campus minister would be the director of a student foundation or student center, while on others, the campus minister would work under the auspices of the local Christian Church with primary responsibility for campus ministry.[33]

There were diligent efforts on the part of both students and campus ministry leaders to move beyond the limitations of earlier views or visions of the campus ministry as they struggled to broaden the concept of the church's mission in the world. Students involved in the DSF were a part of the United Student Christian Council which embraced fourteen national student movements, and was itself included in the World's Student Christian Federation—and they persistently raised questions about the nature and purpose of the modern church. A second question being asked concerned the role of the Christian student in the university—when academic freedom was under fire, when the university seemed like a collection of trade schools, and when specialization led to the fragmentation of learning. A third urgent question concerned the role of the Christian student in the world struggle—seeking to understand the great social issues and to find ways to be faithfully responsive to the demands of justice.[34]

Nevertheless, the language of the *Student Work Bulletin* in both 1953 and 1954 reveals a primary concern for the Christian development of Disciples students. Even when encouraging DSF groups to include working young persons of college age, they were admonished not to lose the flavor of a Disciples college group. And while encouraging the inclusion of non-Disciples, or those who had not made a profession of faith, they were reminded of a primary concern for the spiritual pilgrimage of young Disciples students. Two central motifs were most prominent, that of preparing students for their eventual leadership in the church, and encouraging students as the future leaders of society toward a Christian world view.[35]

In July 1954, a national consultation on student work administration and finance was held at William Woods College. The announcement encouraging the appropriate persons to attend had a note of urgency:

> This Consultation is being called by the Joint Committee on Student Work of the Board of Higher Education and the United Christian Missionary Society, to recommend policies and procedures to solve certain vexing problems in the administration of financing of student work. The importance of this Consultation should be measured by the fact that such a consultation may be held only once in fifty years to clarify principles, procedures, policies and administrative relationships.[36]

It appears that the "vexing problems" were in part a result of the "mushroom" like growth which was reported at the consultation. As the number of centers grew, and the demand for additional centers came from other campuses, the question of more centralized planning and financing became clearly necessary. Also, the lines of accountability needed to be clarified. To whom was the campus minister responsible? A local board, a local congregation, the local pastor, a state committee, or the national office? These issues were addressed at the consultation and recommendations were made to assign responsibility for planning, financing, implementing and accountability:

> Recommendations were drafted for local student work committees, the creation of state departments of Campus Christian Life, and procedures for regularizing the financing of Student Centers and securing more adequate financial support. Most important was the recognition of the growing importance of student work, as the number of college students increases from 400,000 in 1920 to 5,000,000 in 1965. The Consultation group discovered that all agencies and local churches involved had spent nearly three million dollars on student work since 1945, and that this was the first time an effort had been made to study needs, coordinate efforts of the various agencies and make proposals for policies, principles and a long-range goal.[37]

A major change in the administration of campus ministry came in 1955, when the Board of Higher Education of the Christian Church (Disciples of Christ) began to share this responsibility with the Student Work Office of the United Christian Missionary Society. The new Joint Commission on Campus Christian Life was formed as a vehicle through which joint planning, coordination, funding and accountability could be implemented.[38]

These cooperative actions in the Consultation of 1954 and the formation of the Joint Commission on Campus Christian Life would surely have pleased former secretary of University Work, Joseph C. Todd. Year after year he had implored for such cooperation and coordination in his annual reports. The Board of Education had become impoverished during the Depression, and even by 1955 there was a shortage of funds and personnel to carry out the vision of ministry which was carried by the Board. Nonetheless, the events described above are indications of gradual recovery of financial strength and continuing evidence of an inner resolve to relate to the major arenas of higher education—which for the Board of Higher Education—included campus ministry.

In 1956, the earlier recommendation concerning a name change finally occurred. The Student Workers Association, which had been established in 1946, changed its name to the Fellowship of Campus Ministers. These Disciple campus ministers from across the country continued to meet annually. The meetings provided an important sense of identity for this small group of Disciples ministers who were in a specialized ministry of the church. A review of *The Student Worker Bulletins* of that period indicate that some of the most prominent Disciples leaders visited and lectured at the annual meetings. The annual meeting fulfilled several important functions. First, it provided dialogue between the campus ministers and the leaders of the denomination, encouraging a flow of information from the campus to the larger church, and from other manifestations of the church to campus ministers. Second, it symbolized that campus ministry "belonged" in this connectional system, by affirming both the persons involved and the work which they were carrying out. Third, it provided an opportunity for study and reflection about the goals and purposes of the campus ministry in a changing time. Fourth, it provided a time and place for this small band of individuals to share with one another their perils, problems, and progress in the ministry on the campus, thus broadening the perspectives of all.

In retrospect, that period from 1945-1960 was a time of unprecedented growth in the numbers of people enrolled and involved in higher education. It was a time when the church was growing. New churches were established in the suburbs as the nation witnessed the "flight from the city" and the development of suburbia. The positive image of students stemming from the post World War II euphoria and the rapid growth of campus ministry led to an enchantment within the Church for this ministry. By some standards, this was the golden age of campus ministry.

What were the factors contributing to this image of the golden age of campus ministry? There was a spirit of ebullience within the church. World War II had ended, the United States had emerged as a major world power. It was a time of expansive growth for the church, as new congregations sprang up, and new modern buildings were erected. It was a time of major expansion in higher education. It was a period when campus ministry had gained in the number of full-time professionals, and when students were responsive to the programs of campus ministry.

The prevailing expectations for campus ministry in that era were less complex than would be the case in the future. The term "student worker" carries a lot of weight in defining the population targeted for ministry. Although some leaders had a larger vision for campus ministry—the concept of student work prevailed. Furthermore, the work was denominationally oriented. The concept of providing nurture in the Christian faith for Disciples students during their college years continued to be the dominant purpose of campus ministry. This singularity of purpose naturally excluded from serious consideration other aspects of campus ministry. From this perspective then, there was lesser possibility that campus ministry would be seen by many within the church as controversial. It was a time of general agreement and consensus about the goals and purposes of campus ministry in every area of church life—from the campus, the local church, the state missionary societies, and the national agencies.

Still, the seeds of discontent were present even then. The church could not afford to continue the proliferation of denominational centers and foundations on every campus. Increasingly, those involved in campus work were catching the vision of a united church—working toward Christian ends—rather than denominations serving sectarian purposes. As those involved in campus ministry grew in sophistication and wisdom through their experience, the larger issues of higher education demanded their attention as the proper focus for ministry. In this sense, albeit unwittingly, campus ministry had served as a research arm of the church in the discovery of a larger ministry. The campus had provided a laboratory for cooperative experimentation which led to a reconceptualization of the entire campus community as the proper object of ministry, and the issues of higher education as the proper subject from the Christian point of view. Furthermore, as campus ministers and students during this era struggled with the theological questions of the church's role in working toward social justice in the larger society, the groundwork was being formed for a new approach to campus ministry which would develop in the future.

Campus Ministry in Canada: The United Church of Christ

As these events were transpiring in the United States, campus ministry was just getting underway in Canada. To be sure, Canadian students had joined with students from the United States in joint ventures, and as participants in student associations and ecumenical events. However, "the United Church of Canada first became involved in campus ministry in 1955"[39] In its beginning, Dr. Harold Young, Secretary of the Board of Colleges and Secondary Schools, assumed responsibility for the chaplaincy in the United Church and in the Canadian Council of Churches. Although beginning at a later date, it is interesting to note the parallel concerns between these two countries regarding ministry in higher education. Dr. Young reported in 1957 that ministry to university students was likely to become one of the urgent priorities of the church. Following his death in 1958, his successor, Dr. Harold Vaughn, became responsible for chaplaincy. There were at that time four chaplaincies located at the University of British Columbia, University of Alberta, Dalhousie University and University of Western Ontario.[40]

In his first report to the Board of Colleges, 1961, Dr. Vaughan described the campus chaplains as one valuable way in which the church could have visible expression in the university's life. He claimed that:

> These chaplains should give oversight and pastoral counseling to students from the United Church of Christ but should also devote time to the whole student body in co-operation with the Student Christian Movement to preserve the ecumenicity of approach to which the church is committed. He also encouraged chaplains to try to teach a course on religion on the campus.[41]

Such language would have seemed familiar to the Disciples leaders who worked to establish campus ministry in the United States, for in this dual emphasis on teaching religion and providing pastoral care for students, we find a summary of the Disciples aspirations for the church's ministry to the campus.

Para-Church movements and the rise of the cults

No discussion of campus ministry would be complete without reference to the emergence of a variety of other expressions of ministry to students. Over the years these have taken a myriad of forms, from the work of independent evangelists to large scale movements and cults which could in themselves be a subject of research. A number of these movements had their beginning in the decade of the 1950s and developed both in numbers and influence in the succeeding years.

Campus Crusade for Christ

The founder of Campus Crusade for Christ was Bill Bright, who was in his final year at Fuller Seminary and a lay member at Hollywood Presbyterian Church when he caught a vision of his future ministry. While studying for a Greek exam in February 1951 he reported:

> Suddenly, without any warning, it was as if I was in the very presence of the Lord. The sense of his glory and greatness was overwhelming. There in just a few brief moments it was as if the Lord laid out the broad brush strokes of a great canvas that embraced the whole world. At this time and in a very definite way, God commanded me to invest my life in helping to fulfill the Great Commission in this generation, specifically through winning and discipling the students of the world for Christ. It was an intoxicating experience. I was filled with joy.[42]

He became convinced that God did not want him to be ordained, but to begin laying the foundation for his new work immediately. The name "Campus Crusade for Christ" was suggested by professor Wilbur Smith, who taught English Bible at Fuller Seminary. The hallmark of the movement which developed from these beginnings is "aggressive evangelism." Crusaders believe that it is their Christian duty to witness to their faith in Christ with anyone who will listen. Bright's emphasis is on evangelism, he leaves the conservation and development of believers to the churches, once a person accepts Christ as Lord through his methodology. Bill Bright had a growing number of volunteers and a burgeoning staff working full time in the movement, when he decided he needed a tool for evangelism which could be used by staff as well as the newly converted to propagate his particular form of evangelism. This led eventually to the development of the four spiritual laws:

> 1) God loves you and offers a wonderful plan for your life. 2) Man is sinful and separated from God. Therefore, he cannot know and experience God's love and plan for his life. 3) Jesus Christ is God's *only* provision for man's sin— through him you can know and experience God's love and plan for your life; and 4) We must individually *receive* Jesus Christ as Savior and Lord; then we can know and experience God's love and plan fo our lives.[43]

Bright also developed a simple plan for evangelizing college students which he called "capturing the campus," a four stage strategy carried out by his professional staff:

> Phase I is *penetration*, in which staff begin to gather students with leadership potential (those with a "heart for God and a teachable attitude"). The goal is usually to establish a twenty-five to forty person nucleus of potential leaders for ministry. *Concentration* is Phase II. Here staff and student leaders saturate one segment of the campus—most often the freshman class—with the gospel in order to effectively raise up the student leadership capable of executing Phase III, which is *saturation* of the total campus community. Phase IV, *continuation*, maintains saturation continually—"keeping Jesus Christ before the entire campus as a live issue requiring a personal decision.[44]

This movement has spread to virtually every campus in the United States, and one of its principal speakers, Josh McDowell, a traveling representative of Campus Crusade, is said to have addressed an estimated 5 million people on over 540 campuses in more than fifty countries over a twelve year period.[45]

This para-church movement has successfully raised millions of dollars in support of Campus Crusade for Christ's evangelistic goals, with one campaign directed at raising one billion dollars in a five year period.[46] Some of this money has come from contributors who are members of the mainline denominations, including the Disciples, some of whom are more enamoured of this type of evangelistic mission than the campus ministry approach of their own denomination.

Navigators

The Navigators are another evangelistic organization which commonly sponsors work on the major state supported universities. Dawson Trotman is credited with being the founder of this movement which approaches evangelism through the memorization of Scripture.

Inter-Varsity Christian Fellowship

Inter-Varsity Christian Fellowship is a student-directed and staff-facilitated movement, which utilizes friendship evangelism. This is a methodology in which

> a believer builds a relationship over a period of time, and after he or she has won the right to be heard, the opportunity to share the gospel in conversation is a natural result.[47]

A usual pattern for this ministry is the formation of small groups for Bible study and fellowship, in dorm rooms and campus apartments. By 1952 such groups could be identified on 200 American Campuses.

Inter-Varsity had its beginnings in the 1800's in Great Britain, spread to Canada, and became established in the United States after World War II. With headquarters in Chicago, the movement has secured financial backing from business, and from supporters in the major Protestant denominations. In 1951, when 1500 students from across the country attended an Inter-Varsity conference in Illinois during the Christmas break, it was noted that only 8 Disciples students were in attendance.[48]

Two of its auxiliaries are the Christian Nurses Fellowship and the Missionary Fellowship. The former establishes fellowship groups among nurses within hospitals and the latter recruits missionaries. Inter-Varsity holds to a biblical literalism and has its strongest appeal among fundamentalists and conservatives and individuals who seek a more authoritarian leadership.[49]

Fellowship of Christian Athletes

The Fellowship of Christian Athletes is, as its name implies, an organization which relates primarily to college athletes for purposes of fellowship and nurturance in the Christian faith. Small groups of athletes meet on a regular basis for Bible study and for personal testimony concerning their perception of the power of God at work in their lives. Frequently the membership in this group tends to be theologically on the conservative side.

Each para-church movement holds a particular focus which serves as the organizing principle with its distinguising elements and objectives. College students have been regularly confronted with the claims of these organizations and many have chosen to join the movement, at least for a time. Often the demands of discipleship are presented in simplistic terms, and complex issues of faith and action are reduced to simple answers. Younger students, particularly those away from home for the first time, may be vulnerable to the "authoritarian" claims which are so often the hallmark of a movement with a singular mission. Critics have charged that students who become active in these movements do not go on to active church membership.

Campus ministers around the country were frequently enjoined by students, confused and bewildered by the competing claims of the various para-church movements, to help them in the struggle to sort out the vital faith questions. This ministry would become even more important in the decades to follow as cults, both Eastern and Western, drew millions of followers in the 1960s and 1970s.

Summary

The period from 1945-1960 brought significant changes in higher education and in campus ministry. College enrollments swelled with the returning veterans, declined in the early 1950s, and then began a growth spurt which would continue in the decades ahead. More college students were older and a higher percentage were married than ever before. These factors, along with the threats of McCarthyism, the Cold War, and competition with the Soviet Union sparked by the launching of Sputnik, contributed to a serious minded student body. Colleges and universities were busy expanding facilities and hiring faculty and staff in response to these growing numbers.

This was a period of growth for the church as well and the growth was reflected in the establishment of new student foundations and campus ministry centers at public universities. The numbers of full-time professional campus ministers grew from about 200 in 1938 to 1,000 in 1953, then doubled by 1963. Such major growth reflected the growing commitment of the church to provide support and funding for work on the campus. This was a time when most campus programs had a strong denominational identification and only minimal ecumenical cooperation.

There was a clear transition in the Disciples approach as they moved away from the Bible Chair model and toward the student work model. The national organization known as Disciples Student Fellowship flourished during this period, and local Student Fellowship groups sprang up on nearly every campus where Disciples students attended in any numbers. Professionals who had accepted a call to work full-time on the campus on behalf of the church also organized a national fellowship known as the Student Workers Association. The United Christian Missionary Society and the Board of Higher Education developed shared governance for campus ministry through the Joint Commission on Campus Christian Life. This period of enthusiastic support and burgeoning growth contributed to the perspective that this was the golden age of campus ministry.

Yet, there was already a yeasty leaven at work. The Student Workers Association became the Fellowship of Campus Ministers, signifying a broadening concept of ministry. Disciples students were growing more interested in the concerns which they held in common with students of other denominations such as relating the Christian faith to one's life as a student and moving beyond the concern for worship and fellowship to a concern for carrying out the implications of the gospel for social justice. In the decade ahead this ferment for change would continue, and like "new wine in old wineskins" would radically affect the fabric of support and structures for implementation of the church's ministry on the campus.

References

1. Riesman, David, *On Higher Education*. San Francisco: Jossey-Bass Publishing Co., 1980. pp. 44-45.
2. Henry, David D., *Challenges Past, Challenges Present*. San Francisco: Jossey-Bass Publishers, 1975. p. 59.
3. *Ibid.* p. 60.
4. *Ibid.* p. 63.
5. Riesman, *Op. cit.* p. 47.
6. Henry, *Op. cit.* pp. 66-68.
7. Riesman, *Op. cit.* p. 50.
8. *Ibid.* p. 53.
9. Henry, *Op. cit.* p. 71.
10. *Ibid.* p. 72.
11. *Ibid.* p. 90.
12. *Ibid.* pp. 92-93.
13. *Ibid.* p. 101.
14. Riesman, *Op. cit.* p. 58.
15. Henry, *Op. cit.* p. 120.
16. Smith, Seymour, *Op. cit.* p. 75.
17. Underwood, Kenneth, *The Church, The University, and Social Policy: The Danforth Study of Campus Ministries*, Volume I. Middletown, Connecticut: Wesleyan University Press, 1969, p. 75.
18. *Ibid.* p. 76.
19. Personal Communication with Dr. John E. McCaw, June, 1986. (Unpublished)
20. "Annual Report" United Christian Missionary Society, *1946 Year Book* Christian Church (Disciples of Christ) pp. 49-50.
21. "Annual Report" United Christian Missionary Society, *1947 Year Book* Christian Church (Disciples of Christ) p. 50.
22. *Ibid.* p. 50.
23. "Annual Report" United Christian Missionary Society, *1948 Year Book* Christian Church (Disciples of Christ) p. 64.
24. McCaw, John E. "The Student's Claim on the Church" *World Call*. May, 1946. p. 12.
25. "Annual Report" United Christian Missionary Society *1950 Year Book* Christian Church (Disciples of Christ) p. 67.
26. "Annual Report" Board of Higher Education, *1950 Year Book* Christian Church (Disciples of Christ) p. 79.
27. "Annual Report" United Christian Missionary Society, *1952 Year Book* Christian Church (Disciples of Christ) p. 169.
28. "Annual Report" United Christian Missionary Society, *1953 Year Book* Christian Church (Disciples of Christ) p. 191.
29. *The Student Work Bulletin*, Published by the Student Work Office of the Department of Religious Education of the United Christian Missionary Society, Indianapolis. March, 1952. p. 4.
30. *The Student Work Bulletin*, November, 1952. p. 2.
31. "Annual Report" United Christian Missionary Society, *1953 Year Book* Christian Church (Disciples of Christ) p. 192.
32. *The Student Work Bulletin*, November, 1952, p. 7.
33. *Ibid.* p. 9
34. *Ibid.* pp. 16-17.

35. *The Student Work Bulletin*, April, 1953. p. 17.
36. *The Student Work Bulletin*, May, 1954. p. 13.
37. "Annual Report" United Christian Missionary Society *1954 Year Book* Christian Church (Disciples of Christ) p. 214.
38. "Annual Report" Board of Higher Education *1955 Year Book* Christian Church (Disciples of Christ) p. 27.
39. "Campus Ministry: The United Church Story." p. 1.
40. *Ibid.* p. 2.
41. *Ibid.* p. 2.
42. Quebedeaus, Richard, *I Found It!* (The Story of Bill Bright and Campus Crusade) (San Francisco: Harper and Rowe, Publishers) 1979. p. 17.
43. *Ibid.* p. 97.
44. *Ibid.* p. 126.
45. *Ibid.* p. 128.
46. *Ibid.* p. 174.
47. *Ibid.* p. 93.
48. "The Inter-Varsity Christian Fellowship" *The Student Work Bulletin*. Indianapolis: March, 1952. p. 1.
49. *Ibid.* p. 1-2.

Chapter **3**

THE RISE OF CAMPUS MINISTRY AND THE SEEDS OF DISCONTENT (1960-1970)

In the decade of the 1960s there were decisive changes on many fronts in the church's approach to its mission on the state supported campuses. The "student work" which had blossomed in the post-World War II era, evolved into "campus ministry." Individual denominational work on the campuses developed into the ecumenically cooperative work of multiple denominations. State Commissions on Campus Ministry were formed to coordinate the cooperative work at the regional level. Denominations joined to form United Ministries in Higher Education and staff carrying portfolios for their denomination in campus ministry formed a voluntary network to serve the burgeoning needs of campus ministers, local governing boards, and state commissions. National organizations of students like the Disciples Student Fellowship (DSF) merged with others to form a national ecumenical student movement.

Within the Disciples network, the original vision of Joseph C. Todd seemed to be at last taking form. His prayer of lament, "How long O Lord?" over the division of Christendom and the divisiveness of what he then called his own "brotherhood," in addressing the issues related to higher education seemed to be finding fulfillment in the 1960s. The United Christian Missionary Society and the Board of Higher Education discovered new ways to work cooperatively in public higher education. Most importantly, the Disciples, advocates for Christian unity since their inception as a restoration movement, were able to provide leadership in the formation of a new ecumenical approach to ministry in higher education.

The ground work for many of the changes which occurred in the 1960s had been laid in the previous decade. The Disciples, for example, enjoyed the largest attendance ever at the Disciples Student Fellowship Ecclesia in the late 1950s. In 1956, over 520 students had attended the Ecclesia at Estes Park, Colorado. At that meeting they entertained a proposal that the national Disciples Student Fellowship (DSF) consider uniting with several other national student movements. One year later, in August 1957, in an assembly with the theme: "What Are You Willing to Die For?" the Disciples Student

Fellowship voted that this organization should die, and that its membership should unite with three other similar national organizations to form the United Campus Christian Fellowship. The other three denominations were the Evangelical United Brethren, the Presbyterian Church U.S.A., and the United Church of Christ. At this meeting, the proposed merger was scheduled to take place in August 1960.

On April 1, 1959, Parker Rossman resigned and Robert Huber was appointed to the position of National Director of Campus Christian Life. Huber had been serving as campus minister in Indiana, and had formerly been president of the Disciples Fellowship of Campus Ministers. It was agreed upon by the participating parties that the general administration of the National United Campus Christian Fellowship (UCCF) would be carried out by the Director of Campus Christian Life. It was fitting that the initial organizing leadership for this fledgling ecumenical student movement should be provided by the Disciples.[1]

In accord with their previous plans, the Disciples Student Fellowship Ecclesis convened at Stephens College, Columbia, Missouri, and voted on August 26, 1960 to merge into the new fellowship (UCCF). There were no dissenting votes in the uniting assembly in which 700 students, faculty and campus ministers voted to accept the articles of union. Lynn Jondahl, a student at Yale Divinity School, was elected president and expressed the convictions of the new organization in an open letter to the parent communions:

> The negotiations and planning of this union were motivated by the conviction that if we are to carry out the responsibility of the Christian faith we must respond to the unity which is in Christ and to which he calls us.[2]

In the organizing statement of the assembly, the students claimed:

> We, the delegated representatives of the Disciples Student Fellowship of the Christian Churches (Disciples of Christ), of the Student Fellowship Council of the Evangelical United Brethren Church, of the United Student Fellowship of the United Church of Christ, of the Westminster Student Fellowship of the United Presbyterian Church, U.S.A., believing that we are called to unite our campus Christian movements to carry out his mission in our campus life, do now declare ourselves to be one movement, and do take as our name the United Campus Christian Fellowship.[3]

At the time of its inception, the merger was considered a unification of national student organizations, and it was expected that at the local level, denominational student groups would maintain their identity, as is reflected in this comment from the Disciples *Student Work Bulletin*:

> It should be held in mind that there is no recommended pattern for unity on campus. Every local situation is so different that students and churches in the college town must decide locally the types of student organizations which will make possible the most effective campus witness and the reaching of the largest

number of our students. Except upon small campuses we do *NOT* recommend merging DSF groups with other groups. On most campuses we need to increase, not decrease, the number of DSF or comparable groups, in order to reach more students. We do hope, of course, that a broadly cooperative strategy and program can be developed eventually on each campus.[4]

Yet, the drive for unity was powerful. The United Campus Christian Fellowship (UCCF) began with the conviction that the mission of the church demanded a single united witness on the campus. Its founders envisioned a future of ministry in which concerns for denominational prominence, sectarian divisiveness, and competitive programs no longer prevailed. The language of the UCCF statement is reminiscent of the language of earlier Disciples documents in which sectarianism was put away for the essential plea for the unity of all Christians:

> We affirm that in the church of Christ we are members of one body, and we believe we are called to the organic union of our campus Christian movements as a more adequate expression of our unity in the Church, that we may better proclaim the gospel in campus and community life.[5]

It was this theological conviction about the essential oneness of the church and its mission that led to the UCCF covenant.

There were practical realities which reinforced the impetus for cooperation and unity in providing ministry in higher education. Church leaders were also responsive to the changing campus milieu and began to conceive of a new and more comprehensive approach to ministry. By 1960, with the projected growth in higher education, the impossibility of every denomination providing a student foundation on every campus was clearly recognized. Furthermore, if campus work continued to be denominationally oriented, it was also clear that the complex needs and populations of the modern campus would never be addressed. The experience of the past had led to a new vision of the future. In the new future, ministry would not be limited to the undergraduate population, but be extended to the campus community, including graduate students, faculty and administrators. This development had been affirmed by Disciples leaders in the Joint Commission on Campus Christian Life at the time of its official charter in July 1957 when it was claimed that the concept of student work was not an adequate expression of the church's mission— that it must be enlarged to include all components of the campus.

Verlyn Barker's words are eloquently descriptive of the changing tide in the church's ministry in higher education in the early 1960s as he comments on the broadening vision of campus ministry:

> No longer is the term "student work" descriptive of the ministry, nor is the term "student worker" accurate in the portrayal of the role of campus ministers within this ministry and movement. The campus minister is no longer the "director" of the ministry; he [sic] is not hired to "do" the ministry but rather is the one essentially responsible for enabling the Christian community as a

whole to be engaged in the ministry. His task is that of an "enabler" or that of the teaching elder. He assists by preparing others for their mission in their daily life and work. Rather than drawing university personnel into "programs" in the belief that this is the manner in which they witness to their faith, he recognized that university persons are responding to their Christian vocation when they are engaged honestly and openly in study, research, and teaching, and when they are faithful in expressing the power of God's love and reconciliation in their relationships with others. The campus minister seeks to be the theological teacher for those earnestly seeking an understanding of the Christian faith as it is addressed to the ultimate questions being raised in study and research[6]

In a further development of this concept, Donald R. Heiges' article "The Church's Ministry on Campus" appeared in the Disciples *Student Work Bulletin* discussing the mission, objectives and methodology of campus ministry. He claimed that the mission of the church was to minister within the academic community to all participants, both Christians and non-Christian. He saw the basic objective of ministry as the "integration of a person's total experience in terms of the Christian faith."[7] He envisioned the role of the professional campus minister as "the equipment of the saints" for the fulfillment of their task in the university (Ephesians 4:12 and 6:15) This would employ: 1) the provision of the ministry of Word and Sacrament, 2) the ministry of pastoral care, and, 3) the ministry of teaching religion and biblical studies.[8]

With the launching of UCCF, there was a corresponding vision of a new type of ministry, broadly conceived, to encompass every person on the campus within its scope. In this new vision, the campus minister would work in cooperation with the local congregations in a shared ministry with and for the campus community. It was envisioned that on some smaller campus, there might be put one campus minister, yet he/she would represent the mission of the four denominations in UCCF. On larger campuses, with multiple staff, the plan would allow for a staff vacancy to be filled with the most qualified candidate, regardless of denominational affiliation. At the regional level, personnel policies would be developed applicable for the four participating denominations. Policies regarding the nature of campus ministry would be made jointly. At the national level, it was expected that the UCCF Commission for Church Relations would become the representative advisory committee for the higher education agencies of the four participating denominations.[9]

The development of cooperation symbolized by the formation of UCCF was a marked departure from the philosophy and strategy of campus ministry in its earlier years. Each denomination had developed its plans for campus ministry in the light of its own goals, the availability of funds and personnel, independently of other denominations. In the decade of the 1950s most major denominations had increased their investments in campus ministry, and in many cases the number of campus ministers nearly doubled during this period.

However, it became increasingly apparent to denominational leaders that the churchs' funds for expansion could not match the pace of rapidly expanding enrollment. In the early 1960s the first wave of the "baby boom" began to arrive on campus. Enrollment increased dramatically from about 3,570,000 in 1960 to 7,413,000 in 1970.[10] The doubling of enrollment in a ten year period placed incredible strains upon the educational system. There was a rapid increase in community colleges and enrollment in these two year schools first reached the one million mark in 1964.[11] In addition to the increase in numbers of students, the kind of students changed, as the basic assumption developed that every young person should have a college education, even though many students might have been more successful in a different kind of educational environment, or at a later time in their development. As Douglas Hallet reported:

> Fully 60% of those who enter our colleges and universities fail to graduate. They leave school frustrated, unequipped for the jobs our technology is providing. Many end up unemployed or underemployed. . . . Many of those who do graduate from college would have been happier doing something else.[12]

Furthermore, there was an increase in transfer students, as the college student became more mobile, and as more community college transfer students went on to the four year schools. As the enrollment expanded rapidly, there was insuffient housing for students on campus, and more and more students lived off-campus, becoming "commuters" and remaining on campus only long enough for classes and library services and then returning to home or job. More of the students were older, and more of the students were married during this era. Larger numbers of students gained entrance into graduate programs, thus prolonging their excursion in higher education.

As early as 1962, the Joint Commission on Campus Life had gone on record claiming that the issues of ministry in higher education were too big for a single denomination.[13] The Joint Commission began to develop materials to assist local campus ministries in a process of self-study to evaluate their needs and programs and to enlarge the scope of ministry. The Joint Commission secured the cooperation of the Christian Board of Publication in providing a grant in the form of books to twenty campuses to support the development of a library with campus ministry resource material. In those years there was modest support available from the Commission to help establish new campus ministry centers. By mid-point in the decade the Board of Higher Education reported that, in the previous church year, the Disciples had given $486,177.00 through national, state and local sources.[14] Yet, in spite of this, such efforts began to appear as a small drop in a very large bucket.

Fresh enthusiasm for Christian unity, a growing perception of the enormity of the task in higher education, and the development of new forms of ministry all contributed to the excitement of these changing years. As these wheels of change began to roll, other factors contributed to the growing momentum.

Campus ministers had been encouraged by their parent bodies to seek out arenas for the development of a "specialized" and "experimental" ministry on behalf of the church:

> First of all the experiment would in each case attempt to make the Campus Minister (while not sacrificing his regular work and other interests) a *specialist* in this one type of campus work. This would be done by providing him [sic] with all available materials on the subject, by taking him to special conferences, short courses and leadership training courses on the subject, by assisting him to visit campuses where significant work in this area may be underway, and by encouraging him to reflect upon and write about these various experiences he has off-campus and experiments he undertakes upon his own campus. In some cases the "experiments" would be special efforts the campus minister would undertake in his own personal work, in other cases they would be experiments involving the student group, the church, perhaps other student groups and churches and perhaps once in a while the entire campus community.[15]

Such experiments and experiences led campus ministers themselves to confront the theological task of the church in facing and addressing the issues of higher education and the issues of social justice in new ways.

Furthermore, in changing times, the university now provided many of the student services which campus ministries had provided earlier, and the older and more serious students had needs and interests which did not coincide with the type of programming which had traditionally been offered. Still another factor leading to change came from attempts to develop new forms of ministry with graduate students and faculty. Campus ministers commonly discovered that the larger questions of integrating "Christian" concerns in higher education were particularly interesting to faculty and graduate students—somewhat less so for undergraduates. Programs and projects which were offered cooperatively by the participating denominations and which were relevant to student needs and interests evoked enthusiastic participation from students. At the same time strictly denominational or sectarian concerns and programs were not catching their interests.

Campus ministers who experienced the satisfaction of cooperative work with colleagues from other denominations in addressing the tasks of this specialized ministry on the campus frequently felt they had more in common with their campus ministry colleagues than they did with their own denominational colleagues whose focus was primarily in the local congregation. Such positive experiences provided a willing propensity for campus ministers to foster the development of new ecumenical constellations of cooperative work on the campus.

National Campus Ministers Association

In June 1964, the last meeting of the Disciples Fellowship of Campus Ministers was held in a Joint Campus Ministry Convocation with colleagues from other denominations who were participating partners in United Campus

Christian Fellowship. The twenty-five Disciples ministers in attendance voted to merge their organization the following year with the others, to form the National Campus Ministers Association. (NCMA) Thus, in June 1965, the first annual meeting of the NCMA was held in East Lansing, Michigan, immediately following the new staff seminar. The American Baptist campus ministers joined the other four denominations in the NCMA at this time.[16]

In a parallel development, the National Association of College and University Chaplains (NACUC) was formed to provide a similar opportunity for fellowship and sharing of ideas for college and university chaplains on the private and church supported colleges and universities.

Another significant development in ecumenical cooperation took form between 1964-66. After consultation and strategy planning, the four denominations who were participants in UCCF covenanted together to form a new national organization which they called United Ministries in Higher Education (UMHE). Two of the earliest developments in this cooperative venture were:

> 1) a sharing of field staff assignments by area rather than by denominational affiliation, and 2) a common personnel procedure and office for campus ministry placement.[17]

During that year, further consideration was given to the deployment of national staff for the greatest efficiency and the most effective deployment of the financial resources of the participating denominations. The staff of the Disciples Joint Commission on Campus Christian Life noted that "15 Disciple state organizations have linked their state campus ministry administration to a state United Ministry Commission."[18]

The early years of UMHE were rocky going. Not only was this new organization struggling to develop itself as a servant of the parent organizations and to develop its mission and ministry in higher education, it was seeking to do so within a governing body, a National Commission composed (in 1969) of twenty church members representing the denominations and twenty public sector members, advocates of minorities and the "oppressed" in society. Streamlining the organization was a task for the 70s.

The Board of Higher Education Takes on Campus Ministry

By 1968, after careful study and negotiation with the United Christian Missionary Society, on January 1, the Board of Higher Education of the Christian Church (Disciples of Christ) assumed administrative responsibility for the national program of Ministries in Higher Education. The board also created a new commission to oversee this branch of the work, the Commission on Ministries in Higher Education. This commission was charged with the responsibility of advice and counsel concerning the Board's participation in UMHE. In this reorganization, Robert Huber left the United Christian Missionary Society, and joined the staff of the Board of Higher Education.[19]

1968 was an eventful year in many regards. In that year the United Campus Christian Fellowship (UCCF) voted to dissolve itself to become a part of the University Christian Movement. In 1969, at a national University Christian Movement student conference in Cincinnati, during the peak period of the student protest movement, the University Christian Movement voted itself out of existence and the official "student movement" was suspended.

United Ministries in Higher Education

Also, in 1968, only a few years after the original four denominations had signed the covenant to form UMHE, several more denominations elected to participate. By 1968 seven more had joined, including the American Baptist Churches, the Church of the Brethren, the Episcopal Church, the Moravian Church (Northern Province), the Presbyterian Church, U.S., the Reformed Church in America, and the United Methodist Church (which had merged with the Evangelical United Brethren). This new constellation in United Ministries in Higher Education included all major Protestant denominations except the Southern Baptist Church and the Lutheran Churches.

The decision of these denominations at the national level to work together ecumenically is not to be construed as a "top down" movement. The fact is, the "grass roots" movement toward ecumenism in some regions, and on particular campuses, was several paces ahead. Some local ministries had forged new agreements to share resources, buildings, and staff in united or at least cooperative ministries. On some campuses, Lutherans and Roman Catholics also participated in united and cooperative ministries. Some states and regions had already begun to form state commissions which were charged by the participating denominations with the task of planning, oversight, and evaluation of all campus ministry within the region. In many cases denominational funding flowed into the state commission treasury which allocated money and distributed it to each of the local campus boards.

At the national level, UMHE formed a policy board with denominational representation and included persons with background and knowledge from the church, the campus ministry, the university, and the public.

The denominational bodies participating in United Ministries in Higher Education began with the idea that both theologically and practically it was desirable to approach the campus ministry in a united way. This would involve sharing ideas generated in research, the strategic deployment of staff, and creating together those national programs which none might attempt alone, through contributions to a common budget, and using denominationally contributed staff as much as possible.

The UMHE denominations convenanted together in providing field services to existing campus ministry units around the country. Each denomination agreed to provide "loaned staff" to perform such functions. These individuals would form a partnership in which each accepted an assignment for a geographic area in which he/she would provide major responsibility. Such resourcing activities might include consultation to local boards and state commissions, assistance in the search for qualified campus ministers as vacancies arose, and campus reviews in which careful study and analysis were applied to shape a new future in campus ministry appropriate to the findings on a particular campus.

The parent denominations charged UMHE with the task of drawing the church into dialogue with key persons and issues in higher education. It was hoped that through such dialogue, the denominational bodies could keep their constituent members informed and aware of the current developments in academia.

Certain areas of concern for the church in higher education were identified as appropriate arenas for research and development at the national level. Included in the list were: internationalization, urbanization, health and human values, generation issues, and community colleges:

> Internationalization: To engage in analysis and study of the main trends in international education; to isolate the primary issues and concerns that UMHE should confront and to define priorities among the issues; to evaluate the ongoing international program of UMHE and to recommend new projects.

> Urbanization: To relate UMHE to urban studies and ministries and to propose strategy for urban ministries in higher education.

> Health and Human Values: To identify the new human problems in the context of the health professions and their services; to develop methods of clarifying and assisting in solving the problems and to develop change in both the professional attitude and public awareness in relation to the problems.

> Generation Issues: To explore ways of working with alienated youth and to create "generational exposures" for commission members, campus ministers, national and regional staff.

> Community Colleges: To develop resources for state commissions in reference to ministry and relationships with community colleges.[20]

Task forces were formed around each of these to do research, to investigate new possibilities for effective ministry, to implement new programming, and to pass these learnings along to the UMHE network through its communication channels.

Although by no means a perfect vehicle for carrying out ministry in higher education, nevertheless, the formation of UMHE was a significant step forward. It was a sign that a narrow denominational approach was no longer an adequate approach. It announced the dawning of a new era of ecumenical cooperation. It shattered the first layer of isolation which kept the campus ministry separate from the total mission and ministry of the church.

This author served on the UMHE Policy Board as a Disciples representative, and for a period of two years, had the privilege of serving as president for the

Policy Board. Research task forces in national UMHE did in fact provide useful discoveries and insights which could be used at the state and local level.

Health and Human Values

One prominent example was the usefulness of the Health and Human Values Task Force. Under the able leadership of Dr. Ronald McNeur, the task force engaged in inquiry into the extent to which medical education included processes in the curriculum intended to develop in members of the health professions a sensitivity and means of responding to the ethical issues in modern medicine. Secondly, it began to investigate the impact of medical research and its applications in the culture. The work of this task force led to the development of resources and methodologies which stimulated the state commissions to initiate special ministries in medical schools within their own region. Furthermore, encouragement was offered to local operating committees situated next to medical schools to explore new avenues of ministry. Such vitally productive work led eventually to the creation of the Society for Health and Human Values, sponsored by UMHE. Campus ministers were among the first to offer courses in medical ethics, provide pastoral care to students in the health professions, and to serve as lay representatives on Human Subjects Review Committees. These ministers formed a new organization known as "Ministers in Medical Education," which in 1987 continues in existence as a sub-group of the Society for Health and Human Values. The author is the current president of MME, which reports a membership of nearly 200. The Society for Health and Human Values has broadened its scope to include a Nurses Association, an Association of Faculty in Medical Humanities, as well as the Ministers in Medical Education group. A number of extremely useful teaching resources and program descriptions have been produced by the Society and distributed nationwide.

Community College Task Force

The Community College Task Force led to the founding of the community college ministry through encouraging state commissions and local operating committees to take a serious look at providing ministry, usually in conjunction with the local congregations, in serving community colleges. The Community College Task Force undertook research centered upon the community colleges and the most effective ways for the church to approach this unique manifestation of American higher education.

Career Development

Still a third major development growing out of UMHE's research and development was the Career Development Project. Rev. Richard Bolles provided the initial staff resourcing for this program. This noteworthy effort has been extremely valuable to campus ministry. One of the functions which the churches have long expected of the campus minister is that he or she will discuss vocational, professional, or career choices with students from the home churches. Although interested, most campus ministers had very little expertise in assisting students in this way, and too frequently, the colleges and universities were ill-equipped to provide effective help. Richard Bolles developed a training process which many campus ministers have used to develop their competency in this arena, and it has grown to become nationally recognized as the best program in the United States for the training of career counselors. This program has also developed valuable resources, under Bolles authorship, such as *What Color is My Parachute?*, *The Three Boxes of Life*, and *Life Work Design*.

The Trend Continues: Bible Chairs Decline; Religion Departments Grow

Another important change in the late 1960s was the fact that the work of the Bible Chairs had declined in prominence and popularity. Governance and funding had been released from the Disciples' United Christian Missionary Society, and was assumed by local operating boards or trustees. On the other hand, the climate had become much more favorable for incorporating religion in the universities. By the mid-1960s there had been a persistent growth in the numbers of universities which offered courses in religion. As legal doctrines concerning the separation of church and state became clarified, it became possible to establish departments of religion and departments of religious studies, free of any sectarian objectives. Kenneth Underwood commented on this phenomenon in his study (1969):

> In the eyes of students who take work in religion departments, the rapid growth of these departments is an important factor in developing a body of liberal arts graduates well grounded in the history and theology of all major religions and in the emergence of a liberal, ecumenical church leadership. Ninety per cent of the public universities and colleges now offer some courses in religion; increasing numbers of private universities and colleges are revamping their programs in religious studies.
>
> . . . In contrast to several decades ago, theology, sociology and psychology of religion, intellectual and religious historical studies are increasingly regarded in the general faculty as sound, growing, respected disciplines, and not as anachronistic throwbacks to another era. They are seen by their chief advocates (like Robert Michaelsen) as dealing with questions of the nature of the "total culture" and of integrative and dissident forces in it, with the relationship of disciplines in a morality of knowledge and so on—themes which have been neglected by other academic specialization.[23]

This was a far different situation than the era when the Disciples entered ministry in public higher education via the route of the Bible Chair movement. At that time, the interpretation of legal doctrine directing the separation of church and state did not allow for university sponsored departments of religion. In the new age, the university began taking a more prominent role in providing for the scholarly study of religion, the comparison of the religious traditions, and teaching the English Bible as literature.

Having traced the key developments in the Disciples approach to campus ministry during this period of the 1960s, and noting the changes at the local campuses, the formation of state commissions, and the formation of UMHE as an instrument of the participating denominations in carrying out campus ministry, it is important to integrate one's view of such changes in the cultural context of the times.

Key Issues in the Culture Affecting Campus Ministry

There were prominent changes in American society in general during this decade, as well as in the student culture. The 1960s have been characterized as the period of student disaffection with higher education and the values of the culture. Growing use of television to provide news coverage of sit-ins, protest movement speeches and demonstrations brought this picture of unrest into the homes of millions of Americans. Whereas in the past, the older generation tolerated the antics of the "college age" generation with a spirit of benevolent indulgence or tolerant amusement, the 1960s brought a radical change. The sight of long haired youth, dressed in "hippie" clothing, smoking pot, cheering speakers who denigrated the traditional American values, and marching in demonstrations against the "establishment" insulted and inflamed the sensitivities of many in their parent's generation.

Institutions of higher education were caught in a cross fire of criticism. Universities were criticized by the students for contaminated investment policies, for irrelevant courses, and for promoting the military-industrial complex by the very nature of teaching and research. On the other hand, colleges and universities were criticized by older generations for soft policies which tolerated such demonstrations of disaffection, and for leftist faculty who even encouraged students into open rebellion and revolutionary actions.

This was a crucial time as well for the church, its vision of ministry, and its relationships within higher education. Campus ministers were very much involved in student activities during these tumultous times on campuses throughout the country, corresponding to the expanded role of campus ministry. When it appeared to some within the church that campus ministers were involved in student disaffection, and possibly encouraging it, there developed a backlash of resentment and anger which led in some cases to radical cutbacks in the support of such ministries. This was an age of ferment and change, of new wine and new wineskins—a time in which the seeds of discontent were sown. It was a time in which, to use a biblical metaphor, the "tares and the wheat" were sown together. The time of separating the wheat from the tares would be a future issue.

There were many important developments in the culture during this decade, but the following issues will be examined because of their special relevance to and impact upon the church and its witness to the campus. The civil rights movement had a powerful ramifications for change upon the campus, as did the rise of the Black movement. The Vietnam War intensified, resulting in the intensification of the anti-war movement and the organization of student protest movements across the nation. Life-style issues were more prominent than in the 1950s, heightened by more liberal attitudes toward issues such as sexual relationships, abortion, and the use of drugs. The 1960s saw the rise of the feminist movement and the decline of the last vestiges of the parental like role of the university. It was the age of free expression, the Free University Movement, freeway marches, frisbees and flower-children.

Civil Rights Movement

The 1960s saw the rise of the civil rights movement. In February 1960, four courageous Black students staged a sit-in at a segregated restaurant in Greensboro, North Carolina. The four were students at North Carolina Agricultural and Technical College. Their act of bravery caught the attention and spirit of the college generation. Non-violent demonstrations began to spread from city to city across the nation as young people with awakened conscience gave support to their Black brothers and sisters. Other Black students followed the lead of one heroic Black woman who refused to sit in the back of the bus where Blacks had been forced to sit for years in segregated areas of the country. As awareness of these protest movement grew, the cause of human rights caught the attention and the loyalty of many in the student generation.

Youth who had been reared in the church were particularly responsive to the issues of civil rights. They had grown up with admonitions of the Christian faith to "love thy neighbor," the parable of the Good Samaritan, and the example of Jesus who both taught and embodied the spirit of universal love. Many of these same young people who had learned their lessons well in church and Sunday School now saw the opportunity to put their faith into action by working for changes within the culture. In fact, not to act in the face of prejudice, oppression and racial bigotry was exposed more radically than before as sheer hypocrisy.

Campus ministers who had effectively established relationships with key leaders in the student body frequently found themselves called upon to interpret the meaning of the Christian gospel and its demands for creative action in the face of racism. Campus ministers were called upon by activist-students to speak at rallys and to organize campus groups for voter registration activities in the South. Some parents were not pleased with such events on the campus, nor with their own children's participation, nor with the involvement of the campus minister in such activities.

For over 300 years Blacks had not been accepted into the mainstream of America:

In the mid-1960's, this "bondage of the spirit" was broken, and there emerged among black students a deep and intense awareness and consciousness that a Black culture existed. They came to realize that Africa was not a savage land of ignorant people without a civilization; and that black people in American possessed in their own right a history, a life experience, and a world view particularly American, but with roots in Africa rather than in Europe—a culture that could be called "Afro-American."[22]

Black students began to affirm the Black experience, Black pride and Black identity. They also began to realize the need for Black power to continue the struggle now in process against the forces of society which grudgingly gave way to this new beginning.

As the civil rights movement gathered momentum, white students began to learn a great deal from and about Black students as they joined into a common cause to work for social justice. In so doing, these students began to become increasingly aware of white racism, their own, and that of the white society in general. An awakened Black consciousness demanded access and participation in every level of American life. An awakened generation of white students recognized the profound injustices of the past, and demanded an end to white supremacy and the oppression of minorities.

Of course, the civil rights movement was not a Student movement only, but that it involved the entire Black community. Black students formed the Student Nonviolent Coordinating Committee, but the movement involved Black citizens of all ages, and in every part of the country. Dr. Martin Luther King Jr. became the national spokesperson for Black aspirations, and his strategies for overcoming the oppression of racism were based upon a policy of nonviolent tactics.

As the decade began, the Black student movement was peaceful and nonviolent. However, Black students became increasingly impatient with their experiences of the stubborn entrenchment of racist values in the majority culture, and defiant resistance to change. In 1965 Stokely Carmichael led his followers, no longer committed to nonviolence in taking control of the Student Nonviolent Coordinating Committee (SNCC). Increasing numbers of students became more radical in their views concerning change, as they felt the backlash of the white community. Tensions erupted into violence when two young Black students were killed at Jackson State.

In 1968 the National Advisory Commission on Civil Disorders confirmed the allegations which had been made by Black leaders in the findings of their report. A few descriptive terms from that report suffice to summarize the feelings of young Black students which led inevitably to Black student protests.

That Commission found conditions resulting from white racism to be the essential cause of urban disorders. These conditions—"massive concentration of impoverished Negroes," "pervasive discrimination and segregation," and intersection of "segregation and poverty" within "teeming racial ghettos"—are still a vivid and harsh reality to black students and the black masses. In the judgment of that Commission, a number of forces, including "frustrated hopes," "legitimation of violence," and "powerlessness," catalyzed these conditions to produce the disruptions during the summer of 1967. The effects of these disorders and the conditions underlying them have created a new mood among Blacks, especially black youth.[23]

There were at that time, problems related specifically to higher education for the Black community. Proportionately fewer Blacks entered college, and graduated from college, than their white counterparts. In the late 1960s only 58 percent of Black children completed the eighth grade compared to 73 percent of the white children. High school graduates numbered 40 percent of the Black young people, while 62 percent of white youth graduated from high school. Only 22 percent of college age Black youth were enrolled in college compared to 38 percent of the white youth of the same age group. The joint report of the U.S. Census Bureau and the Bureau of Labor and Statistics in 1969 revealed that about one Black male in fourteen age 25-34 had a college education, whereas in the same age group one if five white males claimed a college education.[24]

Half of the Blacks enrolled in college in 1969-70 were attending a predominantly Black college, yet these colleges were among the most impoverished educational institutions in America. To the credit of these institutions, they had survived many hardships and provided a source of hope and access to learning for many who eventually became the Black leaders of their time. Yet, the educational crisis for young Blacks was one of quantity, too few gaining access to higher education—and one of quality, too many Black students attending the poorest and most disadvantaged institutions.

The civil rights movement also expanded to lift up the plight of other minority groups such as Native Americans, Chicanos, and Asians. Campus ministry centers played an important role in providing facilities for meetings and supporting these struggling organizations in efforts to increase the recruitment and retention of minority students.

For the church, seeking to fulfill its mission in the world, here was an arena of social injustice of the most flagrant nature. It would be both false and arrogant to claim that the church provided an adequate response to the problems of racism, or to the injustices which prevented minorities from attaining the quality of education to which they aspired. Yet, the church did respond. On the campus, this response was most often embodied in the personnel and programs of campus ministry. Educational events and opportunities to explore white racism were conducted through the auspices of campus ministry groups. Voter registration projects were among the social action strategies promoted and peopled by ministry leaders and students. Minority campus ministers were more actively recruited and summer internship programs were innovated which gave minority students an opportunity to explore the Christian ministry as a possible career.

The Peace Movement

The world seemed turned upside down for many during the 1960s. Students had for generations been subordinate to their teachers, and particularly after World War II, students had been eager to obtain an education and to take their place in the working world. Furthermore, in the late 1950s, many students had been exceptionally hard working and eager to excel in the sciences in the post-Sputnik era. Only a few years earlier students had been unwaveringly loyal to their country and its causes. Now, all of that had changed.

The civil rights movement, was only a part of the student protest phenomena in the 1960s and early 1970s. The peace movement was another important ingredient. Fear of nuclear arms and the perception that the mightiest nation in the world was illegally interfering with the destiny of one of the tiniest and poorest nations in the world were sources of deep moral concern for large numbers of students.

The United States was involved in a war in Vietnam. Students attending college and universities were given a deferment from the draft as long as they were in good academic standing in their school. For many students of that time, sensitized to egalitarian principles, this presented an ethical dilemma. The shelter from the risks of war which they enjoyed in academia was not available to the poor who could not afford college, to many minorities who had received substandard secondary education, and to others who for a variety of reasons were not eligible for higher education.

This situation prompted many students to criticize the very institution which sheltered them from the draft. Others, who had quite intentionally enrolled in college for the primary purpose of avoiding the draft, were at times like young adolescents—rebelling against the rules and constraints of their parents while enjoying all the provisions and comforts of the home which sheltered them. The campus community proved to be a favorable place to organize resistance against the war. Student leaders found an approving audience in their peer group. Classes drew students together daily, insuring a ready rallying point, and television cameras provided a national audience for protest speeches and demonstrations. All of these factors provided an "apparent" validation of protest actions as newsworthy events.

Campus ministry centers were often called upon to provide "draft counseling" for college students, helping them to clarify their alternatives. This often involved sorting out whether or not the student could sincerely claim to be a Conscientious Objector to war, and if so, to support him in the process of application for the CO status. Frequently, campus ministry centers arranged opportunities for "alternative service" for Conscientious Objectors. Some students did not apply for this deferment, but chose to leave the country.

Many went to Canada and some campus ministers organized teams to visit draft resisters across the border.

The Student Protest Movement

Other issues such as poverty, environmental concerns, and dissatisfaction with the quality of education were issues which fueled the protest movement. Clark Kerr, former president of the University of California spoke of the causes of unrest in his address at the Seidman Lectures for 1970-71:

> . . . The problems on the campus cause some of it, but the greater problems, I am convinced, come from the outside society.
> We have some unsolved problems in America. And we are not going to be a happy nation until we solve them. We have a long drawn out and unpopular war in Vietnam, and we are not going to have campus peace until it is over. We have more poverty than is necessary in an affluent nation, and we are not going to have campus peace until we do something about poverty, more than we have done before. We have less equality of opportunity than the American nation ought to have, and we are not going to have peace on the campus until there is more equality of opportunity for all of our people. Our environment is deteriorating, and there will not be peace on the campus until we do more about the environment. And our institutions, our huge trade unions, our huge corporations and massive bureaucracies, are not sufficiently responsive to the wishes of the people, and we are going to have trouble on the campus until we do something about the responsiveness of our society.[25]

Students have for years been noted for their idealism, but students of the early 1960s were described by their teachers as extraordinarily idealistic. Test scores from that period also indicate that they were among the brightest of student generations.[26] This idealism was focused upon the university itself, prompting the university to demonstrate model behavior in its social policies by boycotting J. P. Stevens products, or grapes, or lettuce. This idealism demanded the university develop affirmative action programs and employ an appropriate balance of minority persons. This idealism demanded a "relevant education." The university was challenged by student activists to give up class time for "teach-ins" with subjects ranging from civil rights to the immorality of the Vietnam War. Colleges and universities were challenged over their admissions policies which had mitigated against the access of minorities into higher education. Many college students volunteered to tutor minority and disadvantaged children in an effort to find practical ways to act upon their belief in egalitarian principles.

Nor were the students alone in their idealism. In the first teach-in, which occurred at the University of Michigan in 1965, faculty joined with students in protesting the war. Faculty were also responsive to student demands for "relevance" by creating opportunities for students to gain academic credit for work which was done away from the campus, but hopefully related to the process of general education. Often these activities were supported by deans of student affairs. Campus ministers, also, were frequently supportive of these involvements in independent study and action-reflection projects. In a number of situations campus ministers provided supervision for students engaged in such learning opportunities. The quality of learning in these independent study projects was usually in direct correlation to the abilities of the supervisor and his/her time and commitment to the students in a particular independent study.

Clark Kerr, in particular, had seen a great deal of student unrest, as the Berkeley campus was a major center for political activists. Simmons and Winograd's description is fairly accurate:

> During the noon hour the Berkeley campus plaza becomes a midway of happenings. You are confronted with a seemingly endless melange of display tables and impassioned speeches and strolling conversations, and almost all of the free space seems to be flooded with a sea of moving people, . . . A small army of youths seated at the rows of tables are handing out pamphlets and seeking donations for racial equality, free speech, overseas children, the legalization of marijuana, saving the giant redwoods . . . sexual emanicaption, slum relief, civil liberties defense funds, Vietnam orphans and Viet Cong blood.[27]

Campus demonstrations had usually been of a peaceful nature, however, a series of events took place at Berkeley which had a profound effect upon the student protest movement, and upon all of higher education. In the summer of 1964 the university started enforcing an old policy which prevented solicitation of money and memberships on the campus. Campus activists resented this, and continued such activities in violation of the ordinance, which led to the suspension of eight students. In the fall of that year, a nonstudent activist was arrested by campus police for trespassing, but students surrounded the car in a spontaneous sit-in and prevented the police from taking their prisoner away for 32 hours.

In reaction to this controversy, Berkeley students organized the Free Speech Movement (FSM). The purpose of the FSM was to protect the right to organize on campus. Only a fraction of the student body were involved in the FSM at the beginning, possibly 2500. These students staged a sit-in to make their cause known. It was broken up after two days when Governor Edmund Brown called in the police. There were many accounts of police brutality and several hundred arrests were made. This event served as a catalyst for the campus, and very large numbers of students and faculty came to the support of the goals of the FSM. A strike was declared against the university and, in a manner without precedent, the activities of the university came to a halt.

In this event, a number of complex factors converged. The matter of civil liberties was one of high moral value for students, and it became connected with a university issue in terms of the degree of freedom for political activity which the university would allow. Tactics learned in the civil rights movement, such as the disruption of normalcy by a peaceful, nonviolent sit-in were incorporated in student protest activities for the first time. When the university called in the police, the university appeared to be repressive, and when the police resorted to unnecessary force and violence it appeared to collaborate this notion. Furthermore, the police action resulted in provoking a large number of students and faculty who quickly became involved in political protest activities. This larger number of participants brought campus liberals and radical leaders together, where often in the heat of the activity, the radical leaders would assume leadership and become spokespersons for the group. The Berkeley situation combined two important factors, the defiance and rebelliousness of youth combined with idealism in the pursuit of issues of social justice.[28]

In the year of the Berkeley disturbance, the great minority of the 849 colleges responding to a national survey reported protests:

> But almost all of these protests were of the pre-Berkeley variety—traditional, single issue protests, many of them conducted off campus. More than a third of campuses reported off-campus civil rights activities, and just over one fifth had on-campus protests against the Vietnam War. A variety of other issues stimu- lated protests on campus, including the quality of food, dress requirements, dormitory regulations, controversies over faculty members, censorship of pub- lications, rules about campus speakers, and the desire for more student partici- pation in university governance.
>   After 1964-65, however, this pattern began to change, and students increas- ingly related campus issues to broader political and social isues, and these broader issues to one another. As they did, the Berkeley invention began to spread to other campuses.[29]

So, the unrelenting problems of racism, the continuing war in Vietnam and the conviction that the American system is repressive became the three major issues which fueled the continuation of student protest. Violence esca- lated on both sides. By the end of the decade of the 1960s, after 1967, the political views of radical students grew more extreme. In 1969 the Students for a Democratic Society (SDS) split between the more peaceful branch which deplored violence and terrorism in achieving its goals, and the more violent branch which spawned the Weathermen who advocated violence against both people and property in achieving their goals. Eruptions of campus violence resulted in the injury and death of a number of students, most notably on the campuses at Kent State and Jackson State. Confronta- tions between radicals and police at the Chicago Democratic Convention appeared on national televison, shocking the nation with the violence and brutality characterized by both sides, but particularly of the Chicago police.

A brief review of the history of American colleges provides a reminder that student protest is not a new phenomenon. However, the years immediately preceding this period of tumult were quiet by comparison and students of the 1950s had been called the "silent generation." The campuses were unusually peaceful. Few, if any, were prepared for the events of the 1960s and 1970s.

When the decade of the 1960s began, student protest was restrained and nonviolent. Student workers in the civil rights movement were admired and praised by most for their courage and idealism. Most students at that time were either uninvolved politically, or committed to peaceful and nonviolent reform within the system. When the decade ended the American public was fearful and angry about the escalation of protesting students. As for the students, many had increasingly fallen into despair over the possibility of peaceful change and had come to accept a more radical course. However, it must be emphasized from the beginning that the vast majority of students in that period were on the continuum between conservative and liberal—and that only a small minority were hard core radical extremists. Nevertheless, by decade end, there had been a significant increase in episodes of violence on a number of campuses. The week following the Kent State killings nearly one third of approximately 2,500 campuses experienced some form of protest activity.[30]

The Feminist Movement

The women's movement also had its beginnings in the 1960s and continued to develop in strength and influence during the 1970s. It became clear that the leadership in the Black movement was predominantly in the hands of Black males. Likewise in the anti-war movement, the leaders were predominantly male and women were often relegated to supportive subsidiary positions. However, in the 1960s, this began to change. The language of egalitarianism and the success of various minorities in claiming a greater "piece of the action" provided a climate in which bright and articulate women began speaking out about the role of women in America.

In the field of higher education, women began to demand access to schools of medicine, engineering, and law—fields in which women had for generations remained in the smallest minority. Still other women initiated affirmative action plans which opened up construction jobs. Women became pole-climbers, telephone line repair persons, firefighters, and policewomen. Women in increasing numbers began to apply for postbaccalaureate degree programs and sought positions of leadership in academia. More and more women entered business and competed with men in the marketplace.

The church has long been an institution in which women have had an active role. Women began to protest, however, that in the Protestant Church the ordained leadership had always been predominantly male, and in the Roman Catholic Church, exclusively male. Gradually, the numbers of women entering Protestant theological seminaries began to grow until currently about one half of all seminarians are female. Campus ministry centers provided support and encouragement to many of the women returning to higher education as older students. Day care centers were established, often in nearby campus churches, so that mothers could return to the campus to complete their education, to seek an advanced degree, or to prepare for a new vocational direction. Christian theology offered a strong argument in defense of egalitarianism between the sexes.

The period of the 1960s and early 1970s did not involve all students in activism, by any means. Students, for example, in pre-medicine and pre-law programs recognized the requirement for excellent grades and continued to work hard, as did their predecessors, to win admittance to the professional schools. Thousand of students turned out on the larger campuses for demonstrations and marches, but for many, these were occasional activities and they lacked the commitment required to continue the work on a day-to-day basis. The more pervasive theme was the development of a counter-culture movement which did more universally involve the college age generation of this period.

The Counter-Culture

It is interesting to look at pictures taken during the 1960s and early 1970s. The "radical" dress and hair styles of that period no longer seem radical in this generation. For the post-1950s male generation who wore their hair in crew-cuts, the long hair on their male counterparts in the 1960s seemed radical. Blue jeans, the more faded the better, became the apparel of choice for both men and women students, a definite break with tradition. Women students whose mothers had teased their hair, grew their own long and straight. Blacks who had straightened their hair for years began to wear it natural, Afro-style. Convention was out, diverse and colorful style was in. Girdles and bras became unfashionable among college women who adopted a more relaxed and natural style of dress. Suits and ties were out. Flowers were definitely in.

These were the most superficial trappings of the counter-culture, of more significance were some of the underlying ideas or philosophies. Whereas earlier generations had been concerned with upward mobility and the importance of work, this generation began to resist such notions, and to value leisure, recreation, meditation, and the life of the spirit. "Dropping out" came to signify that one has dropped out of the "rat race" of making work the predominant theme of one's life and "getting ahead" materially the consummate goal. The prevailing mood was one of introspection, which was often mediated by the use of street drugs. The most common was "pot" or marijuana, but young people experimented with LSD, "speed" or amphetamines, hashish, and to a lesser extent, harder drugs like heroin. Alcohol continued to be popular among many.

The voting age requirement was lowered to 18 years, and the new age of majority hastened the emancipation of college age students from some of the traditional sources of authority. Sexual mores were changing. For many, sexual activities were more openly discussed than in former generations. The advent of the birth control pill gave women of college age access to a relatively safe and effective means of contraception. The automobile gave college students both mobility and privacy and allowed a greater degree of autonomy regarding sexual expression and experimentation. The role of the university as "parent" took an even more radical decline in this period. Women in dorms no longer had a "curfew" by which they had to be inside the building. For the first time, co-educational dormitories began to be in vogue, usually with men's floors and women's floors and a common dining facility shared by all. Amongst college students, the stigma against homosexuality began to decline, and gradually those with a same-gender sexual orientation began to "come out of the closet" and to acknowledge their sexual preference openly. Even before the *Roe v. Wade* decision in January 1973, many states had liberalized abortion laws. The availability of low cost, medically competent abortion may also have supported a more permissive view toward sexual expression outside of marriage. It is also true that the climate of the times supported the liberalization of abortion laws. On any number of campuses, female students with unwanted pregnancies turned to campus ministers for counseling and assistance in considering alternatives. Campus ministers who chose to support women in their decision to obtain an abortion, and who provided post-abortion pastoral care, drew sharp criticism from church constituents who were adamantly opposed to abortion.

The student counter-culture placed a high value on personal autonomy and "authenticity," living in harmony with one's natural feelings and intuitions. Individuals found a common cause with others in rejecting the work ethic, materialism and the conventional mores, dress, and conventions of the majority. The new culture called for a return to nature, the enjoyment of sensation, living in the moment. The President's Commission on Campus Unrest offered the following analysis:

> Its aim was to liberate human consciousness and to enhance the quality of experience; it sought to replace the materialism, the self-denial, and the striving for achievement that characterized the existing society with a new emphasis on the expressive, the creative, the imaginative. The tools of the workaday institutional world—hierarchy, discipline, rules, self-interest, self-defense, power—it considered mad and tyrannical. It proclaimed instead the liberation of the individual to feel, to experience, to express whatever his unique humanity prompted. And its perceptions of the world grew ever more distant from the perceptions of the existing culture: what most called "justice" or "peace" or "accomplishment" the new culture envisioned as "enslavement" or "hysteria" or "meaninglessness." As this divergence of values and of vision proceeded, the new youth culture became increasingly oppositional.
>
> And yet in its commitment to liberty and equality, it was very much in the mainstream of American tradition; what it doubted was that America had managed to live up to its national ideals.[31]

Campus Ministry's Mission:
Misunderstood, Mistrusted, and Maligned

These years are of particular significance for ministry in higher education, for many of the attitudes toward students and toward ministers in higher education appear to have been influenced by the events of that era. There was a great deal of public backlash against those identified with the student generation. The majority of adult Americans were dismayed and outraged over the incidents of violence and disruption which occurred on the campuses of the nation. Still others were confused and angry at the counter-culture life style. Many failed to distinguish between the issues, and many failed to distinguish between peaceful protest and violent disruption. There was growing disenchantment with the student generation and even with higher education itself. Laws were quickly passed barring financial aid for disruptive students, requiring dismissal or suspension of disruptive faculty, and requiring jail sentences for those who denied access to university property to those who should properly have it. In some states disfavor was shown by purposefully withholding appropriations, or reducing appropriations for higher education.

Many church leaders and church members found themselves affected by these feelings of backlash. In some cases, these feelings were directed toward those involved in campus ministry during those tumultous times. Some campus ministers, I believe a small minority, had become caught up in the movement and had lost some of the objectivity so valued in adults who work with a student population. Some of these were young ministers recently graduated from seminary, and not much older than their student constituents. Some were so convinced of the idealism of students in challenging the moral injustices of our society that they became confused concerning the just ends being sought and the means to attain those ends.

On the other hand, the vast majority of campus ministers provided a most valuable source of mature and wise leadership, often in situations which were explosive and potentially dangerous. These campus ministers were not alone, but were joined by large numbers of students who had a moderating influence on mass marches and demonstrations. On many such occasions campus ministers and students trained in nonviolent tactics in campus ministry centers, accompanied marching students while wearing black or white arm bands as an identifying mark, and exerted leadership in discouraging and quelling any destructive or violent behaviors of participants in the march.

Many of these campus ministers were seen by folk in the local churches on the evening news, marching in a student demonstration, with no informed perception about the valuable role which was being enacted. Others were disturbed because campus ministers in this period seemed to be moving out of the familiar roles of pastoral and priestly function. Some were concerned that the church-related students whom they imagined the campus minister was there primarily to serve, were being neglected, while radical campus activitists claimed the time and attention of the campus minister as well as the use of the Christian Campus Center for a meeting place. Others were unsympathetic to some of the issues which campus ministers addressed, racism, the Vietnam War, or the shortcomings of higher education, and concluded that such views were unAmerican, unChristian, or simply unpalatable.

Just as the universities felt the public backlash, so also campus ministry centers encountered negative reactions from other manifestations of the church in terms of reduced budget allocations, reduction of full-time staff positions, and in some situations the campus ministry program was simply closed down.

Disenchantment

There were several contributing factors to the loss of favor and general disenchantment with ministry in higher education which developed in this period. One major element was due to the fact that an older generation of persons in the church who had received their education during the late 1940s and 1950s were both confused and outraged with the student protest movement and with any person or institution which seemed to support such activities. Since campus ministers appeared to be involved, there was disapproval by implication in some instances.

A second consideration which led to disenchantment was related to the reaction of the older generation to the counter-culture of the student generation. The apparent flaunting of traditional values by college age students was difficult to accept by a generation of parents who had worked hard to make life easier and more pleasant for their children. These parents through hard work and savings had provided a more affluent lifestyle for their children than most of them had enjoyed during their own developing years. Having indulged their children materially, they were now resentful at the seeming lack of appreciation of their offspring, and the repudiation of the very system which had provided for their material well being.

Campus ministers were often identified with the counter-culture movement. After all, they were among the first to wear longer hair, to grow beards, to dress informally or in the more colorful and nontraditional garb of the student generation. Some were rumored to have experimented with marijuana and LSD. Campus ministers seemed to be "joining" the opposition, rather than campaigning against the counter-culture, and this resulted in strong reactions of disapproval from many corners.

A third factor in the disenchantment with campus ministries sprang from the growing absence of consensus about the mission and the methods of such a ministry in a rapidly changing era. At the risk of oversimplification, it seems fair to say that the primary vision of the Disciples' mission in public higher education in the preceding years had been with students.

Furthermore, the methods employed were designed to nurture and develop the faith of college students, when possible to invite those outside the household of faith to respond to the "good news" of God in Christ, and to cultivate future leaders for the church and society who were grounded in the basic JudeoChristian values. The programs of ministry in higher education had been focused primarily upon campus life: vocational counseling, courses aimed at upgrading the student's understanding to theology and the Bible, opportunities for worship, fellowship, and social activities.

During this time, in a new way, the issues of what it meant to be a student and a Christian were merged with the larger issues of what it meant to be a responsible citizen in the world, grappling with the issues of race, war, nuclear proliferation, environmental degradation, higher education, and human sexuality. As students confronted these important moral issues and began to work for change, they found the culture unresponsive to change and resistant. Impatient with idealism, many in the student generation begin to believe that even the church was complicit with the rigid and inhumane values of the American system.

As campus ministry programs began to focus upon the major issues which were rocking the campus and the nation, they were moving into new waters, unawares perhaps, of the rocky shoals. Campus ministry centers were among the first to provide counseling for students with a troubled conscience about whether or not they could conscientiously participate in the Vietnam War. They were often the chief reference source for students' appeal letters to the draft board seeking a Conscientious Objector status. In other situations, campus ministry sponsored discussion groups which examined the war in Vietnam and took issue with our country's position with regard to the Tonkin Gulf Incident and the invasion of Cambodia. For parents of these young people who had fought in World War II, sometimes called the "good war," these activities appeared to be acts of insubordination to the values of home and country.

A fourth factor in the disenchantment was also related to the growing breech between the expectations of the folk in the home church and the expectations of those engaged in campus ministry about the nature of ministry in higher education. With any change, there is a "lag time" between the cutting edge of change and the rest of the world. To some extent, many of the good church people in local congregations expected that the campus ministry would provide a "home away from home" for their young people. Such a concept was especially important in a time when parents were nervous about sending their young people off to the turbulent campus at all. Parental concerns were many and centered on such issues as a campus environment which seemed to promote lax sexual standards, easy access to marijuana, and a rebellious attitude against the values of God and country.

A fifth factor in the disillusionment with ministry in higher education lies in the naivete of campus ministers about the urgency of interpretation and dialogue with other manifestations of the church. This led to misinformation, misunderstanding and a growing loss of confidence. (Although, this is not to place the entire burden for communication on the campus ministers, nor to assume that there was fertile ground for accepting the news from the campus.)

In retrospect, one might ask, how could this happen? In that era, the predominance of Disciples campus pastors were in the early years of their ministry; younger, less mature and not quite as seasoned by the trials and tribulations of experience in ministry. They had felt the backing and support of the church at large in accepting a ministry on the campus. They had been encouraged to be creative, innovative and experimental in developing new paths and patterns for ministry to the academic community. Few were prepared for the "backlash" of negative opinion as most segments of the established culture reacted against the "protest generation" and those individuals and institutions associated with it. Long haired and bearded campus ministers were a symbolic target for criticism.

On campuses where diligent attempts were made to provide feedback and communication to pastors of local churches as well as judicatory leaders and lay persons there was considerably more positive rapprochement. At the University of Washington, for example, an annual clergy conference was sponsored by the campus ministers in which clergy from all denominations were invited to the campus where they were briefed on the campus scene. During the two day-long conference they heard not only from the campus ministers, but from student body leaders, campus activitists, university faculty and administrators, as well as participants in the campus ministry program. Many visiting pastors arranged to take students from their home parish to lunch or to visit them at the dormitory. On several occasions the entire conference adjourned from its regular schedule in time to observe an on-campus demonstration which drew as many as 10,000-12,000 students during the noon break.

These experiences were valuable sources of insight and helped equip local pastors and judicatory leaders in interpreting the campus scene to their constituencies. Furthermore, campus ministers who took time to initiate speaking opportunities in local churches where they could interpret and inform the congregations made a positive contribution toward better understanding of the culture and context of ministry on the campus.

Nonetheless, in some situations, even when communication was crystal clear, there was outright disagreement and disparagement about the changes which were developing in campus ministry. In spite of some particular bright spots of understanding and support, the climate in the church was generally less hospitable toward ministry on the campus by the end of this era, than at its beginning. The luster had faded, disenchantment and disillusionment were to be the challenge for the near future.

References

1. "Annual Report" Board of Higher Education, *1960 Year Book* Christian Church (Disciples of Christ) p. 91.
2. "Annual Report" United Christian Missionary Society *1961 Year Book* Christian Church (Disciples of Christ) p. 247.
3. Earnshaw, George L., editor, *The Campus Ministry*. (Valley Forge: The Judson Press, 1964). Verlyn L. Barker, "The United Campus Christian Fellowship." p. 277.
4. "Merger Schedule" *The Student Work Bulletin*, February, 1959. p. 13.
5. Earnshaw, George, *Op. cit.* p. 293.
6. "Annual Report" Board of Higher Education, *1957 Year Book* Christian Church (Disciples of Christ) p. 20.
7. Heiges, Donald R., "The Church's Ministry on Campus" *The Student Work Bulletin*, September, 1958. p. 7.
8. *Ibid.* pp. 7-8.
9. Earnshaw, George, *Op. cit.* p. 298.
10. Stephens, Michael D. and Roderick, Gordon W., *Universities for a Changing World*. (New York: John Wiley and Sons, 1975) W. Wilcox, "The University in the United States of America" p. 37.
11. Eurich, Alvin C., *Campus 1980*. (New York: Delacorte Press, 1968) p. 134.
12. Viser, Festus J., editor, *The University in Transition*. (Memphis: Memphis State University Press, 1971) Clark Kerr, "Higher Education in America and its Discontents" p. 26.
13. "Annual Report" Board of Higher Education *1962 Year Book* Christian Church (Disciples of Christ) p. 89.
14. "Annual Report" United Christian Missionary Society *1965 Year Book* Christian Church (Disciples of Christ) p. 190.
15. Rossman, Parker, "Joint Commission on Campus Christian Life Pilot Projects for 5 Year Experiments" *The Student Work Bulletin*, February, 1959. p. 16.
16. "Annual Report" United Christian Missionary Society *1965 Year Book* Christian Church (Disciples of Christ) p. 190.
17. "Annual Report" United Christian Missionary Society *1966 Year Book* Christian Church (Disciples of Christ) p. 259.
18. *Ibid.* p. 260.
19. "Annual Report" Board of Higher Education *1968 Year Book* Christian Church (Disciples of Christ) p. 107.
20. Underwood, Kenneth, *The Church, The University, and Social Policy, Volume I*, (Middletown: Wesleyan University Press, 1969) pp. 337-338.
21. *Ibid.* pp. 245-246.
22. The Report of the President's Commission on Campus Unrest. (New York: Arno Press, 1970.) p. 92.
23. *Ibid.* p. 103.
24. *Ibid.* p. 106.
25. Viser, Festus, *Op. cit.* p. 19.
26. Riesman, David, *On Higher Education*. San Francisco: Jossey-Bass Publishing Co. 1980. p. 68.
27. Simmons, J. I. and Winograd, Barry, *It's Happening*. (Santa Barbra: Marc-Laird Publications, 1966) p. 1.
28. Report of President's Commission, *Op. cit.* pp. 25-28.
29. *Ibid.* p. 29.
30. *Ibid.* p. 18.
31. *Ibid.* p. 62.

Chapter **4**

THE CHURCH'S MINISTRY ON THE MODERN CAMPUS: CENTER FOR LIFE-LONG LEARNING (1970-1985)

It all began in 1893 with the Bible Chair movement, when Disciples brought to the state institutions courses in Bible and religion. This ministry evolved from there to "student work" and, in the decade of the 1960s, to "campus ministry." In the period from 1970-1985, the prevailing concept of the church's mission continued to evolve and came to be regarded as "the church's ministry in higher education," signifying a widening vision.

Robert Huber, who had served as administrative executive for the Disciples' work in campus ministry during the turbulent 1960s, resigned to take a staff position at the University of Michigan. On June 15, 1970, he was succeeded by Barton Updike who continued to serve as "loaned" staff to UMHE and to administer Disciples' work in campus ministry through the Board of Higher Education. When Updike resigned to enter graduate school in the spring of 1973, he was succeeded by Arla Elston in October 1973. Ms. Elston resigned this position in 1974.

The seeds of discontentment which were sown in the 1960s were sprouting and taking root in the early 1970s. It was not an easy time to be a national executive in campus ministry. Another barometer was the budget. Annual reports in the *Year Book* of the Christian Church (Disciples of Christ) between 1969-1974 reveal significant reductions in the funding of "Campus Christian Life" (the designation used to describe activities related to campus ministry which were included in the Board of Higher Education Budget).

1969	-	$64,701.
1970	-	$52,150.
1971	-	$45,791.
1972	-	$40,869.
1973	-	$25,860.
1974	-	$22,070.[1]

During the early 1970s, reports from the Board of Higher Education noted, not only the reduction in financial support for campus ministry, but a reduction in the number of job openings for Disciples campus ministers as well. Signs of the times can be gleaned from the explanatory notes regarding these changes. The reduced funding was attributed to inflation while more women and minority persons were filling vacancies in campus ministry positions. In 1973 the distribution of Disciples in campus ministry was as follows:

48. . . . Disciples Campus Ministers and College Chaplains of which
21. . . . served on state supported campuses
 8. . . . were congregationally based, serving state campuses
 3. . . . served private institutions
16. . . . served Board of Higher Education member institutions[2]

It is an interesting fact that during these troubling and sometimes traumatic years of campus unrest and turmoil, the writers of annual reports made sparse mention of any difficulties and generally wrote in a positive vein concerning campus ministry. In 1974 there was a brief allusion to the difficult times in the comment ". . . Although church-related educational institutions and campus ministries confront many problems, there are encouraging signs . . ."[3] This mild report was a far cry from the former days when the pen of Joseph C. Todd so graphically described the problems related to the church's work in public higher education.

The flavor of campus ministry can be savored in the following description from 1974:

Although numbers of campus ministry positions are few, candidates for those positions are encouraged among Disciples. The Board is at work to increase the numbers of Disciples engaged in campus ministry. University town pastors have expressed a need for structured communication with each other and an opportunity to share their concerns . . . Ministry continues to shape itself around the needs of persons and society. Many campus ministers find themselves engaged in nearly limitless hours of counseling. Growth groups and values clarification events emerge from these kinds of endeavors. Gatherings of identifiable student groups have increased in number.

Two visible issues on campus today are equality for women and ethics in professional life. Women are the "new learners" on campus. They are engaged in equipping themselves to assume areas of leadership just beginning to open for them. Women Centers are increasing in number at universities and colleges; campus ministry has been the group providing initiative and space for such centers. Ethics and human values in decision making are receiving increased attention through campus ministry. "What is the moral use of knowledge?" is a question raised in many forums provided by campus ministries. Medicine and law are particular professional areas where campus ministry is giving attention to providing forums for raising theological/religious questions.[4]

1974 was also notable as the year in which the Disciples held a Consultation on Campus Ministry. In August of that year, forty-six campus ministers and general staff of the Christian Church (Disciples of Christ) met for three days at Washington University in St. Louis. The featured speaker was Parker Palmer, a sociologist at George Washington University, who was engaged in a study of campus ministries in a project funded by the Danforth Foundation. The objectives of the conference were 1) to provide a study document interpreting campus ministry to all manifestations of the church, 2) to maintain a support system for Disciples campus clergy, 3) to strengthen the ecumenical thrust of the Disciples, and 4) to work "in all ways possible to develop a better understanding of this unique ministry in the church."[5]

John Butler, a former campus minister at Washington State University, followed Arla Elston as Executive Director of Higher Education Ministries for the Board of Higher Education. While in this office from 1975-76, he continued the pattern of serving in the nation-wide network of UMHE staff on loan from the participating denominations while attending to the oversight of Disciples campus ministry programs. Butler reported that in 1976 there had been an over-all decrease in campus ministers serving state supported campuses in the UMHE network. Whereas it was reported in 1974 that there were 1,100 UMHE campus ministers serving on 1,000 campuses,[6] by 1976, Butler could identify only 740 UMHE campus ministers working on 453 campuses.[7]

William L. Miller, who had been President of the Board of Higher Education since 1968, resigned effective June 1977. Howard Short was the interim president until the end of the year and during his term of service the former Board of Higher Education was restructured to become a general administrative unit of the church to be known as the Division of Higher Education. On January 1, 1978 Dr. D. Duane Cummins assumed the reins of leadership as the first President of the new Division. By July 1978 Dr. Cummins and the Division had called Lawrence S. Steinmetz as Director of Ministries in Higher Education.

How did Disciples view campus ministry by the time of this important shift in structure and leadership? The following words from the transitional report are illuminating:

> Many in the Christian Church (Disciples of Christ), when they think of campus ministry, have images that are at least a decade old and were not generally true even in the 1950's and 1960's. . . . Their concept of the church's ministries in public higher education is even less accurate. Not only does the church's campus ministries need to be accurately understood; they need to be supported.[9]

The Disciples had long prided themselves as leaders in the ecumenical movement stemming from the very origins of the movement which was intended to restore unity to the church. How were the Disciples doing in ecumenical campus ministries by now?

> We have approximately 25 Disciples engaged full time in ministries at public-governed colleges and universities. Because of our ecumenical stance with other denominations which covenanted along with us to form United Ministries in

Higher Education, the vast majority of our ministers are ecumenically supported. Even if our theology were not sound, our pragmatism would force us
to be united. Disciples are among the poorest fiscal backers of the church's
ministries in public higher education. The BHE has been engaged in this
pattern of higher education ministries in public institutions for 62 years, and
there are still those among us who feel that these "new" ministries are of a lesser
order. Over seventy-six percent of the persons enrolled in degree credit courses
in the United States were in public-controlled colleges and universities in 1975.
The church must strengthen its witness within these academic communities.[10]

These candid descriptions of the Disciples are reminiscent of the prophetic
tradition of Joseph Todd and reminders that problems of definition and
acceptance which troubled him in his long tenure of work in university ministry
remained unsolved decades later.

The Danforth Commissions Study of Campus Ministries

The Disciples, along with most major denominations, were interested in a
serious examination of campus ministry, its mission, goals, objectives, and
methods. Just such a study was initiated when, between the years of 1963 and
1968 Kenneth Underwood, sponsored by the Danforth Foundation, undertook a major study of the church's ministry in higher education. Although
nearly completed, Underwood died before he could finish this lengthy treatise,
and the remaining work was finished by his friends and published in 1969 as
a report entitled *The Church, The University, and Social Policy*, in two
volumes. Volume I was the report of the Director, and Volume II consisted of
the working and technical papers. Also, in November 1969, a report of the
Commission on the Danforth Study of Campus Ministries was published
under the title: *New Wine* (an interpretation of *The Church, The University
and Social Policy*). *New Wine*, for which William L. Kolb was the principal
author, was an attempt to present in a brief and readable form a summary of
the process of prophetic inquiry which was both used and described by
Kenneth Underwood.

In the early 1970s these documents were being read and reflected upon by
nearly everyone associated with campus ministry. Underwood's method of
"policy research" had a powerful influence upon the shape of ministry in
higher education in the ensuing years and is particularly deserving of comment in an analysis of this period. The author hoped the process which he
described would be one through ". . . which the church and the university can
reform ministry to campus, and in so doing may point the way to the
reformation of all ministry."[11]

Underwood sought to take seriously what he had learned from campus
ministers about their own perceptions of their work—that they were engaged
in a reformation of campus ministry. At first he called his method "policy

research" and sought to combine his own ethical commitment and reflection with competent methods of research. He called these methods of study and reflection "prophet inquiry":

First, the Study took seriously the self-conceptions of those being studied . . . Thus he planned to evaluate the ministers in terms which were in part legitimized within their own faith and work.

Second, the procedures of the Study and the possibilities envisioned were designed to invite responses on the part of those studied.

Third, a basic method of the Study was the use of colloquia in major centers of higher education—the colloquia being made up of clergy, students and faculty, and other professionals. In studying themselves and others in relation to campus ministry, these people were themselves researchers as well as the subjects of research.

Fourth, the more technical instruments of social research, particularly surveys, were used but not for the purposes of manipulation or to reduce religious categories to other modes of causation or experience.

Fifth, where case histories were used, the individuals studied were themselves involved in the process of reflection and research and are described as they changed their ways of thinking and acting during the course of the Study.

Sixth, the purpose of the research was to indicate possibilities for changing ways of thinking and acting in campus ministry, and to suggest what responsibilities may be assumed by campus clergy and others in the church and higher education for influencing the profession, the laity, the church, higher education and the major institutions of the larger world. . . .[12]

Although Underwood was profoundly interested and ethically committed to the exploration of new forms of ministry in a rapidly changing world which was discovering vast quantities of new knowledge, his fundamental concepts of ministry were grounded in historical perspective. He held that the roles of pastor, priest, prophet and king were "foreshadowed in the Old Testament, and were fully embodied in Jesus Christ, and are historically normative for the Christian community thereafter."[13]

This four-fold model of ministry can briefly be described as follows:

The pastoral role is that of caring for individuals; the priestly role is proclaiming the faith and its gospel and of carrying out ritual acts which affirm the central tenets of that faith; the prophetic role is judging the justice and humaneness of the social order and pointing to the changes required if these values are to be present; and the kingly role is governance and the organization of activities for the care of men in the world through responsible corporate action.[14]

Underwood believed that there was a logical consistency in viewing each of these four roles of ministry as being necessary and inextricably bound together in any adequate accounting of the meaning of ministry. Although differing individuals may emphasize one of these aspects more than the others—he held that the roles could not be separated without a grave distortion. He believed that in his day

> the prophetic and governing ministries have been neglected, and that this neglect has led to the failure to care for human beings and to shape the social order to the ends of justice and humaneness, as well as to severe distortions of the priestly and pastoral modes of ministry. For Underwood there had to be an unbreakable unity of the modes of ministry. In this unity the proclamation of the majesty of God and the recognitition of good and evil in the world are forever linked with responsible action in history for the sake of the individual and social lives of men in the world. Only in this way can proclamation of the faith and pastoral care escape irrelevancy or worse, and prophecy and governance escape sentimentalism or despair.[15]

Such a ministry affirmed the gifts of both clergy and laity. It elevated each beyond "individual" ministry and incorporated the acts of individuals into the ministry of the "church." Yet, he also affirmed the activity of non-Christians who also committed themselves to informed action toward justice and humaneness in the social order.

The actual form and content of such a ministry must be shaped by the temporal context. This meant that ministry must be based upon disciplined knowledge of the institutions and issues of the world. "Thus he frequently stressed technical scientific knowledge in the social sciences and in the natural sciences to correct the overstress in much of the church and in the liberal arts colleges upon the humanities as being the sole source of knowledge relevant to the world."[16]

The arena which was of particular importance for Underwood was the university. He recognized the university as the place where new knowledge was being generated, but also the arena where the technical disciplines and the humanities disciplines could enter into dialogue and confrontation. He saw the task of the university as being a partner in prophetic inquiry as a part of its rightful ministry to the world:

> It is only if the university accepts the importance of this task of uniting humanistic, ethical reflection and technical knowledge in continuing inquiry that the professions may be educated and the institutional structures within which they carry out their tasks reshaped for the sake of a more humane world.[17]

Underwood saw campus ministry as a precursor for all ministry in the future because of its close relationship to higher education. It was his belief that:

> . . . as all ministries recover the mode of prophecy and governance, they will be forced to do what campus ministries are beginning to do; relate themselves increasingly to the technical, scientific, and humanistic knowledge of the university in order to carry out their functions. All ministry will increasingly require knowledge of the professions and of the aesthetic, social, and technological issues of the urban-technical society. It will require knowledge of the roles and responsibilities of professionals in corporate life as they relate to the decisions which must be made for the sake of a humane world.[18]

As more and more campus ministers, local boards, state commission members and others related to the administration of campus ministry became familiar with Underwood's extensive research and concurrent recommendations, his work had quiet but profound ramifications. Here was the most extensive study of campus ministry which had ever been done, covering a span of six of the most turbulent years in campus life from its inauguration in 1963 to its publication in 1969. Herein was a description of some of the most creative and competent ministries in current higher education. And here was a definition of ministry which had a historical and Biblical grounding, yet a modern interpretation which was theologically sound and rationally defensible.

The Danforth Study of Campus Ministries became a "plumb-line" in the continuing "remodeling" or reformation of ministry in higher education during the 1970s. The four-fold model of ministry described by Underwood was a paradigm which was adopted by many, or served as a measuring device to evaluate existing program by a significant number of others. Events in the late 1960s and early 1970s had created many and sometimes radical changes in campus ministry. Some campus clergy had lost, or perhaps had never found, a cohesive definition of ministry in higher education. For many, Underwood's model appeared attractive amidst the ambiguous alternatives of the day.

Pastoral

In many situations, the campus minister would typically be involved in the first two modes described by Underwood, the pastoral and the priestly. This was natural as, through the years, students have turned to campus ministers for counseling and pastoral care. The self-criticism implied in prophetic inquiry encouraged the campus pastor to guard against a narrow, individualistic approach and to help students look at their situation theologically, socially, economically, politically, and psychologically.[19] For example, many students who were involved in the student protest movement engaged campus ministers in dialogue about current issues and criticisms of the university and the establishment. The campus minister who "compartmentalized" might interpret the appropriate pastoral approach to such a student as one of "acceptance." On the other hand, the campus minister who recognized the inter-connectedness of these four modes of ministry could move beyond unquestioning acceptance to a position of creative criticism and questioning of all parties in the dispute, including the students. Such enlightened pastoral care could have helped students avoid the trap in which some found themselves, of seeing only the most simplistic answers, and adopting an anti-intellectual or anti-establishment position as the only alternative.

Others in that time made the mistake of seeing but two alternatives and found themselves caught in a needless dichotomy between "dropping out," and "radical" activity. "Dropping out" in this context meant a retreat from society, seeking an individual existential solution to the problems of the world by finding a place in which to escape. Such a retreat could be into drugs, passivity, personal meditation, or a retreat to the countryside to live the simple life. On the other hand, "radical" activity implied revolutionary activities designed to break down the institutions of society in the belief that they could not be reformed by any other less radical means.

Unfortunately, in some cases, campus ministers were not themselves prepared to offer critical insight into the issues of the day, and found themselves over-identifying with the students. Some faculty who might also have offered this critical element into the dialogue were carried away with the intensity of student protest and missed the opportunity to deepen the critical probing of the issues and the alternative solutions. The Underwood Study identified this tendency toward individualism and subjectivity as a high cultural value in America. He came to believe that the missing, or weaker element, was the capacity to develop policies which changed the institutions of America to make them more humanistic and capable of timely and just response to the needs of the people. He strongly believed that the Christian gospel offered just such a hope.

During those critical years of student protest, other more conservative clergy did not side with the students, but with the administration. Unfortunately, many of these were equally uncritical, and missed the opportunity to use their rapport with administrators to help broaden and deepen their view of these issues. Still other campus ministers seemed to have grasped the insight that the situation demanded not only a religious world view, but an informed constituency who truly understood something about the structure of the university, and the operating principles of the institutions of America. These ministers invited students and faculty to join with them in an exploration of the demands of faith, informed by the actual realities of the institution, in a consideration of practical strategies which had the best possibility of being translated into just and humane changes.

Priestly

The second mode of ministry with which ministers are most familiar is the priestly function. In fact, for many, preaching and administering the sacraments have been the central aspects of religious life. Underwood believed that when worship is cut off or separated from authentic wrestling with doubt and from serious grappling with the ethical issues of the day—it was not true to the gospel. Jeffry Hadden, a sociologist at Case Western Reserve University, did some interesting research during the 1960s concerning the cleavage between clergy and laity. He noted that many in the laity saw the church as a source of comfort and help, especially during confusing times of rapid change. He observed that many in the clergy, and some laity, saw the church as a place of challenge, where the faithful were rallied to wage war against social injustice.

These apparently opposing points of view had led to a "house divided," within the church.[20]

It was observed in the Study that, on the campus, the ministers were generally more liberal than the students who gathered for worship, not just in the conservative traditions, but in the mainline denominations as well. Thus, the content of worship was often divorced from the context of prophetic inquiry and disciplined involvement in changing the causes of social injustice. Often, in fact, these more conservative students claimed more of the campus ministers time and energy. Yet, Underwood claimed:

> . . . there is on most campuses a constituency of young people revealed in the Study, who, though not deeply committed, are accessible to a proclamation of the faith and to worship within a context of doubt, prophetic inquiry, and effective governance related to the world. This constituency offers to the campus clergy the varied perspectives and experiences needed to explore the meaning of contemporary Christianity along with various other religious and ethical options. . . . There is a religious complex of beliefs on which new institutional structures can be built—a radical monotheism that makes the ethical dimensions of faith a test of religious seriousness.[21]

The church is a voluntary institution, challenged by the task of providing opportunities for growth through involvement in the causes of social justice for those who come primarily for comfort. Yet this educational task is an important part of the priestly ministry.

Prophetic

The role of prophetic inquiry is as old as the fifth century prophets who railed against the religiosity of their times and challenged the people on their way to worship to "let justice roll down like waters . . ." Prophetic inquiry in our time begins with a fact or a situation which dehumanizes, or possibly one which offers the promise of encouraging and enhancing humanity. It leads to inquiry, to investigation, to research, in order to learn more about it. The second component in prophetic inquiry is that of the prophets of old, discerning the will of God in the present moment. "Prophet inquiry raises the explicit, concrete questions of what men are seeking to do with their energies and resources and what ought to be done with them."[22]

Rightly regarded, prophetic inquiry is an activity which should claim the commitment of the church and the university, optimally an activity which should be done cooperatively. Some campus ministers have been leaders in opening the resources of the university to the church, and those of the church to the university, in the common service of humanity.

Governance

Underwood observed in his study that campus ministers (and ministers in general) have less experience and competency in the governance mode of ministry than any other. Historically, campus ministers who worked in a denominational setting primarily geared toward student work found themselves separated from the centers of governing power within the university and from the persons who grappled with the issues of governance. In an earlier time, this mode of ministry was clearly outside the self-identified prerogatives of ministry:

> . . . without any conception of their own governing roles, there is a lack of recognition that the success of the ministry of prophetic inquiry and the ministry of governance requires creative relationships with those who have power and authority in the university as well as in other institutional structures. . . . Governance is a possible mode of ministry for campus clergy if they are prepared to lead their own constituencies and are willing to locate the centers of significant institutional change and reform both in higher education and the larger community.[23]

James Brubacher has likened the university to the church, claiming that prior to the end of the nineteenth century the purpose of knowledge had been to glorify God. Since the turn of the century, however, the explosion of knowledge has moved higher education from its ivory tower to the center of social and ethical issues. In the modern world, young people who pursue answers to the perennial questions, seeking to understand the self, the universe, and one's ethical duties in society, turn to the university, rather than to the church:

> . . . we must turn to the university rather than the church or even the government, because the success of our individual and social behavior rests ultimately on what we are convinced is true about our nature, the universe, and our destiny in historical time, about good and evil and how to differentiate between them, and about truth itself and how to distinguish it from error. In earlier times and places the appointed custodians of the answers to these questions were hierarchies of priests and dynasties of rulers from kings and emperors to courtiers, civil servants, and commissars. Today all these must give way to the universal company of scholars.[24]

The modern challenge of the university is to move beyond fact to wisdom. "But wisdom involves values as well as facts. It emerges from knowledge when what is true about the nature of things is reshaped to human need and oriented to human hope."[25] In these ideas we find a convergence with the ideas of Underwood about "prophetic inquiry." In this inquiry, scientists project new ideas and new alternatives which, when acted upon actually change to some degree the kind of world we live in. Geneticists, for example, in understanding the genetic code may unleash the power of humans to change themselves.

Brubacher finds such parallel values in both the church and the university that he refers to the "university as church" in an increasingly secular society. In this paradigm, he sees the university taking on some of the functions which have historically been assumed to be the role of the church. Faith in human intelligence takes on a religious quality. Or, with Dewey, "faith in the continued disclosure of truth through scholarly investigation is more religious in quality than any faith in a completed revelation."[26]

It is fascinating to recall that those pioneers who originated campus ministry followed their young people to the state supported universities with the conviction that the church was the repository of a rich historical tradition and the gospel held the design for shaping the future of individuals and communities after the spirit of Christ.

In an interesting shift, Brubacher describes the modern university as the one institution in society which seems to promise community, and offers a sense of reverence for the historical traditions and ideas of the past while searching for new knowledge in the present, and contemplating the design for human community in the future. The unifying principle which holds the university together is not so much the common body of knowledge, but the process of seeking knowledge. Clark Kerr has often suggested, the university has lost its integrative power and has become a "multiversity." Yet, intuitively, most people yearn for the ability to integrate specialized knowledges into wholeness. In this sense, the university has achieved ecumenicism more easily than the church. Unified by the spirit of inquiry and the common reverence for truth, freedom, and human dignity, people of all the world with diverse theological views can share this "secular faith" and work cooperatively together.[27] How much more, even than before, the church must manifest this complimentary and ecumenical spirit in its approach to ministry in higher education.

The university, like the church, has a moral influence upon the student. The church has pursued this task with intentionality. In the university, it may happen more by accident than design. Yet, the best moral decisions are influenced by knowledge. Knowledge of alternative choices and knowledge of the consequences one might rationally expect to follow from one's choices is basic to moral decision making. Furthermore, the choices which are prized are those which are in keeping with one's most deeply held values. Where are values to be taught? They will be "caught" to a large extent in the campus environment, through the curriculum, through the leadership and mentorship of the faculty, and through peer influence of classmates. Is this not a place of convergence for university and church?

In discussing the nature of the university's mission, we discover that the language is very much like the language and terms used in discussing the mission of the church. In reality the university has not really supplanted the church, but rather, in this arena we find a commonality in mission. This notion is underscored by the Underwood study, and affirmed by Brubacher when he claims:

> Although the university seems to be assuming some of the church's responsibilities, there is no reason to expect it to supplant the church altogether. The church still has an important role to play.[28]

In addition to the generally accepted roles of the university in teaching and research, a third function, that of prophetic inquiry, is mandated. Since prophetic inquiry is an essential part of the church's mission in the world, this offers a fruitful ground for convergence between the university and the church:

> As seedbeds of innovation and dissent, they [colleges and universities] constantly explore alternatives to conventional wisdom and operate as an ethical forum for lay society. Whereas piety and virtue once defined what the institutions of higher education should teach, today the clergy has lost much of its authority to fill these words with content. Consequently, the university, as a secular church, now fills them with such elastic values as "social concern," "democratic or humanistic values," or, even more flexible, "socialization."[29]

Some have suggested that the university must now be what the church has always been—the conscience of society, and an agent for social reform. Henry Steele Commager makes the claim that, along with the church, the university finds its mission in serving the wholeness of humankind:

> The university is the most honorable and the least corrupt institution in American life. It is, with the church, the one institution that has, through all of our history, served or tried to serve the interests of the whole of mankind and the interests of the truth. No other institution can perform the functions which the university performs, no other can fill the place which it has for long filled and with such intelligence and moral influence.[30]

It should be noted that such a view of the university, and of the church, imply an underlying assumption of instrumentalism. That is to say, intelligence and truth are not just ends in themselves, but are to be used for the resolution of problems of all sorts in the world; that the spirit of justice can best be served by applying the power of knowledge in support of the dignity and wholeness of persons.

Changing Trends in the Student Body

Any attempt to characterize a "student generation" is bound to fall short of any universal description, and may not even describe the majority of students. Still, these generational images are useful as they describe emerging trends. What can be said about the student generation between 1970-1985?

Arthur Levine, senior fellow at the Carnegie Foundation for the Advancement of Teaching in 1980, published a description of today's college student in his book, *When Dreams and Heroes Died.* This little volume presents a concise but valuable comparison of the 1970s student with the 1960s student. He claims that three significant differences stand out: 1 (an increase by 42 percent in the number of students, from 7,976,834 in the fall of 1969 to 11,669,429 students by 1979; 2) a change in the composition of the student body, with an increase in the percentage of minorities, women, and older students attending, many of them beginning in the community college; 3) and a change in the character of this student generation which is more career oriented, more self-concerned, more oriented to material success.[31]

This generation of students is the first to grow up with television as a constant companion throughout their lifetime (the Sesame Street Generation), they come from homes with a higher than ever rate of marital disruption, their schools have been less secure and more dangerous than in other generations, they have been exposed to more violence, and they are disillusioned with society, as though their dreams and heroes have died.[32]

The top reason for attending college listed by freshmen in this student generation was to get a better job, and 85 percent of all undergraduates reported in 1976 that they were attending college with a specific career in mind. More students were studying business, preparing for a career in the health sciences, agriculture and the technical fields. Many students limited their hours in general eduation and increased their electives in areas which might enhance their careers. As might be expected, there was a corresponding decline in interest in language and the humanities. Competition accelerated and there has been an increase in cheating on exams and thefts from the library in many institutions of higher education. Grade inflation which began in the 1960s continued in the 1970s.

On the other hand, this generation of students revealed themselves to be less adept at reading, writing, and arithmetic and 25 percent of college freshmen admitted to needing remedial instruction in these fields. Yet, in the face of this, students in the 1970s were generally more satisfied with their college or university experience than those in the preceding generation. Students in the 1970s viewed themselves as consumers of higher education and it is predicted that this phenomenon will continue the remainder of this century as demographic conditions will be favorable to students and not to colleges.[33]

During the 1970s there seemed to be a proliferation of religious groups associated with the campus, yet a general decline in student interest in religion. Those which seemed to be especially popular were those which offered a more authoritarian doctrine, apparently appealing to young people who were searching for something to believe in:

Nevertheless, religious commitment among college students seemed to be dropping. Although the majority of freshmen (58 percent) believe that the nation's churches are doing a good job, some freshmen feel that organized religion is responsible for considerable dishonesty/immorality (18 percent) and that it should have less influence (12 percent) (Bachman and Johnston, 1979, p. 86) Attendance at religious services is down slightly in comparison to the late 1960s. Eighty-four percent of freshmen went to services at least occasionally in 1978 versus 89 percent in 1969 (ACE/UCLA Surveys; 1969, 1979). Even more to the point, students in the 1970s are twice as likely to say that they are opposed or indifferent to religion (30 percent) as that they are deeply committed

(15 percent). At the same time, the proportion of college students who state no religious preference has risen noticeably (15 percent in 1969 versus 21 percent in 1976) Carnegie Surveys; 1969, 1976).[34]

It would appear there is a correlation between the shift in education to the training of the mind and the approach which students take to religion. The mind-set which is most comfortable with the technical disciplines in the curriculum seems also to espouse a preference for authoritarian religion. When the mind is closed to open exploration, it becomes a haven for dogmatism, religious and otherwise. Furthermore, there seems to be a correlation between the drive toward individual success in a climate of pessimism about the larger society and the popularity of religions which stress individual salvation, individual success and prosperity, with little apparent concern for issues of social justice. Such individualism is depicted in the following excerpt from an oft-repeated conversation reported from campuses across the country:

Interviewer: Will the United States be a better or worse place to live in the next ten years?
Student: The U.S. will definitely be a worse place to live.
Interviewer: Then you must be pessimistic about the future.
Student: No, I'm optimistic.
Interviewer (with surprise): Why?
Student: Because I have a high grade point average and I'm going to get a good job, make a lot of money, and live in a nice house.[35]

The 1979 Carnegie Study revealed that a high of 91 percent of the students felt optimistic about themselves, while only 41 percent felt optimistic about the country. They identified a long list of apprehensions, including nuclear war, a poor economy, growing pollution of the environment, a shortage of energy, increase in crime and the decline of morals, and much more. In Levine's analysis, today's undergraduates are like passengers on the *Titanic*, determined to go first class, if fate has doomed them to such a future. Such fatalism gives rise to a sense of justified hedonism on the one hand, and on the other, may be a factor in the rising suicide rate, the second leading cause of death in students of the 1970s.[36]

Is the need for the church's ministry in higher education less apparent, or less demanding, than in those early days of its inception? Throughout this volume the oscillations of students from one generation to another have been noted. Students of the 1970s and early 1980s exhibited tendencies toward those patterns of behavior which are typical of individual ascendancy. In times of individual ascendancy, as opposed to community ascendancy, students are less serious about academics and more interested in social activities. Personal freedom is accentuated and supported by more liberal attitudes. Students are less activist, and their politics are more middle-of-the-road. Students are more susceptible to authoritarian religious movements. They are also more interested in the material offerings of the culture and less interested in movements of social change.[37]

Levine has described this generation of students as on the average:

- self-concerned and me-oriented
- nonideological
- disenchanted with politics
- moderate in political attitudes
- liberal in social attitudes
- weak in basic skills
- career oriented
- competitive
- diverse in lifestyles and background
- concerned with personal development (physical and spiritual)
- optimistic about their individual futures
- pessimistic about the future of the country
- interested in material success
- friendly and pleasant
- pragmatic[38]

For campus ministry which sees "prophetic inquiry" as essential to its mission, this student generation provides an authentic challenge. The proclamation of the gospel and the power of the risen Christ to transform narrow individualism into loving concern for one's neighbor awaits an adequate witness on the campus.

The arena of concern for campus ministry is not confined to students. There are problems in the governance of higher education which have led to disillusionment and discontent among college administrators and faculty. The rate of increase in enrollment has declined. Even apart from inflation, many colleges and universities have experienced a decline in actual dollars from the state funds. Faculty and staff salaries have suffered from inadequate adjustments. Building maintenance has gone wanting. A recent survey of college teachers reveals that almost half are unhappy over low salaries and poor prospects for advancement and might leave their positions within the next five years:

> Of 5,000 college teachers polled by the Carnegie Foundation for the Advancement of Teaching, nearly 40 percent of the four-year college instructors said they might leave their posts within the next five years. More than 50 percent of the teachers of the two year schools said they would leave by then. About 40 percent of the teachers said their morale is worse now than it was five years ago, according to a study released yesterday. There are about 700,000 jobs for teachers at the nations 3,300 colleges. . . . Nearly one-fifth of teachers said if they had it to do again, they would not become college teachers.[39]

Only a few years ago, the idea of universal access to higher education was broadly supported. The theological underpinnings of campus ministry's governance agenda in this arena were founded upon convictions about the equal worth of each individual and the claim for equal opportunity in access to learning for each individual. The fostering of this attitude was in fact followed by an era of unprecedented growth in enrollment. The costs of maintaining such a position were many. The enrollment rate and the inflation rate were growing faster than the Gross National Product, and led to a situation in which a larger portion of the GNP was required simply to maintain the program quality which had been developed by the late 1950s. The issue of quality will be on the forefront of higher education's future agenda, and how to improve or even maintain quality in the face of imminent scarcity.

Community Colleges

A new arena for campus ministry developed with the rapid expansion of community colleges. Since these smaller colleges are "in the community," much as the local congregations have their lives "in the community," those exploring possibilities for new ministry envisioned a fresh opportunity for the local congregation to become partners in serving the community colleges.

In terms of "access" to college, one of the most significant and revolutionary changes in higher education was taking place in the two-year community colleges. Although the junior college or community college has been here since the turn of the century, in the 1960s and early 1970s there was a phenomenal growth in the numbers and enrollments of community colleges. By 1975 there were 1200 community colleges serving over four million students.[40] By 1985 the number had grown to 1219 community colleges and nearly five million students, with 63 percent of all first and second year college students beginning in the community college.[41] The average age of these students is about 25-27.

These colleges were established in small towns and in urban areas to make access to higher education a real possibility. These colleges were close enough to the communities where students lived so that they could continue to live at home, work full or part-time, and still attend college. Community colleges developed an open door policy so that no one who wished to attend would be excluded. Teachers gave their highest priority, not to research, but to teaching, and developed policies to enable students to be successful. This was justice in governance.

As we have seen, higher education in early America had been the prerogative of the affluent and those of social position. With the advent of the land grant colleges higher education was broadened to include the bright upwardly mobile young people headed for professional careers. With the growing commitment to egalitarianism in higher education, the community college opened the door to a new kind of student and offered a new kind of curriculum.

These New Students included many of the ethnic minorities and students from blue-collar families, many of whom had performed at the lower end of the scale and had suffered the defeats of academic failure in their secondary educational experiences:

Most of the New Students are Caucasians whose fathers work at blue-collar jobs. A substantial number, however, are members of minority ethnic groups. Most parents have never attended college, and the expectation of college is new to the family. The New Students themselves have not been especially successful at their high school studies.

Fundamentally, these New Students to higher education are swept into college by the rising educational aspirations of the citizenry. For the majority, the motivation for college does not arise from anticipation of interest in learning the things they will be learning in college but from the recognition that education is the way to a better job and a better life than that of their parents.[42]

We have seen how the church played a vital role in establishing church-related colleges in the founding of America. With the rise of the state universities, the church innovated the Bible Chair, and later the campus ministry. With the rapid development of the community colleges, the church is again faced with a major challenge of addressing a relatively new system in higher education.

It is clear that the traditional approaches to ministry that have been developed on the larger state university campuses are not appropriate for the community college. New models of ministry must be developed which respond to the unique context of the community college. Indeed, considerable creative work has already been done in exploring and demonstrating new approaches to this work. William E. Hallman has edited two very useful volumes which provide a wealth of information for anyone interested in developing a partnership of common ministry between the church and the community college. (*So There's A Community College In Your Town*, 1976; and *The Challenge of the Community College to the Church*, 1980) Also, Betsy Turecky, co-editor of *Church and Campus Calling*, 1985, has had considerable experience in creating a team ministry to work within the Community College System in Dallas, Texas.

Mary Alice Geier, who brings a wealth of experience to the community college ministry, claims that the local church is ideally situated to provide the first line of ministry. Both the church and the college are in the community. Local churches and pastors might best work out an ecumenical approach toward cooperative work. At times such work will be involved with students and teachers in direct services. In other times the church as a system will find its greatest avenues of service in responding to the systemic issues of the community college:

The first ministry of the local church should not be to race to the campus with chaplains and religious centers, but to march to the local school boards and state legislatures to lobby for high standards of education in these institutions.[43]

From this perspective, since the community colleges were intended to be within commuting distance for the majority of the population, nearly every congregation is now a college-related church. The UMHE Community College Program National Advisory Committee has developed a considerable bibliography to assist local churches and denominational leaders in imagining ministry within the community college. The modern community college embodies a new concept in higher education; the church is challenged to respond with new concepts of ministry to this special arena of higher education.

Mark Rutledge, a campus minister in New Mexico, points out in a recent essay on new staffing patterns in community college ministry, that there is no single model which is universally applicable. Rather, each situation invites a careful analysis through which the goals of ministry may be established. Professional leadership is usually required in the initial stages of development. Local churches play a major role in the conception, development, and maintenance of community college ministries. Ecumenical partnerships or cooperatives seem to insure consistency over the long pull, as a larger number of local pastors and volunteers provide a greater pool of energy, ideas, talents, and connectional relationships.[44]

C. Freeman Sleeper, Vice President-Dean of the College at Roanoke College, Salem, Virginia claims that the response of the churches to community colleges "needs to take place within a framework of reflection which is informed by educational and social theory, as well as by theology."[45] The church and the community college are both moral communities—seeking to identify and promote a notion of personal and social responsibility in the light of certain basic values around which there is at least some agreement, even in a pluralistic culture. Dr. Sleeper believes that the churches and the community colleges are natural allies in this task, and that each can enrich the dialogue as we help students address the meaning of human responsibility, not only in today's world, but in the future as well.[46]

The Variety and Diversity of Campus Ministry

Today, there is great variety and diversity in the form and expression of the church's ministry in higher education. Campus ministers serve on private and church-related colleges as employees of the institution. Campus ministers serve on state college and university campuses, funded by the church. Local church pastors and lay volunteers serve in campus ministry in many settings, including the community colleges, private colleges, and state universities. Some campus ministers are "generalists" and serve a broad constituency with a wide spectrum of needs. Other campus ministers can best be described as "specialists" because they have narrowed and concentrated the focus of their ministry upon a particular issue, or a special constituency.

Campus Ministry at Private and Church-Related Colleges

In earlier times, when church-related colleges were established by denominations and attracted a large percentage of students from within the founding body, it was unusual for the college to provide a chaplain or a campus minister.

This was because the faculty was often composed of some members who were also ordained clergy. They were usually available and often eager to provide pastoral care for students as well as to provide leadership for chapel services and occasions of worship on campus. Such faculty envisioned the teaching of values as an integral part of their mission, and along with Alexander Campbell, saw the development of moral character as a higher priority than the development of intellectual skills.

In time, the availability of college professors grew and the numbers of clergy-faculty declined. Students from various denominations began attending in greater numbers, as did non-religious students who chose the college for reasons other than its denominational affiliation. As these shifts arose in the nature of the campus community, more and more colleges began to employ a campus minister who was formally charged with carrying out a mission which had been informally fulfilled in former days by the faculty.

The campus minister was frequently called the "chaplain" of the college, and had responsibility for the religious life of the student body. Often this included the oversight and supervision of the chapel services, pastoral counseling, interfacing with local churches of the region, and occasionally teaching formal courses in religion or administrative duties in the office of student affairs.

Currently, most denominational colleges attract a very heterogeneous student body, and members of the supporting denomination may be a tiny minority of the enrollment. The role of the chaplain, or campus minister, has changed with the times. A narrow sectarian approach would be quite out of place on the modern campus where the campus minister has an equal concern for students without regard for their denominational heritage. Furthermore, on some of the larger private and church-related campuses, denominations other than the founders often support campus ministry staff and programming. The role of the campus chaplain, employed by the college, frequently includes coordinating an ecumenical ministry which is quite similar to ecumenical teams which serve on the state campuses. Naturally, there are additional responsibilities unique to the particular campus which will claim the attention of the college chaplain.

Case Studies of Campus Ministry at Disciples-Related Colleges

Currently, within the church-related colleges of the Christian Church (Disciples of Christ) some employ full-time campus ministers, others are served by part-time campus ministers and local church pastors who dedicate a portion of their time to campus work. The following case studies are descriptive of the variety of ways in which campus ministry was originated in Disciples colleges. Given the unique circumstances of each institution there was no general or universal pattern in the establishment of such ministries.

Transylvania University

Established in 1780, Transylvania University is the sixteenth oldest institution of higher education in the country and the home of the first medical and law schools founded west of the Allegheny Mountains. During its first century, the school was influenced at different times by various religious groups; such as Unitarians, Presbyterians, Baptists, Episcopalians and Methodists. In 1865 the dream of John B. Bowman to found a "great non-sectarian Christian University" became a reality as Kentucky University with a confederation of colleges, including a College of the Bible, opened its doors and initiated the relationship of the Disciples of Christ to Transylvania University.

With the College of the Bible on the Transylvania campus an intentional religious presence persisted without a formal campus ministry program. However, this changed when the seminary moved to a new location in the early 1950s.

In 1955, President Frank Rose created a new office, Dean of Morrison Chapel, and called Dr. Irvin E. Lunger (B.A. Bethany College; M.A., B.D., Ph.D. University of Chicago), pastor at University Church of Disciples of Christ at the Unviersity of Chicago, to fill the post. Before he could construct the parameters of this new position, Dr. Lunger moved to the office of the Academic Dean in 1956 and subsequently to the office of the President in December 1957.

Although the debut of the first Dean of Morrison Chapel was indeed auspicious, the architect for campus ministry at Transylvania was Dr. Benjamin F. Burns, the second Dean of Morrison Chapel. Called by President Lunger from the pastorate at Austin Boulevard Christian Church in Oak Park, Illinois in 1962, Dean Burns (B.A. Transylvania University; B.D. University of Chicago; D.D. Eureka College) forged a unique ministry among Disciples church-related colleges.

Heretofore campus ministry was an adjunct responsibility of a faculty member, usually a professor of religion. At Translyvania that model was reversed. Dr. Burns was intentionally called as a minister with adjunct teaching responsibility. Furthermore, Dr. Burns expanded the ministry to include the entire university community. Campus-wide ministry was instituted at Transylvania.

The focus and range of campus ministry under the leadership of Dean Burns is best expressed in a summary paragraph in the brochure "Transylvania and the Church":

Transylvania's commitment to the Christian tradition is expressed in the presence of a Chistian minister as a member of the college staff. The Dean of the Chapel is a witness for the Christian faith within the total life of the college. He is the presence of the Church in the classroom, in faculty meetings, in policy-making bodies, and dialogue with students, faculty, and administrative officers. He also performs many of the traditional functions of the ministry in counselling, directing programs of religious interest, conducting worship, and performing a ministry to the sick, bereaved, and troubled among the faculty and student body. The Dean of the Chapel constantly seeks to lead a program on campus that is supplemental to rather than competitive with the programs of local churches.

After serving as Dean of Morrison Chapel for eighteen years, Dr. Burns retired in 1980.

In 1985, President Charles L. Shearer called Paul H. Jones (B.A. Yale University; M.Div. Texas Christian University; M.A. Vanderbilt University) as the third Dean of Morrison Chapel. The primary responsibilities of the new Dean are to continue a campus-wide ministry, to teach half-time in the department of religion, and to act as a liaison with Disciples and community churches.[47]

Atlantic Christian College

The office of chaplain was first inaugurated in 1961, at Atlantic Christian College. The pioneering chaplain was Rev. Dan Hensley.[48]

Drake University

Drake University serves as an example of a Disciples college which never initiated a chaplaincy program. However, in 1962, campus ministry at Drake University was begun in a cooperative effort through the Iowa State Commission on United Ministries in Higher Education. Since that time, campus ministry has been a function of the UMHE Commission.[49]

Midway College

The campus ministry program at Midway College began with the actual founding and mission of the Kentucky Female Orphans School in 1847, by the Rev. Dr. L. L. Pinkerton. Dr. Pinkerton was the minister of the Midway Christian Church and, with the help of some elders in that congregation, started a school for the purpose of educating orphaned females. The school established Pinkerton High School in the late nineteenth century. The Institution remained the Kentucky Female Orphans School until 1942, when Midway Junior College was established. The last high school class graduated in 1973.

The spiritual needs of the campus were traditionally met by the Midway Christian Church. In the 1800s, the students were expected and required to attend services at the church. As the school became more sophisticated and grew in size, the Christian Church minister would conduct services on the campus as well as at the church. When the Midway Christian Church employed a Student Associate Minister, that person served one-half time as the campus minister. Russell T. Zigler served in that capacity for approximately eight years.

When Bert Cox left Midway College as the President, Dr. Nelson Hoffman was named in that capacity. When Mr. Zigler left as campus minister, a committee decided that perhaps they needed a conservative and stable theological viewpoint. President Hoffman announced that the candidate for campus minister need not necessarily be affiliated with the Christian Church (Disciples of Christ). The search led to the employment of the first female campus minister who served part-time while attending Asbury Theological Seminary.

On July 1, 1985, Dr. Robert Botkin began his presidency at Midway College and his first major appointment came in the form of a campus minister. The criteria announced in the search were:

1) A full-time, 12 month appointment
2) Ordained minister in the Christian Church (Disciples of Christ)
3) Female

The national search, using this criteria, led to the hiring of Rev. J. Ellen Barnott as Campus Minister/Assistant Dean of Student Affairs. The majority of her time is spent counseling, planning chapel services and implementing campus ministry program, with some time devoted to responsibilities in the Office of Student Affairs.

This new appointment has worked out beautifully. Looking to the future, there will be continuing changes as Midway College looks for ways to strengthen ties with the Disciples. Students are still encouraged to attend services at Midway Christian Church and graduation exercises are traditionally held there. A new chapel, contributed by the alumnae of Midway, seats 250. Chapel services are held twice each month, at 11:00 a.m. on the second and fourth Wednesdays. Although chapel and church attendance are no longer required, encouragement and transportation are provided to assist students who desire to do so, to become integrated into the local congregations. Inter-faith fellowship meets each Monday evening for Bible study and prayer, and special services are offered appropriate to the church year. The campus minister is a member of several ministerial associations in the area and the college participates in community church events. The campus minister preaches regularly in churches across the state, conducts seminars, and interprets the work of campus ministry at Midway College.[50]

Chapman College

Chapman College began its 125 year journey as a small college named Hesperian. Founded on March 4, 1861, the very day of President Lincoln's inaugural, Hesperian College was the fulfillment of a dream for several committed church people who believed in education and especially Christian education. Located in Woodland, California, the tiny college accepted members of both sexes and all races; a radical concept at that time.

In 1934, the college's most generous benefactor, Charles C. Chapman was honored when the name was changed to Chapman College. Mr. Chapman was a banker and rancher in Orange county. Chapman is the seventh oldest educational institution in California, although it moved to its present location at Orange as recently as 1954.

Religious life and religious education have received priority attention at Chapman. The required weekly chapel service was at the heart of campus life. The services were usually coordinated by the Chairman of the Religion Department, utilizing the Disciples pastors from the area as speakers, as well as faculty and special guests. Although faculty were hired without regard to their denominational affiliation, the college sought in its hiring practices to employ persons who expressed a commitment to religion.

Rev. Willard Learned was the first chaplain to be hired at Chapman, in 1953, with a joint appointment as chair of the Religious Department. He came to the college with experience as a local church pastor, a missionary, and a military chaplain. He retired in 1961, and was followed in a brief ministry by Dr. George Tolman, who had a joint appointment as pastor of the First Christian Church at Orange, and part-time campus minister.

Rev. Carroll Cotton succeeded George Tolman in 1961, and became chaplain and head resident at the men's dormitory. Dr. Cotton was an alumni of Chapman, where he had been student body president. He had only recently graduated from seminary when he began this ministry during the turmoil and turbulence of the 1960s, and he brought a fresh contemporary approach to the campus.

In 1963, Dr. Cotton became the Dean of Students and Rev. Clinton Campbell succeeded him as chaplain, with a joint appointment as associate professor of sociology. During this time of student revolt, and following widespread campus consultation, the decision was made to continue offering chapel services at a period in which no classes were scheduled, but to cease requiring chapel attendance.

In 1965, Dr. William Carpenter was called as chaplain and professor of religion. He was respected as an excellent teacher and innovative campus minister. In 1968, he brought Rev. Jon Lacey to the campus as seminary intern. Dr. Lacey served as assistant chaplain until 1973. Bill and Jon provided important leadership for the campus community in a difficult period, helping resolve confrontations between minority students at Chapman and the local police; facilitating dialogue between students and administration over such issues as civil rights, the anti-war movement, and the student protest movement.

Bill Carpenter resigned in 1973 to become Dean of Golden West College in Huntingon Beach. He was succeeded by Dr. Kent Hoffman, who had served one year as assistant chaplain at Chapman, and was completing his Doctor of Ministry degree at Claremont. Hoffman served until 1975 when he was succeeded by Rev. Dennis Short. Mr. Short had previously served as Associate Regional Minister in the Pacific Southwest Region. He was familiar with the churches of the region, and was known as an advocate for social justice.

Dennis Short initiated a program for persons considering the Christian ministry called "Models of Ministry." In the eleven years since its inception, the Models of Ministry Program has brought over 300 persons to a three day conference at Chapman College to consider the professional ministry. In the fall of 1985, in an expression of support for ecumenical campus-wide ministry, Chapman hired its first full-time Roman Catholic chaplain, Maryloyola Yettke. Ms. Yettke is a graduate of the Graduate Theological Union and the Jesuit Theological Seminary of Berkeley and teaches in the Religion Department as well as serving as college chaplain.

Culver-Stockton College

Culver-Stockton, in its 133 year history, since 1853, has had but one college chaplain, Rev. Thomas Walmsley. He held this position during the 1960s when most campuses were experiencing turmoil and student unrest. After a short tenure as chaplain, Walmsley resigned, and the college chose not to refund or renew this position.

For a time, Professor John Alexander served as Dean of the Chapel with a secondary portfolio to organize programs and activities in the area of campus ministry. The title was strictly honorary while the function was similar to that being performed by faculty persons currently in charge of the Religious Life Committee.

Culver-Stockton College is currently seeking a $250,000.00 endowment ($40,000.00 has been committed) to permanently underwrite the position of college chaplain and a program in campus ministry. Faculty are simply unable to carry out the more extensive responsibilities and programming which are hoped for in the new campus ministry position. Over the duration of its life as a college, Culver-Stockton has utilized ordained clergy-faculty on a rotating basis to perform the tasks of campus ministry. One test of the effectiveness of such a program is attested to by the large number of graduates who have chosen the Christian ministry. The major focus of the clergy-faculty leadership through the Religious Life Committee has been on preaching, teaching, pastoral care and service to the campus community. Ministers from the local churches in Canton, have on a rotating basis, conducted chapel worship. It is now evident, however, that there has been a steady decline in the effectiveness of the program due to insufficient leadership. Weekly chapel services are poorly attended, life adjustment counseling services are minimal, individualized Bible study is not provided, spiritual focus is poorly communicated and Christian fellowship activities are few.

The college chaplain of Culver-Stockton will be hired on a full-time basis with responsibility in the following areas: 1) 50 percent of the chaplain's time is to be spent in direct ministry as leader of the Religious Life Committee and campus ministry program, i.e., leadership in weekly chapel, coordination of church year and religious life cultural events, providing opportunity for Bible study, counseling, visitation among students, crisis intervention, value clarification, and modeling Christianity as a life-style; 2) 25 percent of the chaplain's time is to be spent in pre-ministerial instruction, relating with student congregations, and providing counsel and advice to persons heading into full-time Christian vocations; 3) 25 percent of the college chaplain's time is to be spent in church relations, i.e., regional and general assemblies, leadership for the Church Advisory Council, visiting with area congregations, supply preaching on Sunday, and building relationships with the local congregation in Canton.[52]

Eureka College

The first chaplain at Eureka College was Paul Murphy who came to the position in 1960. Prior to that time the religious activities on the campus had been directed and coordinated by various members of the religion faculty. Royal Humbert and Chester Crow had worked with the pre-ministerial students in the *Koinonia* program and the chapel services had been planned by such faculty persons as Howard Kester and Norma Brown.

Dr. Murphy, who served from 1960-1965, worked under a contract in which one-half of his time was devoted to the activities of chaplain and one-half to teaching. He reported his duties as follows: director of student employment, parents advisory committee, chapel, convocation, Focus, pastoral counseling, committee responsibility, preaching and various congregational and community services which were performed off-campus.

He was succeeded by Dr. Daniel Cobb, who served from 1965-1966. Dr. Cobb also divided his time between campus ministry activities and teaching.

Dr. Walter Sikes served in 1966. He had retired from Christian Theological Seminary and Vanderbit and accepted an invitation to come to Eureka as chaplain and teacher. This promising ministry was interrupted by his death in November 1966.

Dr. Charles Emerson served for two years as chaplain and teacher of religion, from 1967-1969. In the fall of 1969, Glenn Riddell came to the campus as Coordinator of Religious and Cultural Affairs. One-half of his time was spent in teaching and one-half in chaplaincy. He served as college ombudsman and worked in developing the curriculum. In 1977 the title was changed once again, and Riddell became chaplain, with responsibilities in teaching, religious life, and church relations.[53]

The following description of religious emphasis at Eureka carries something of the flavor of campus ministry's perspective:

> The students at Eureka College are exposed to a religious emphasis which is uniquely relevant to their own lives because it is more persuasive than authoritarian, more experience-centered than dogmatic. They are encouraged to develop an appreciation for the rich diversity of religious traditions and are supported in their efforts to strengthen and deepen their faith. Students are expected to gain an understanding of the spiritual roots of our heritage and to wrestle with contemporary issues in which the Christian challenge to secular values is most clearly visible. They are given numerous opportunities to participate in activities which enrich faith, bring the satisfactions of meaningful service to society and develop responsible churchmanship. They are challenged to explore all fields of human knowledge and to reflect upon their meaning in the light of the spiritual and ethical insights of religion. A student who takes full advantage of the opportunities offered . . . will not only be intellectually equipped for a professional career but will have also grappled with the faith and value systems which provide the basis for a meaningful and satisfying life of personal growth and service to humanity.[54]

Such an approach to campus ministry at the college level offers a serious challenge to any professional chaplain and represents a worthy undertaking for any college. Other important campus ministries are occurring at Disciples-related colleges. These case studies are offered as brief illustrations how such ministries developed and examples of the diversity of these ministries.

Disciples Serving in Community College Ministry

The work of Rev. Jerry M. Miller serves as an example of one Disciples campus minister who has developed a creative ministry at the community college level. Mr. Miller's particular interest and expertise centers around ministry with the aging in his work on the ecumenical team at the Dallas Community College Ministry, Dallas, Texas. At this relatively new ministry site, pioneered by Rev. Betsy Turecky, there is no space provided on the campuses, and the ecumenical campus ministry team works out of an off-campus office. Jerry has developed the Emeritus Institute, providing life-long learning and self-enrichment classes for older adults. The instruction, drawing upon community college resources, is occurring in local churches.

A significant number of Disciples ministers in local churches situated near a community college are involved in community college ministry. The opportunities for ministry in this context provide one of the greatest challenges to the church in the next decade. To a large extent, the possibility of developing the community college ministry depends upon the health and vigor of the local church, and the willingness of lay volunteers to become involved with the pastor in serving the community college.

Disciples Chaplains Serving in NonDisciples-Related Institutions

The Disciples have a few campus ministers serving as the chaplain or campus minister at church-related institutions of higher education which are not affiliated with the Disciples. John R. Langfitt, at Winter Park, Florida is one such case, as is Diane Moore at Watham, Massachusetts, and Brent P. Waters at Redlands University, Redlands, California.

The Illinois Disciples Foundation

A Disciples minister, Rev. James B. Holiman, has for many years served at the Illinois Disciples Foundation on the campus at Champaign, Illinois. The history of this Foundation is interesting as it represents a type of work which Disciples began which was divergent from the pure Bible Chair. The foundations usually combined educational work with an activity program. The first of these foundations to be established by the Disciples was at the University of Illinois, in 1916:

> By 1923, this Foundation had a staff of five full-time workers serving the needs of the more than 800 Disciples students enrolled in the university. These workers included two assistant pastors, a chaperon of Bethany House (a rooming house for Disciples girls), an instructor in religious education, and a promotional secretary. This work was carried on in close cooperation with the University Place Christian Church at Champaign.[55]

Although the Disciples were involved in a number of foundations in earlier years, the others have by this time lost their particular identity and, most typically, have merged into ecumenically sponsored ministries.

Disciples Bible Chairs

The Bible Chairs, through which the Disciples began their ministry in higher education, have all been closed except for the Bible Chair at the University of Texas in Austin. Today, Bible Chairs are looked upon as an anachronism. Most universities have developed their own departments of religion, or departments of religious studies. The University of Texas at Austin is a notable exception, and this is largely due to the fact that the Bible Chair continues.

Disciples strategy for the future should be to support the development of religious studies within the university. For example, Cotner, a former Disciples Bible Chair now funds a professorship in religion, but turns the governance of this program over to the University of Nebraska.

Disciples Campus Ministers Serving Ecumenically in State-Supported Higher Education

The majority of Disciples campus ministers are currently serving on state college and university campuses through programs which are supported ecumenically. Even though some of the enthusiasm for ecumenical ministries has waned in the mid-1980s, the Disciples have encouraged ecumenical cooperation at every level. As recently as the fall of 1985 the Executive Committee of the Division of Higher Education of the Christian Church (Disciples of Christ) affirmed that every encouragement should be given to avoid a "denominational" approach to campus ministry and to work positively toward ecumenical cooperation.

United Ministries in Education

During this period under consideration, 1970-1985, there were significant changes in United Ministries in Higher Education. Verlyn Barker exercised strong leadership in calling for an end to exploration and the need to formulate a plan of action. National UMHE articulated its purpose as follows:

> Persons in their societal context are the controlling forces of UMHE which, as a Christian ministry, works redemptively by conserving those values which contribute to wholeness and struggling against demonic and dehumanizing forces. All actions of UMHE are to be tested against this purpose.

The Plan of Ministry which developed from this purpose was two-fold, the National Ministry, which undertook tasks which could best be accomplished by a national agency, and the Nationwide Ministry, which was a shared ministry of resourcing and encouraging the state commissions and the local units of campus ministry.

In 1979-1980 another significant change occurred when United Ministries in Education was formed by the uniting of United Ministries in Higher Education (UMHE) and Ministries in Public Education (MPE).

By 1982-1983 it had become clear that UME, if it was to continue in existence, needed a more streamlined organization. A task force reviewed the history of UME and its antecedents and identified three future alternatives: 1) to substantially modify the operating structure, 2) to dissolve UME, or 3) to continue according to the original basic policies document. The task force and the committee of denominational executives found agreement in the decision to preserve UME, but to radically restructure its organization. The following rationale was affirmed in making this decision:

> 1. UME can offer a means for expressing the unity of the Church's mission through the abiding ecumenical commitment it has established among its participants.
> 2. UME can fulfill a valuable role by monitoring events in the educating arenas of our society and helping the denominations a) to understand these events, b) to respond to present developments, and c) to anticipate and shape a future course.
> 3. UME can develop and resource a functioning network of contacts within the denominations and across the society.
> 4. UME can generate selected programmatic ministries from a national base to address public policy issues and special areas in education.[56]

Table 3. entitled "Proposed Operating Structure For United Ministries in Education" provides a graphic description of the current structure of UME.[57]

Currently, Dr. Lawrence S. Steinmetz, Vice-president of the Division of Higher Education for the Christian Church (Disciples of Christ) is treasurer for United Ministries in Education, and 50 percent of his time is devoted to the mission of UME as the Disciples' "loaned staff." Dr. D. Duane Cummins, President of the Division of Higher Education, serves as the Disciples' denominational executive, representing the Division as the appropriate agency for collaboration and cooperation with other like divisons of the supporting denominations.

The pool of contributed staff for UME has declined during the past decade. Considerable work is now being undertaken by a UME team to develop a proposal for a National Network which would utilize the services of contributed staff and especially qualified local campus ministers to provide resources and leadership for the support and development of campus ministry in the future.

Dr. Steinmetz continues to provide leadership through the Division of Higher Education for the Disciples Ministries in Higher Education. One of the most important tasks involved in his portfolio is the administration of Campus Ministry Program Grants. Since 1979, the Division of Higher Education has made approximately $9,000.00 available each year with which to fund new and innovative programs with seed money grants of not more than $1000.00 each. These grants are available to all Disciples campus ministers, and to UME ministries in which Disciples participate.

A few examples of recent grants help disclose the creative programming which campus ministers are initiating across the country. Dr. Steinmetz reported that special consideration is given to proposals which address the stated priorities of the Christian Church (Disciples of Christ); "Peace with Justice," "Hunger and Human Rights," and "Renewing Congregational Life":

ESTABLISHMENT OF AN EMERITUS INSTITUTE AT BROOKHAVEN COMMUNITY COLLEGE $700.00 Granted. Georjean Blanton, Greater Dallas Community of Churches' Community College Ministry, Dallas, Texas—to initiate an Emeritus Institute on the Brookhaven campus. Patterned after the Emeritus Institute established successfully on the campus of the Eastfield Community College in 1982 (for which a Campus Ministry Program Grant was awarded in 1982), this second Emeritus Institute is designed to offer ten six-week courses to provide for older adults opportunities for continued learning and a means for active participation and contribution to the society in which they live. Community college faculty will participate in providing leadership.[58]

WORKSHOP TO EQUIP STUDENTS TO BE CAMPUS MINISTRY ASSOCIATES –$500.00 – Erwin R. Bode, Indiana office for Campus Ministry, Indianapolis, Indiana—for a workshop to train student leaders to participate in peer campus ministry. Through the use of case study presentations, small group discussions, program opportunities, model building . . ., and the establishing of a peer ministry state-wide network in Indiana, the goal is to equip and support these students for evangelism and development of social outreach by students for students as an extension of the work of the professional, full-time campus ministers in Indiana.[59]

LATIN AMERICA EXPERIENCE—A REVERSE MISSION –$500.00 – James Nielson, The Common Ministry at Washington State University, Pullman, Washington – to provide scholarship aid for students to participate in a ten day seminar at the Cuernavaca Center for Intercultural Dialogue on Development in Mexico. . . . The goal is to offer participants the opportunity to explore their convictions concerning poverty and injustice in Latin America through visiting with people who are involved in the struggle, and struggling to survive . . . and to assess the effects of United States foreign policies in Latin American countries.[60]

BLACK STUDENT MINISTRIES
–$575.00 - Robert A. Geller, United Campus Ministry at Colorado State University, Fort Collins, Colorado – for a Black campus ministries program designed to provide greater awareness of Black cultural heritage for Black students enrolled at CSU and to provide for these students opportunities for religious experiences on campuses and in the community.[61]

STUDENT INTERNSHIP
–$750.00 – Jo Garceau, Thruston Community Ministries in Higher Education, Olympia, Washington—to hire a student intern for nine months during the 1982-83 year to assist the campus ministry by performing a peer ministry with students at Evergreen State College.[62]

These examples are offered to indicate the rich diversity of programming which is taking place on campuses across the country where Disciples campus ministers and lay persons are involved in ministry. Dr. Steinmetz also serves as editor of a newsletter entitled *Footnotes**, a quarterly publication from the Division of Higher Education. Each year the campus ministry program grants are reported in *Footnotes**, and back copies of this helpful newsletter will reveal a wide range of creative programs.

In this chapter, we have reviewed events of importance in the period from 1970-1985 in the church's ministry in higher education. During this period the Danforth Study had a profound shaping effect upon ministry. The community college ministry gained recognition and engaged a growing number of local congregations and local church pastors. The problems of inflation and a slowing economy brought financial problems to campus ministry, combined with some of the results of the backlash of disillusionment from the previous period of disenchantment. Disciples campus ministers in this period are serving on church-related and private college campuses, in the community colleges, and in the state colleges and universities. As shown in the grants for local programming, descriptions of regional cooperation, or programs of national significance through UME, such ministries have a vital role in the lives of the participants in the campus communities.

References

1. "Annual Reports" Board of Higher Education, *Year Books*1969—1974. Christian Church (Disciples of Christ).
2. "Annual Report" Board of Higher Education, 1973 *Year Book* p. 77.
3. "Annual Report" Board of Higher Education, 1975 *Year Book* p. 103.

4. *Ibid.* p. 106.
5. *Ibid.* p. 103.
6. *Ibid.* p. 106.
7. "Annual Report" Board of Higher Education, 1976 *Year Book* p. 107.
8. "Annual Report" Board of Higher Education, 1978 *Year Book* p. 142.
9. "Annual Report" Board of Higher Education, 1977 Year Book p. 102.
10. *Loc. cit.*
11. *New Wine*, A Report of the Commission on the Danforth Study of Campus Ministries. (An interpretation of *The Church, The University and Social Policy, Two Volumes*) William L. Kolb, Chairman. St. Louis: Danforth Foundation, 1969. p. 5.
12. *Ibid.* pp. 7-8.
13. *Ibid.* p. 9.
14. *Ibid.* p. 9.
15. *Ibid.* p. 9.
16. *Ibid.* p. 12.
17. *Ibid.* p. 15.
18. *Ibid.* p. 14.
19. *Ibid.* p. 20.
20. Underwood, Kenneth, *The Church, The University, and Social Policy, Volume II*, Connecticut: Wesleyan University Press, 1969. "The House Divided" by Jeffrey K. Hadden. p. 276.
21. *New Wine.* Op. cit. p. 24.
22. Underwood, Kenneth, *Op. Cit. Vol. I.* p. 220.
23. *New Wine.* Op. cit. pp. 27-28.
24. Brubacher, John S., *On The Philosophy of Higher Education*, San Francisco: Jossey-Bass Publishers, 1982. p. 129.
25. *Ibid.* p. 130.
26. *Ibid.* p. 130.
27. *Ibid.* p. 132.
28. *Ibid.* p. 135.
29. *Ibid.* p. 135.
30. *Ibid.* p. 136.
31. Levine, Arthur, *When Dreams and Heroes Died.* San Francisco: Jossey-Bass Publishers, 1980. pp. 6-7.
32. *Ibid.* pp. 21-26.
33. *Ibid.* pp. 59-83.
34. *Ibid.* p. 98.
35. *Ibid.* p. 103.
36. *Ibid.* p. 103-104.
37. *Ibid.* p. 123.
38. *Ibid.* p. 131.
39. *Seattle Times*, October 15, 1985. p. A-9.
40. Hallman, William E., editor, *So There's A Community College In Your Town*, New York: UME Communications Office, 1976. p. 1.
41. Turecky, Betsy A., *Church and Campus Calling*, Dallas: UME Communications Office, 1985. "A Preview of Coming Attractions at Your Community College," Betsy Turecky. p. 38.
42. Hallman, *Op. cit.* p. 6-7.
43. *Ibid.* p. 58.
44. Hallman, William E., editor, *The Challenge of the Community College To The Church.* Valley Forge: UME Publisher, 1980. pp. 122-138.
45. *Ibid.* p. 17.
46. *Ibid.* p. 17.
47. Personal Communication, Paul H. Jones, June 4, 1986.
48. Personal Communication, Dan Hensley, September 7, 1986.
49. Personal Communication, Dale Miller, June, 1986.
50. Personal Communication, Ellen Barnott, June, 1986.

51. Personal Communication, Dennis Short, June, 1986.
52. Personal Communication, William R. Kennedy, June 26, 1986.
53. Personal Communication, Glenn Riddell, June 27, 1986.
54. Riddell, Glenn, "Religious Emphasis at Eureka College" pp. 7-8. (an unpublished paper)
55. Rossman, Parker, "Background of Bible Chair Study" October 5, 1972. p. 5. (an unpublished paper)
56. Report of the Policy and Planning Committee on the Question of Restructure to the Policy Board of UME, November 17-18, 1983. p. 5.
57. *Ibid.* p. 11.
58. Steinmetz, Lawrence, Editor, *Footnotes**, VII/1 Spring-Summer 1985. p. 6.
59. *Ibid.* p. 6.
60. *Ibid.* p. 7.
61. Steinmetz, Lawrence, Editor, *Footnotes**, IV/2 Summer 1982. p. 4.
62. *Ibid.* p. 4.

Chapter **5**

CASE STUDIES IN
DISCIPLES CAMPUS MINISTRY

CASE STUDY ONE: A MINISTRY IN TRANSITION TOWARD
AN ECUMENICAL MODEL
Rev. Thomas R. McCormick
Disciples Campus Minister
University of Washington
Seattle, Washington

When I entered campus ministry, January 1, 1966 at the University of Washington, I accepted a call to work on behalf of three denominations committed to a common ministry: The Baptists, the Disciples, and the United Church of Christ. I joined my senior colleague, Rev. John Ross, an American Baptist campus minister. My initial assignments was two-fold: 1) to nurture the community of students who gathered for worship and community life at the Koinonia Center, and 2) to explore future avenues for ministry which transcended the traditional student-ministry model.

I had previously served a small congregation for five years, following graduating from seminary. I began to realize that a campus minister could easily devote his/her full time as a pastor to a student congregation, and indeed, the students seemed to expect that this would be the case. I devoted myself to this aspect of my assignment. The student group grew to about 50 or 60 fairly regular participants, and seemed to plateau at about that number. We were engaged in worship, social and recreational events and pursued a variety of community service activities. I taught Bible Studies, conducted elective classes in theology and religion, provided counseling, and accompanied student work crews to the White Swan Indian Mission and a variety of other local projects. In this model, there was simply insufficient time to pursue the broader issues in higher education.

I hoped to learn more about campus ministry from the older and more experienced campus clergy at the other denominational centers. There was, in addition to our Koinonia Center, a Westminster Center, a Wesley Foundation, a Canterbury Club, a Newman Center and a Lutheran Student Center. Further exploration revealed that the activities of each were nearly identical, with the exception of a few identifiable denominational marks particularly discernible in worship and liturgy. The denominational model resulted in duplication of program and basically ignored the larger issues and populations of the campus.

In carrying out the second mandate of my job description: "exploring future new avenues of ministry," I began a dialogue about the possibility of an ecumenical approach to ministry which would provide for an ongoing student community with opportunities for worship in keeping with the polity of the supporting denominations, and the reassignment of staff to a variety of new forms of ministry.

In the late 1960s a great deal of enthusiasm was generated around this idea by the campus ministers and the local operating committees. By the end of that decade these explorations resulted in the formation of a new organization which embraced all mainline denominations. The Campus Christian Ministry at the University of Washington had as its founding members: 1) the American Baptist Church, 2) the Christian Church (Disciples of Christ), 3) the Episcopal Church, 4) the Lutheran Church (ALC/LCA) 5) the United Presbyterian Church, 6) the Roman Catholic Church, 7) the United Church of Christ, and 8) the United Methodist Church. The next logical step was to embark upon a fresh study of the campus and the surrounding community in an effort to discover the most pressing needs and thus to identify the priorities for mission. At that time, four or five regional UMHE executives were available for leadership in such projects. William Hallman, Richard Bolles, Bill Shinto and Sam Kirk composed the leadership team for the University of Washington campus study, with the assistance of Verlyn Smith from the Lutheran Church's Western Regional Office.

The study itself involved the campus ministers, local boards, students, faculty, administrators, local pastors, and a variety of other categories of persons whose ideas could be useful in shaping ministry. It proved to be a inherent value as it involved a number of people in some exciting considerations and dialogue about the future of campus ministry. There was functional utility in the study as well, and a number of recommendations were made. The campus study identified arenas for ministry which had never been undertaken before, and for which there existed no coherent plan nor program. In careful dialogue, staff were reassigned to initiate new forms of ministry, and some were assigned responsibility for the ongoing life of the student religious community.

One colleague, for example, was assigned to relate to the disenchanted and disenfranchised political radicals and activists. This led eventually to a fine piece of work in organizing these individuals into a loose knit "community," harnessing their energies into constructive projects such as the creation of the U-District Center, a community organizing headquarters.

Another began a new work with university faculty, to discover ways in which the campus ministry might serve their needs. This led to a monthly faculty forum where issues in higher education could be discussed among faculty colleagues and campus ministers. At one of these monthly forums the topic under consideration was "What is the Shape of a Liberal Arts Education Today?" A senior faculty from the College of Arts and Sciences remarked, "I have been on the faculty here for 12 years, and it's interesting that the first discussion on this topic was called by the campus ministry."

Still another arena which was identified was that of "Human Values in the Health Sciences." Pacific Avenue is a natural boundary between "upper campus" and "lower campus" of the University of Washington. The former is the liberal arts campus and the latter is the home of the health sciences. It was remarked during the study that to the best of anyone's knowledge, "no clergy had ever set foot south of Pacific Avenue." Such was the affinity for religion and science. The Health Sciences was home for a premier medical school, a first class nursing school, a school of dentistry, with programs in physical therapy, and many more. The medical school was also in the top three in the country as a recipient of federal research funds. This was a new arena for mission in higher education. I was willingly assigned to Human Values in the Health Sciences. In seminary, I had taken a full measure of courses in Pastoral Clinical Training and was somewhat familiar with the hospital setting. I began my work there by interviewing 50 faculty in the health sciences, including the foremost researchers, teachers and clinicians. In making these appointments, not one of the 50 denied me access, and in most cases I was quite graciously received. Not only did I meet fifty faculty members, I also learned a bit about their life-work and research interests. Furthermore, my help was solicited for three tasks. I was invited to conduct a seminar for medical students in death and dying, another in human sexuality, and a third in medical-ethical dilemmas. I willingly volunteered my services in response to these faculty requests and my new campus ministry was underway.

This new involvement led me to request first hand observation in the delivery of clinical services, and opened a new field of literature for my independent study. I observed in surgery everything from brain surgery to the removal of ingrown toe-nails, from kidney transplants to open heart surgery. I observed electro-shock therapy (ECT) in the psychiatric ward and respirator dependent patients in the Intensive Care Unit (ICU). I observed the care of premature newborn infants in the Newborn Intensive Care Unit, (NCIU) and sat in on discussions concerning genetic counseling and prenatal diagnosis. Eventually, I came to believe that my effectiveness could be enhanced if I took time out to further my own education. In 1972, I enrolled in a Doctor of Ministry program studying ethics, at Southern Methodist University. I was also awarded a fellowship in the ethics and human values program at the Institute of Religion and Human Development: Texas Medical Center, Houston, Texas.

In 1974, the Department of Biomedical History at the School of Medicine, University of Washington, invited me to accept a one-third time appointment on the faculty. My job-description called for me to create a program in medical ethics. It was to be geared particularly for the School of Medicine, but I was encouraged to develop classes which could be interdisciplinary in nature. The first classes in bioethics were offered in Autumn Quarter, 1974, with about 20 students in attendance. In 1985, over 250 students participated in bioethics classes thru this program.

In 1980, I was for three months a Fellow in the Ethics and Human Values Program at the University of Tennessee, Memphis. There I had the opportunity to make rounds in the clinical setting and teach ethics in a variety of clinical services. Upon returning to the University of Washington, I began teaching ethics in three clinical settings: the Neonatal Intensive Care Unit, Children's Orthopedic Hospital, and the Prenatal Diagnosis Clinic at University Hospital. I was invited to serve on the Human Subjects Review Board, the committee to investigate the ethical issues in beginning a heart transplant program, and the Ethical Advisory Committee for the *in vitro* Fertilization Program at University Hospital. The opportunities for me to become involved in the policy and decision making arena seemed to multiply. The opportunities for me to provide clinical teaching and consultation were more numerous than I alone had time and energy to fulfill.

In 1979, the Dean of the School of Medicine was approached by a number of graduating medical students who presented information on ways in which they believed medical education could be "humanized." Most of these were students who had participated in my ethics classes, and in support groups to enhance "coping" with the pressures of medical school. The latter I had offered in my role as a campus minister. Included in the list of suggestions was the recommendation that two one-half time counselors be employed by the School of Medicine to provide counseling and support groups for medical students—due to the very stressful nature of medical education. The next recommendation identified Margi Anderson and myself as the counselors whom the students preferred be hired. The Dean responded positively, and in 1979 the Campus Christian Ministry Board graciously released more of my time so that I could continue to teach ethics one-third time, and begin a counseling program for the School of Medicine one-half time, with the remainder of my time under the direction of the CCM board. In 1985, the Dean requested that I give full-time to the School of Medicine. He wanted me to accept a new position which he was creating, The Director of Counseling Services for the School of Medicine. From this new position I would coordinate the counseling services, and add to my responsibilities the task of helping students through programs designed to assist them with making career decisions, that is, which pathway in the broad field of medicine to choose: primary care, a sub-specialty like opthalmology, radiology, anesthesiology, etc., or a career in academic medicine. I accepted this position two-thirds time, and continue to teach bio-ethics one-third time. I continue my relationship with the Campus Christian Ministry as an "adjunct campus minister" (with a salary of $1.00 per year).

My purpose in sharing this story is to dramatically illustrate the possibilities for ministers in higher education to become involved in new arenas of ministry. Our ecumenical configuration provided administrative approval and financial support for launching an entirely new ministry. The nature of this ministry seemed to dove-tail so nicely into the perceived needs of the School of Medicine, that they "institutionalized" a program which had been created by campus ministry. I could never have done this as a "denominational campus minister" providing pastoral care for my student group. This is the kind of ministry which can only be performed in a team relationship in which other priorities of the supporting denominations are being provided for by other members of the team.

Other team mates were, in the meantime, creating new programs within the campus community and providing leadership within the loosely-knit student community which gathered for worship, study and social action at the Center. Each week began with worship on Sunday evening. For a time Catholics and Protestants worshipped together, breaking into two separate groups to celebrate the Lord's Supper, and returning for the closing hymn and benediction. Later, a general Protestant service was devised which was held separately from the Roman Catholic Mass. Rev. Lucy Forster/Smith coordinated this. The Protestant ministers all participated, and students representing a broad variety of denominations worshipped together. Through this, a great deal was learned about one another's traditions. This basic group also met on Thursday evenings for supper and a presentation-discussion on some aspect of "what it means to be a Christian in the modern world." This was the developing community in formation.

Another staff team member, Rev. David B. Royer, United Church of Christ, received training from Richard Bolles and began a Career and Life Planning Program at the Campus Christian Ministry. This program has proven extremely valuable, as the university had cut back such services due to funding difficulties. Each quarter, students ranging from freshpersons to PhD's and post-doctoral students participate in some aspect of career planning or leaning how to move to a more suitable career choice.

Still another staff team member, Rev. Susan Morris, licensed in the United Church of Christ, developed a program to provide premarital counseling and pre-marriage workshops to nurture young couples in attitudes and practices most conducive to a healthy marriage. She has recruited a cadre of 40 volunteers, (20 married couples) who are willing to receive continuing-education and provide primary leadership for at least one weekend-long Marriage Preparation Workshop each year. Currently, one such workshop is conducted each month of the year, with 10-12 couples participating. Last year over 250 individuals from the campus community participated in this program. Local churches which rim the campus have come to realize that their busy pastors do not have sufficient time to provide in-depth preparation for couples planning for marriage, and many pastors now refer all couples who come to them for a wedding, to participate in our Marriage Preparation Program. An example of campus ministry and local congregations working together in a common cause.

Rev. Jon Nelson, a Lutheran campus pastor, and Rev. Tom Forster/Smith, a Presbyterian campus pastor, teamed up each week to take a group of university students to the state prison at Monroe. There, discussion sessions were held on every imaginable topic, from marriage in prison, to racial conflicts and prejudice within prison walls. In the process these students came to learn a great deal about our Justice System as well as the factors within our society which lead to crime and imprisonment.

Rev. Richard Younge, an Episcopal priest has provided continuing leadership in working with faculty. In addition, he has provided counseling for gay students on campus and their families. In the light of the recent outbreak of AIDS, and the many fears which have developed concerning the spread of this deadly disease, Rev. Younge planned a conference on AIDS. Co-sponsorship was arranged between the Campus Christian Ministry, the School of Medicine, the local Council of Churches and the Dorian Society. Through this vehicle a special opportunity was provided for the religious community in Seattle to learn more about the disease, to investigate some of the ethical issues surrounding the care and treatment of AIDS victims, and to explore religious issues such as the use of the common cup in communion.

The Roman Catholic staff members have provided leadership for a Catholic student parish. Their primary efforts are centered in the celebration of the mass daily and 4 times on Sunday. In addition they teach classes such as "What Catholics Believe," and "Bonehead Bible."

Most recently, this ecumenical ministry in higher education has been threatened by a variety of factors. The Roman Catholics have announced that they must pull out of the corporation due to severe financial problems. The Episcopal Diocese, upon learning of this, have also announced their intention to withdraw from the ecumenical campus ministry. The loss of these two major denominations will be a considerable blow to this witness of unity and oneness in ministry in higher education. Perhaps, even more importantly, this may be a manifestation of that trend we have earlier identified in the current religious context: "a renewed emphasis on denominationalism." There is further evidence of this trend in recent actions of the Wesley Foundation

Board which set the stage to reduce Methodist money supporting ecumenical campus ministry and increase direct support of the local University Methodist Church's Campus University Program.

The current challenges in ministry in higher education are considerable. We are challenged to communicate our theology of the church's mission in higher education back to the church at every manifestation, local, regional, general and ecumenical. We are challenged to assist those agencies of the church which administer, fund, and evaluate campus ministry to the responsible stewardship of the trust that has been given to them. We are challenged to re-examine the tendencies toward denominationalism, and to create opportunities for strong ecumenical partnership for mission in higher education. Such challenges pertain to the underpinnings of ministry in higher education. The most exciting challenge of all is to create new programs and forms of ministry which will truly serve the coming age.

CASE STUDY TWO: "MINISTRY FROM A PERSPECTIVE OF THREE UNSIMILAR CAMPUSES"
Rev. Jon A. Lacey, Disciples Campus Minister
Michigan State University
East Lansing, Michigan

My first experiences in campus ministry were a direct extension of the ministry I had experienced in the local church, particularly in the persons of youth ministers who usually turned out to be students—or recently graduated students—all of whom, parenthetically ended up at some point in their careers as college chaplains. And at Chapman College at that! Carroll Cotten, Bill Carpenter, Dennis Short—all role models in ministry—in more ways than they probably know, all friends. Dennis Short remains Chaplain at Chapman College; Bill and Carroll are in higher education administration in California colleges.

By circumstance each of these persons added a dimension to my ministry which I still cherish and seek to develop—that campus ministry is a ministry of the church, above all else. It is not peripheral to the church's ministry; it is not auxiliary, it is with the many other ministries of the church—general and specialized—the ministry of the church. This remains true for me, and is perhaps heightened today, as denominations pull away once again toward "other priorities." This is one of the most crucial issues of the church in higher education. In meetings of committees charged with overall fiscal policies of regions, frequently agendas roll round to "budget reductions" and more likely than not the allocations for higher education ministry are targeted: reason, they are "icing" on the cake, rather than the substance of the loaf. I'll fight with my last breath against the notion that campus ministry, deeply involved in developing tomorrow's leaders of congregation and world, is an easily dispensed with frill to other more "essential" ministries.

Campus ministry, for me, has been a varied and rich experience in ministry of the Christian Church (Disciples of Christ) though it has often been spent in the ecumenical arena. Disciples have wisely worked cooperatively with others from the beginning, seeing the ecumenical thrust of campus ministry as an essential ingredient to holistic ministries.

I began professional campus ministry in 1968 at Chapman College in Orange, California with Bill Carpenter. As an internship in my doctoral program at the School of Theology at Claremont, I contracted for 9 months—which stretched into 4 years—to be a chaplain in residence, meaning I discovered that they would not have to pay me much and I would have the benefit of the close proximity of students. That was a valuable feature of campus ministry which I have missed in my two succeeding campus ministries—first of the engineering and mining campus of the South Dakota School of Mines and Technology at Rapid City, and then on the campus of Michigan State University at East Lansing, Michigan. Three campuses: one a small, church-related campus; one a technical college in the midst of the Wild West; one a major land-grant university with a heavy thrust toward agriculture and international education.

Each of these campus ministry experiences has offered its gifts, challenges, and problems. Chapman College offered the relationship of the Disciples in a formalized way, at a time when it was rejecting—or its students were—the traditional, required religious courses and chapel attendance—and was seeking to integrate spiritual values and offer religious disciplines, while keeping faithful to the liberal arts traditions of broad general education. These were years of the opposition to the Vietnam War, complete with mock cemetery with students names on the sunken lawn, but also of the growing political conservatism of the Orange County area. They were also years when the college finally took ownership of a former Episcopal Church near campus to house the religious center of the campus—a place for many marriages, ecumenical worship, workshops on church vocational choices, draft counseling, problem pregnancy counseling, etc.

South Dakota School of Mines was a new experience for a liberal arts-trained campus minister, but my hesitancies were offset by a group of beautiful people who supported me in ministry and personally as the "California boy" sought to adjust to South Dakota (whose travel department slogan that year was "South Dakota, of all places!") As things turned out, it was "of all places" a place for a unique ministry. Wounded Knee and the Indian's confrontations with government authorities drew me in rapidly as a "free" minister with few developed institutional loyalties, but with an interest in relating Christian ministry to crisis times. Environmental issues of mining and engineering and alternative energy sources—particularly coal gasification—

focused issues of campus life, as did "death and dying" issues after the catastrophic flood of June 9, 1972, the day of a Kubler-Ross conference focusing on the issue.

South Dakota also served to highlight for me a central issue of campus ministry—that campus ministry must be collegial and supported by a community. For most of my time at SDSM&T I was the sole campus minister; by the end of my time there not only was that true, but I had moved to a position of regional campus minister serving Black Hills State College, St. John's Nursing School, the National College of Business, and SDSM&T from a base in Rapid City. "Lone ranger" is not my style.

Funding crisis as a regular diet of the campus minister can be debilitating; it was for me. Reductions in force were the name of the game, with campus ministers being asked to supplement their campus ministry salaries with other work. That and a desire to be further West for family reasons—you may notice here an anomaly (East Lansing is a lot of things, but is not west of Rapid City!)—set the scene for saying yes to the call to United Ministries in Higher Education at Michigan State University, a call to a team campus ministry with a woman, a United Methodist clergyperson, Diane Deutsch.

MSU had several attractions for me. Opportunity to work with a clergy-woman; to work in a team relationship; to work on a large campus; to work on a campus with a large number of international students and scholars. It also had a long history of involvement with socially significant issues, housing as it still does, the East Lansing Peace Education Center, and it had a strong history of relationship with other manifestations of the church.

So I was called as co-director, co-worker in campus ministry on a large campus with many opportunities for growth of ministry and for my growth as a minister. Opportunities have been shared with others seeking similar experiences including developing staff positions for experience for seminarians in campus ministry which have benefitted 3 Disciples clergy now in active ministry, offering campus experience in ministry to 3 US-2's from the United Methodist Board of Global Ministries, and building peer-ministry models for developing ministry skills among undergraduate students. Along the way I have focused professional efforts on family ministry, including divorce adjustment and counseling of troubled marriages, especially upon the "disposable marriage" so prevalent in professional and graduate schools. With the Episcopal chaplain, Rev. John Mitman, I have developed a series of brochures and residence hall presentations on "Cults: conversion or coercion?"

Not unlike other ecumenical programs and ministries, United Ministries in Higher Education at MSU has faced—and is facing—its share of the financial crisis and crisis in confidence of the church in its higher education ministries. Frequently heard are the words: "We don't see anything happening," with an emphasis on the words "we" and "see."

Campus ministry styles are quite varied, as they should be. There is a renewed interest in visibility, in numerical accountability, in what amounts in many cases to wanting more "taking care of our own." When campus ministry ONLY pays attention to these thrusts, it imperils its life by trivializing the Gospel mission to "set the captives free, heal the sick, feed the hungry" which is at the heart of all of the church's ministries. When campus ministry IGNORES these thrusts, it risks moving itself to the margins of the church into obscurity, if not death itself. Campus ministry, as I see it, walks this line of faithfulness and accountability. Both are attributes that the church strives for.

Finally, I am in campus ministry today because it is for me one of the exciting ministries of the church in the 1980s, threatened thought it is. Campus ministry is integral to the church's FULL ministry of the Gospel of Jesus Christ. It is, as Paul has written, a part of the Body which has an unquestioned right to its life as a part of the Body. As part of that Body, however, I believe that the change that it has been undergoing is but the beginning. There are serious questions about campus ministry's survival in its present forms. For me there are no questions about its survival. For many in campus ministry today—and hopefully for more to come—campus ministry is a part of a holistic vision of the church's ministry.

CASE STUDY THREE: "MINISTRY TO MINORITIES IN
A DUAL SETTING"
Rev. Dwight Bailey, Disciples Campus Minister
University of Texas and Huston-Tillotson
College
Austin, Texas

In July of 1985 I accepted a position through the Wesley Foundation of Austin to be the Campus Minister/Chaplain of the University of Texas/ Huston-Tillotson College Minority Ministry Project. The position sought "the skills of a person who can maintain and build a program of counseling, support, and resource services on two campuses, while keeping in mind the long range goal of working a joint relationship, where possible, with minority constituencies on both campuses." This ministry was to take place on two campuses with a 75%/25% split in time usage. I was to spend the bulk of my time in the development of a stable ministry on the Huston-Tillotson College campus but I was also to make a concerted effort to maintain ministry with minorities at UT. Let me add that this program began in the fall of 1980 with the hiring of Claudia Highbaugh* as the first campus minister/chaplain to the project. The arrangement was between the Wesley Foundation of Austin, Huston-Tillotson College, and the United Campus Ministry of Austin, an ecumenical campus ministry serving the University of Texas. This ministry provided an office, telephone service and secretarial assistance for the campus minister/chaplain at UT and served as a center for ministry to the minority students on these campuses.

*Claudia Highbaugh, a black Disciples of Christ clergy, served the position for four years 1980-1984; before leaving to serve a church in Orange, CA.

The Challenge

Before accepting the position in Austin I served with the United Campus Christian Foundation of Normal, Illinois with responsibilities that included work with minorities as well as working with the total population on two campuses (Illinois State University and Illinois Wesleyan University). These were two predominantly white institutions with similar student populations and with basically the same type of needs among the black students on both campuses.

I began with the belief that the situation in Austin would be much the same as Illinois. I was very grateful to Claudia Highbaugh for providing me with insight to the unique characteristics of the Austin position. In one of her reports Claudia stated:

> the demands and needs of taking seriously the tasks on two campuses that are very different, having basically two different sets of assumptions and work styles, are great. The need on a private church-related campus (Huston-Tillotson) is for a person that can minister to the whole campus and relate to the denominational bodies. . . . In a small church-related college the chaplain works hard to strengthen and promote religious studies in the learning community/religion department.

She continues to say in regard to the university:

> "The University requires a very ecumenical and informal kind of availability and outlook. There is every indication that a campus minister should float around and perform different kinds of tasks in various places. A chaplain needs to be far more stable."

SETTING ONE: HUSTON-TILLOTSON COLLEGE

Let me introduce you to the setting for this ministry. Huston-Tillotson College is the first part of the setting for the minority ministry project. Huston-Tillotson is located in east Austin in the heart of the black and Hispanic middle-lower neighborhood. Historically, Huston-Tillotson is one of the few traditionally black colleges remaining in this country. The college is a result of the merger of Tillotson College and Huston College in 1952, resulting in Huston-Tillotson College. The mission of Huston-Tillotson is to provide educational opportunities for black Americans and other ethnic groups. The population of Huston-Tillotson is about 500 students; of these approximately one fourth as international students.

When I received the notice of the position vacancy I was excited about the possibility of working in the capacity as a chaplain in a church-related institution. One of my career goals was to be a chaplain in a church-related institution. I felt that my previous experiences in campus ministry and in the local church pastorate would provide the needed background to do a good ministry.

After one year as chaplain I knew my dream was being realized. I loved it! First of all I was able to design and lead worship, which is important to me. Initially this took place with the oversight of a group called the Fellowship Hour, a student led organization that conducted worship on a regular basis. But the worship was not balanced enough to attract a large number of students. It basically appealed to a group of the more church-going oriented students who wanted to have a worship experience during the week. They were sponsored by a Christian staff person who worked in the business office name Donnie Scott. In the first semester it was my job to develop a working relationship with the Fellowship Organization in order to begin providing a worship environment that was benefitting the college. I am glad to say that the personalities meshed and I was able to work with the Fellowship Organization to provide support initially and as the semester progressed I was able to provide worship design and leadership. The community started the year with about 20 in worship and rose to a high of 75+ in that first semester and the second semester there were as many as 100 in a couple worship services. The average attendance was about 65-70.

In the role of Chaplain the pastoral care aspect is very important to the church-related college not for students alone but for faculty and staff as well. In my first semester I had regular sessions with individual faculty and staff as well "on the spot" care-giving as I visited from office to office in the college. Pastoral care was much needed due to the great loads that faculty and staff carry in fulfilling various functions on the campus. It is expected that each person will work in their own area of expertise and in addition take on committee assignments for formal work of the college as well as the informal functions. At times the faculty and staff are over worked and under praised.

As I envisioned my role in providing a presence of ministry to the Huston-Tillotson campus I saw a community aware of its own calling to the church as well as the inter-connectedness with the even larger expression of the church. The campus which was originally begun by the United Methodist Church and the United Church of Christ is now populated primarily by Baptists (National, Progressive, Missionary), Catholics, Church of God in Christ students, Presbyterians, along with the Methodists and United Church of Christ students of wide spectrum to encompass with information about the larger church.

The approach used to share about the wider expression came in various ways. The Annual Charter Day Observance (similar to a convocation with visiting dignitaries from supporting denominations providing the students with a picture of the larger church. The Chaplain's office also sponsored a revival on campus bringing in various speakers that represented the religious diversity on the campus. To further identify the larger expression of the church I had my installation service held on the campus at Huston-Tillotson to signify the common bond of church and higher education.

An ongoing concern at the college is the need to develop a ministry with the international students. Although Huston-Tillotson is a predominantly black school many international students attend; it is like having a mini-United Nations right on campus. Since a large portion of these are Muslim ministry takes on a care and concern giving enterprise. Whenever a crisis occurs I try to give support not out of a paternal mode but as a genuine expression of my faith to theirs. When one of the Muslim faculty members experienced death in his family, I made myself available and the offer was received and appreciated. Living the Gospel is more desirable than just talking the Gospel. My concern for the international students has prompted me to be involved with a new ministry in the community that seeks to serve the needs of non-Americans.

The setting of ministry at Huston-Tillotson is a world unto itself. Now let us journey approximately 10 blocks west to the other setting in this dual ministry—the University of Texas.

SETTING TWO: UNITED CAMPUS MINISTRY AT THE UNIVERSITY OF TEXAS

The University of Texas is one of 14 components of the University of Texas System. There are 11 colleges in the University of Texas-Austin academic offering for undergraduates. Nearly all of the colleges and schools offer graduate programs at the masters and doctoral levels. The present enrollment of the Univesity of Texas-Austin is 48,000 students and of that number 1643 (3.5%) are black and 4273 (8.9%) are hispanic. The American minority representation on the University of Texas campus is low; the administration is giving special attention to the recruiting and retaining of minorities. The students at University of Texas are high achievers and highly motivated.

The approach to ministry to black students at University of Texas is one of working through the structures of the university. My primary entrance into the life at University of Texas came through the Dean of Students office. Upon arriving at Austin, Wayne Bryan, director of the United Campus Ministry Association (UCMA), introduced me to the Dean of Students, Beverly Tucker and part of her staff, Suzan Armstrong-West and Sam Taylor, three very concerned individuals about the ministry to the black students at University of Texas. Through the Dean of Students office I was to touch base with the student program office and find the name of black organizations. I found in the file left by my predecessor contact names for two organizations and called these individuals to meet and hear about life at the university. After meeting with the contact persons I visited meeting of the black Gospel Choir's rehearsal and the Black Student Association. There were other groups that I wanted to be involved with but due to time allotment I chose to deal with the choir and to keep in touch with the Dean of Students office for one-time opportunities for ministry. One particular "one-time" opportunity for ministry occurred when I was asked to assist the Dean of Students office, the Black Student Association and the Counseling Center in an event on communication between black males and black females. The program was a huge success and I worked with other professionals on the university campus as a colleague. The campus minister on the secular campus has to establish himself as a professional, demonstrating the skills and training that places him on par with those in the university.

The ministry to black students at University of Texas is a part of a larger ministry called United Campus Ministry of Austin, an ecumenical ministry that is sponsored locally by the United Methodist Church. The United Presbyterian Church, Christian Church (Disciples of Christ) and the United Church of Christ, UCMA has as its basic support system board members from the university, supporting churches, and the business community. I included this statement to show that the ministry to black student is a unique focus of a total ministry to the university.

As a closing statement I would like to re-affirm the joy that has been mine as I minister in such a cacophony of settings. There are clashes in styles as I travel from one side of the interstate highway that separates the wealth of University of Texas from the meager resources of Huston-Tillotson College but they are bearable as long as I am able to serve the students, faculty and staff in both settings. There are days when I long for more time and more staff to get the task done but never do I wish to give it up.

CASE STUDY FOUR: "CHAPLAINCY AT
A DISCIPLES-RELATED COLLEGE"
Rev. Dennis Short, Chaplain
Chapman College
Orange, California

I was hired on June 1, 1975 and accepted the position with a great deal of enthusiasm. The opportunity to return to my Alma Mater was exciting. I was fortunate that during my first month on the job I was asked to participate in an Assertion Training workshop with seven faculty and seven members of the Student Development team. This provided an excellent way to get acquainted with key people on campus as well as gain an "assertive" skill which I would need in later years. We formed seven teams and taught assertiveness each week to a group of twelve entering students. This not only helped me get to know a small group, but the process was successful in increasing the students retention—nine of twelve graduated from Chapman.

I am a product of the fifties and sixties a formative time in which I developed primary concerns about Civil Rights and peace. I graduated from Chapman in 1964 with a major in philosophy and a minor in sociology. I graduated from Christian Theological Seminary in 1968 with an emphsis in social ethics. I was then called to the Pacific Southwest Regional Office of the Christian Church (Disciples of Church) with responsibility for social concerns and urban ministry. I brought these commitments to my work at Chapman with the realization that I was weak in the area of pastoral skills. During my first summer at Chapman I attended the 17 day LaJolla Program of the Karl Rogers Institute to increase my counseling and pastoral skills. Another very helpful pastoral training program for me was as faculty of the Western Academy of Church Life and Mission. This provided yearly training and application of group work and theological skills.

These pastoral skills were used to the fullest soon after my coming to Chapman. In the Fall of 1975, Chapman developed a serious financial crisis and almost went bankrupt. Many employees were let go and each remaining employee was required to take a 10% pay cut. Chapman was also forced to cut off its relationship to the World Campus Afloat. This wonderful approach to global education was a real boost to faculty and administrators who sailed and worked as part of their jobs at Chapman. Losing the ship and 10% of our salaries brought campus morale to an all time low. My grief counseling was sorely tested.

The 1975-76 academic year was a difficult year with two or three all campus meetings held to update the community. In the late Spring of 1977 the Trustees announced the calling of a new President, G. T. "Buck" Smith. Buck and his wife, Joni, came to Chapman that summer and greeted the employees at an all campus meeting. Before that meeting they asked me to meet with them in the Chapel for a brief service of prayer and inspiration. I happened to choose one of their favorite scriptures for the service. Both are active Christians and this service helped establish a very good relationship which has grown in the intervening years.

The leadership of Buck Smith and the Trustees turned around the morale of the college almost immediately. He implored the campus community to help raise $1,000,000 in his first six months and found a donor to match that amount. The announcement was a great celebration for the College and I played an important role in putting that all-campus convocation together. Since that time, President Smith and the College have raised over $50,000,000 to put the college on solid financial ground.

The Religion in Education Committee was a very important group for me and the campus ministry in the late 70's. This group of six faculty, three Student Development staff, the Deans of Students and Faculty and the College President were one of the primary groups which directed the ministry on the campus. Formed by Chaplains Carpenter and Hoffman, this group focused its attention on the need to and the ways to teach values on our campus. This group gave me and the campus valuable input and direction until its demise in 1983. A key leader of this group was Dr. Fred Francis, Head of the Department of Religion. A graduate of Lexington Theological Seminary and Yale, Dr. Francis led in the writing and publishing of the following statement which is presented to new faculty and prospective staff to explain who we are as a college related to the Christian Church (Disciples of Christ).

Statement of the Religion In Education Committee

Through its founding communion, the Christian Church (Disciples of Christ), the distinctive spiritual heritage of Chapman College has been shaped by the idealism of Christian tradition, the religion of the Enlightenment—particularly the empiricism of John Locke, and the lively hope of the American frontier. This is a rich legacy of free inquiry, reason, historical criticism, the new sciences, social reform, and the unity of human kind.

The founding of Chapman by the Christian Church was expressive of that communion's characteristic impulse to create schools and publish critical journals. The enthusiasm for the life of the mind carried with it the questioning of dogma, creed, and ritual. Truth was to be found in the restoration of simplicity of life and the renewing power of reason. No persons were to give assent to received doctrine simply because of authority, but they were to test assertions for themselves.

Because of this heritage, Chapman College does not prescribe religious beliefs for students or faculty, though the founding vision continues to animate the College with a commitment to the renewing love personified in Jesus Christ. The College seeks to provide a value-centered education, a full chaplaincy program, and a strong religious studies curriculum, thereby preserving for its students in each generation this heritage of liberty, personal responsibility and self-transcendence.

Dr. Fred Francis also provided the idea and much of the direction of "Models in Ministry." This two and one half day workshop for persons considering the ministry has been hosted at Chapman since 1963. Over three hundred men and women have attended these workshops sponsored by the Disciples, the United Churches of Christ, and three seminaries in the Pacific Southwest. Dr. Francis was a moving force in this event until his untimely death in 1984.

The Chaplaincy at Chapman has always worked closely with the Office of Church Relations and I have been very fortunate to have worked with four excellent Directors of Church Relations: Charles Severns, Waymon McReynolds, Dennis Savage, and Vernon Ummel. In fact, I served as Director of Church Relations for a couple of years before Dennis Savage came to Chapman in the early 1980's. Chapman is fortunate to have an excellent Church Relations Committee of the Board of Trustees made up of Trustees, Faculty, Disciples clergy and the Director of Church Relations and the

Chaplains. This group meets five times a year and provides valuable leadership to the college.

A key part of my work at Chapman has always hinged around my work with student assistants—the Chapel Staff. I inherited a fine staff of two Jewish students, one Catholic and one Protestant student from the former Chaplain Kent Hoffman. To this group I added two students I had previously worked with in local churches and summer camps—LaTaunya Bynum and Cameron Malotte. I have always sought the goal of having an ecumenical and racially mixed group, believing: "who you are says more to me than what you say."

The Chapel Staff is a support group which plans, promotes and implements religious programming on the campus. It is a training ground for ministry, both clergy and lay. It also provides an opportunity for the Chaplain to have a closely knit team to give feedback on campus wide issues. The smallest Chapel Staff I've had was four and the largest was ten. Students work from three to ten hours per week and are paid a small stipend. Regularly planned activities have included weekly chapel, mass, fellowship, morning prayer and at least one retreat for students each semester. One group has also worked with Hillel, the Jewish student organization, to celebrate the major Jewish Holidays—especially Passover. Our Interfaith Passover service, led by a Rabbi, has drawn up to one hundred participants.

Chapman has traditionally had a large number of International Students. When I began in 1975 we had over 50 Saudi Arabian and over 50 Iranian students. These two groups composed almost 10% of the student body at that time. Both groups were devout Moslems and they expressed a need for a place to pray. I arranged for a Moslem Prayer Room on campus. It didn't take long to realize that I needed two Moslem prayer rooms—one was Sunni and one was Shiite. We had quite an active Saudi Moslem group until the Saudi government built their own Universities in the early 80's and stopped sending their students to the U.S.

Chapman is fortunate to have a racially mixed student body. 15% are International students, 6% are American Black, 10% are American Hispanic and 8% are American Asian. These numbers have remained fairly constant during my 10 years here with the Asians increasing and the Blacks decreasing in recent years. I have worked very closely with the Black Student Association and have served as Advisor for the Mexican American Student Association (MECHA). For a number of years Chapman's Black and Brown employees served as advisors but the College has not done very well in its minority hiring practices in the 80's. I strongly believe that ethnic students need role models and advisors from their own ethnic group as well as from other groups.

During my first year at Chapman, I often noticed the different ethnic groups kept to themselves in the college dining room and at the dorms. I shared this concern with Sonia Eagle Diaz, Professor of Anthropology, and the two of us developed a course called Cross Cultural Experience. We limited the class to 1/5 American Hispanic, 1/5 American Black, 1/5 American Anglo, 1/5 Internationals, and 1/5 other. In the ensuing four years, some 250 students went through this class which opened their eyes and their hearts to what is now referred to as the Rainbow Coalition. Some prejudice and racism remains, but I feel that quite a dent was made in this serious problem.

I also developed a class entitled *Practical Aspects of Ministry* for preministerial students to learn some youth work, administration and time management, and counseling skills. This often coincided with their involvement as youth workers in local churches and definitely augmented their academic education—and kept some of the less academically inclined students interested in ministry. I'm very proud of the 25 students who have taken this class and gone on to the finest seminaries in the United States.

Peace Studies and Peace Education are also strong interests of mine and I'm pleased to have been participant in the committee which devleoped our Peace Studies minor here at Chapman in the late 70's. The college owes much to the efforts of Dr. Paul Delp, Emeritus Professor of Philosophy for this program. In his retirement, Paul continues to eat his meals in the college dining room and talk with students about the importance of working for peace. I had the pleasure of teaching two classes in Peace Studies and look forward to supporting this program for as long as it exists. I also helped develop the very active Peace Club at Chapman and have served as its advisor.

I have also been very active in regional and local efforts for peace and social justice. After the 1981 General Assembly of the Christian Church (Disciples of Christ) urged the creation of Shalom Congregations, I helped Orange First Christian to become the first Shalom Congregation in this region. I was also chosen to become the first Chair of the Regional Peace and Justice Task Force, and served from 1982-85. My proudest accomplishment has been the Co-Founding of the Orange County Interfaith Peace Ministry in 1981. That organization has worked closely with Chapman to "make a difference" in one of the most conservative counties in the United States—a county very dependent on military contracts.

The College and the Chaplaincy were very fortunate to have Ms. Rita Brock as Assistant Chaplain from 1977 to 1980. A 1972 graduate of Chapman, Rita had received the Cheverton Trophy as the outstanding student upon graduation. While at Chapman, Rita was working on her Doctor of Ministry at The School of Theology at Claremont and her Ph.D. at Claremont Graduate School. Rita, a dynamic preacher and teacher of Puerto Rican and Japanese descent, was an excellent role model for female students who were considering the ministry.

Other key persons in the development of the campus ministry at Chapman are Jody Bullock, who served as secretary from 1970 until 1980, when she became the full-time wedding hostess for the College, and Audrey Anderson, who has served as secretary from 1980 until the present. It is not a coincidence that both women were educated at Disciples schools. Jody received her Bachelor of Religious Education from Northwest Christian College, and Audrey studied for the ministry at Texas Christian University before getting her BA degree in Elementary Education from the Univesity of Colorado. Both have provided valuable ministry to students, the Chapel staff and the Chaplains.

In 1981, I saw the need to further develop my skills in counseling and embarked on a four year program of study toward my Masters in Counseling Psychology, receiving my M.A. in May of 1985. This program not only deepened my skills, which I use regularly, but it put me into deeper contact with our excellent Psychology Department and enabled me to see the needs of our graduate students in a whole new light. I also gained new insight into what it means to be a student in the 80's. I encourage Chaplains to continually take classes as well as to teach classes.

Chapman has been fortunate over the years to have had an excellent relationship with Orange First Christian Church. In many ways it has been the campus church with an excellent music program and ministry to college students. In the past few years, under the leadership of Dr. Ben Bohren, it has been especially helpful. In 1984, Dr. Claudia Highbaugh was added to the pastoral team. She and Ben have started an excellent Disciple Student Fellowship which involves some 20 Chapman students each week in its program. My wife and I have been very active in Orange First since coming to Chapman, serving as Co-Chair of the Elders in 1984 and 1985.

In the past few years, Chapman has sought to be on the cutting edge of helping the church understand and relate to the ethnic groups in its community. I helped write a proposal which enabled the Division of Higher Education to grant Chapman funds to utilize its students in helping six Disciples congregations better relate to their communities. While the Church and Cultures Project was not the success we had hoped for, it accomplished many of its goals. It helped churches and students to a clearer understanding of many of the difficulties in this area of Church life.

Chapman has been quite sensitive to the needs of its Roman Catholic constituents since the late 1960's. In 1962, a Roman Catholic Advisory Committee was formed under the leadership of the Dean of the Faculty and Religion Professor, Cameron Sinclair, and Dr. Fred Francis, Head of the Religion Department. Their desire to find a Professor of Catholic Studies and my desire to find a Roman Catholic Chaplain culminated in the hiring of Maryloyola Yettke in 1984 on a part-time basis. A graduate of the Graduate Theological Union and Jesuit Theological Seminary at Berkeley, Ms. Yettke provided such fine leadership that she was hired as full-time Chaplain in 1985. During the spring semester of 1986, Ms. Yettke served the campus full-time, enabling me to go on sabbatical.

My sabbatical was very helpful in providing rest, perspective and renewal of skills. I recommend such sabbaticals to all Campus Ministry Centers. Highlights were a General Assembly of the World Student Christian Federation (WSCF) in Mexico City and a trip to Spokane, Washington, to visit with former Chaplain, Kent Hoffman. The WSCF Conference was attended by over 150 persons from 60 countries. It gave me an excellent perspective of the ministry of the church throughout the world. I was especially inspired by the Christians I met from El Salvador, Mexico, Cuba and Nicaragua. The Theology of Liberation is defintely changing Latin America.

Another highlight of my years at Chapman was the beginning of a Fall Faculty retreat at a conference grounds away from the campus. After two or three years of discussion, President Smith and Dean Sinclair decided to change our half-day faculty meeting to a twenty-four hour retreat in the mountains. This event does an excellent job of integrating new faculty (who come four hours early for a special orientation), but also builds a sense of unity among faculty and administrators in kicking off the year with a sense of enthusiasm. I open each retreat with a ten minute meditation and update of personal concerns and celebrations of the college community. Maryloyola or I also take five minutes at the beginning of each faculty meeting to share community concerns and celebrations.

Building and maintaining community is one of my primary tasks at Chapman. It is done in large gatherings like Faculty Meetings as well as one-on-one contact with members of the campus community. I report to the dean of Student Development and am very fortunate to have an excellent Christian Dean to work with in Susan Hunter Hancock. She has built an excellent team of persons dedicated to serving, guiding and directing Chapman's students. Chapman is fortunate to have many fine administrators who see the need to educate our students in a "caring and value-centered community" (one of the stated goals of the college).

In the last three years, I have come to really appreciate the value of a long ministry. I've experienced the joys of many ordinations, weddings and Marriage Encounter experiences with members of the Chapman Community. I've also experienced the joy of handing my oldest son, Mark, his diploma at the May 1986 Commencement as well as enjoying his performance in many plays and musical events. In July of 1985, I experienced the joy of my wife, Linda, coming to work at Chapman's Center for Human Interdependence and look forward to Linda and my youngest son, Steve, continuing their education at Chapman this Fall. I have also felt the pain of having students I've grown close to graduating and moving away and close faculty and staff leaving the college. Perhaps the most painful have been the death of Religion Professor Fred Francis and Drama Director Henry Kemp-Blair, as well as the deaths of seven other members of the Chapman community in the 1985-86 academic year. College Chaplaincy is both difficult and rewarding. It allows one to celebrate both the joys and sorrows of life.

CASE STUDY FIVE: "THIRTY-ONE YEARS IN MINISTRY
AT IOWA"
Rev. Sally Smith, Campus Minister
University of Iowa
Iowa City, Iowa

Half of my life has been spent as a campus minister—in one place. For 31 years I have shaped and been shaped by my ministry in Iowa City, Iowa, home of the University of Iowa. The most constant element in this ministry has been "change," which I would like to describe for you in several broad areas.

Ministering to "Our Own"—Mission "For Others"

I was employed in 1955 by the Iowa Society of Christian Churches to work half-time as a student worker. My other half-time job was with First Christian Church in Iowa City doing Christian education. We tried to provide a home-away-from-home for Disciples students through Sunday night supper meetings, Friday night ping-pong and recreation, occasional retreats and small groups for prayer or study. There was a strong sense of community among the students, but not much sense of mission. A few of the students and I were challenged from time to time to consider some of the larger issues in the world as we participated in Disciples Student Fellowship (DSF) Ecclesia annual conferences, state conferences, United Nations Seminars, and especially the Student Volunteer Movement Quadrennial Conferences at Athens, Ohio.

We came back from these events and tried to spark some enthusiasm among other students, but the response was not very encouraging. I remember one fellow passing a petition around protesting the failure of local barbers to cut the hair of black students, but he couldn't get anyone to sign it. Students were more concerned in the late 50's with their studies when assignments got tougher in response to the Soviet's Sputnik.

Along came the 60's and everything changed. The civil rights movement took off, along with the sexual revolution, and then came the Vietnam war and the women's movement. Students got into doing their own thing, and they weren't into gathering in groups planned by someone else. Sunday night suppers gave way to coffee houses, and our campus ministry sponsored the Mugwump Coffee House where students were free to drop in as they chose for refreshment, occasional music or poetry readings, and conversation. This was also the time when graffiti became quite popular, and so the walls were covered with quotations and personal expressions that occasionally had to be painted over at the insistenace of campus ministry board members.

The coffee house became possible when our campus ministry moved out of the churches where we had been housed into our own property. Students had proposed a coffee house in the basement of one of the congregations but they weren't quite ready for such "offbeat" activity. The basement of the campus ministry house was ideal. It was one way to keep in touch with students who were suddenly living in a rapidly changing society where no one was quite sure of the rules, or if there were any.

In one of our two campus ministry houses we started a daycare, since there was very little offered in Iowa City at that time, and surveys indicated a pressing need. We felt this would be a good ministry for student families who were trying to get an education, make a living, and raise children all at the same time. Melrose Day Care is about to celebrate its 20th birthday. It is licensed for 50 children, and even though there are now many day cares in the city, it has a reputation as one of the best.

Our campus ministry has had a continuing concern for student families in recent years. For a time, when funds were available, we had a part-time staff person working in this area, offering study and interest groups for student wives and mothers, planning orientation sessions for new student families, and raising the consciousness of congregations for the needs of these persons.

Another group that we have ministered to in recent years is international students. The Office of International Education and Services at the University asked us if we might organize a loan closet, and we did. We gather donations of furniture and other household items from our congregations and others, and then loan them to international students while they are in Iowa City. I have carried stacks of mattresses, and even couches, on top of my car, and students have made good use of them.

A couple of years ago someone gave us an old van which helps in picking up furniture and help my car as well. We also use it to take student families to the grocery store once a week. University housing for families is on the edge of town without easy access to grocery stores and some families do not have cars, especially international students. So this has been a valuable service for them, and often an enjoyable outing.

One program or area of concern often leads to new developments. We have tried to help congregations to be more aware of international students and their needs, and we have promoted the University Host Family program. A number of church families have "adopted" international students, and it seems that more of them are finding themselves welcomed into the life of congregations. We have just recently held an Iowa International Peace Camp with about 50 participants, mostly students from 16 different countries. It was a great experience in global community and we plan to hold another camp next year, and to try to create more global community on our campuses. The Division of Higher Education helped the Peace Camp to happen through one of its grants. Another of their grants helped to get the van in better working order.

Student generations change, and in recent years they have been ready to gather again. Once more we have Sunday night suppers with retreats and prayer groups. Most of this happens through the ministry of local congregations, with some encouragement, counsel, and coordination by the campus ministry. Students are also welcomed as full participants into the life and programs of congregations where they worship, sing in the choir, help with church school and youth groups, serve on church boards and committees.

The difference now from the late 50's is that there seems to be a broader understanding of what the Church is to be about. Both congregations and students are concerned for world peace, the environment, women's issues, world hunger, and more. This, to me, is a very encouraging sign.

From Denominational to Ecumenical Ministry

When I was a Disciples student worker I usually felt quite comfortable with my own little group of students in my own church. On the few occasions that campus ministers from the various denominations gathered we approached one another rather tentatively, feeling out the kinds of programs others had, and the numbers who participated. Our main activity together was Religion in Life Week, which was just one week long, but which took nearly a year to plan and to evaluate at monthly meetings.

In the early 60's our students went to the Disciples Student Fellowship (DSF) Ecclesia Conference to consider a proposal to unite with several denominational student fellowships. After a week of study and deliberation they voted to become part of the United Campus Christian Fellowship. On our campus that meant coming together with the Presbyterians and the United Church of Christ, and we were all very hesitant about associating with "strangers." Furthermore, this union came at about the same time students were not gathering well for any activities, so our united fellowship group was a fairly small one.

The next step was more fruitful, however. We decided that we needed to have more than a united *student* fellowship. We needed to be a united *ministry*. Boards at the local and state level wrote by-laws, campus ministers spent time together in planning program, and some good things began to happen. I discovered that it was great to work with a team, and that together we could do all kinds of things which no one could do alone.

About the same time, campus ministers from most of the mainline denominations began to gather frequently for a variety of reasons. We did some study together, shared information, and offered some joint programming. One of the first serious efforts we undertook together was a lay studies program, where three or four groups of students covenanted to study theological papers and to discuss them together over supper. Out of this program the Lutheran campus ministry established their Christus House Community, a live-in group that engages in disciplined study and activities, and which still continues.

We initiated an orientation program for incoming students, and after a couple of years, the University developed its own program. Now the campus ministers are invited by the University to participate in its orientation program.

During the 60's when student lifestyles underwent dramatic changes, we invited clergy and others from around the state to come to the campus for "exposure experiences." We arranged for them to visit with all kinds of students: draft resisters and ROTC students, gays and straights, those in communes, student families, counter culture people, those who were into taverns and rock music, and more. In more recent days we have organized conferences for clergy and others on "faith development" and on cults, to increase their ability to understand and relate to young adults.

Campus ministers try many programs—sometimes they succeed and often they don't but we keep on trying. One of our biggest successes was the Changing Family Conference, which was initiated by the UMHE. We had $1000 in our budget for a speaker and found out we could get Margaret Mead. We put together a conference, and to our amazement had 500 participants show up. Encouraged by our success we launched a series of annual conferences which reached 1500 participants at the peak and generated enough income to be self-sustaining. People from other campus ministries and the University were welcomed into the planning process. Eventually the University took over the leading support for the conferences, but all interested persons are still welcome to be involved.

Campus ministers were involved in the civil rights movement. Four of us west to Jackson, Mississippi to participate with the chaplain and students at Tougaloo College in their efforts to integrate the churches. It was a tremendous learning experience for us and we spoke to many persons about it upon our return. The coming summer, a few students went South to work in the Freedom Movement and I returned for a couple of weeks to help with voter registration and other efforts by the National Council of Churches.

During the time of the Vietnam war when students protested, disrupting life in the University and the town, campus ministers were heavily involved. We helped to rally students, faculty, administrators and others to monitor the activities, and tried to interpret what was happening to our churches and others. We tried to be present with the students as they agonized over the war, and we participated with many of them in the political processes that hoped to bring an end to the war.

Campus ministers from the major Protestant denominations and the Catholic and Jewish faiths now meet weekly for mutual support, to share information and to do some joint programming. We do some things as a total group, like promoting the Oxfam Fast every November. We do other things according to whoever is interested, like the Life Work Planning Workshops the Methodist campus minister and I do every year. When campus ministers leave and a new candidate is being interviewed, campus ministers are always asked to meet with those persons being considered.

We've come a long way from our denominational ministry and the Church has become far more effective and outreaching in the process.

Dwindling Financial Support

Finances are probably the biggest ongoing headache for campus ministry. I'd like to suggest a couple of factors which I believe have contributed to our dwindling finances. The first was our move to ecumenicity. When our campus ministries united it was almost like a marriage where the parent bodies felt we were now on our own, or at least we had a lot of in-laws, and they no longer needed to support us in the same way. Unfortunately, campus ministry does not have a constituency to draw upon for income, as congregations do, but depends upon the larger manifestations of the church for support.

Another factor which may have added to the "disowning" of campus ministry by the denominations was the desire by campus ministers to be recognized as a legitimate ministry in its own right. Prior to our union, our campus ministries had been housed with the local congregations and the pastors were our "bosses." They were the top administrators of campus ministry even though their time and responsibilities were chiefly in other areas of church life. Campus ministers, who gave all of their attention to their area of expertize were unhappy that they did not have the authority to go along with their job descriptions. So, when the opportunity came, they moved out of the churches and into their own centers. In our case this came when the Presbyterians had capital funds enough to purchase two adjacent properties for campus ministry. Unfortunately, this move suggested to local congregations and pastors that they now had very little responsibility for any ministry to students, and it probably caused more division between campus ministry and the source of its funding.

Another factor which added to the loss of financial support was the campus itself in the 60's. The Church looked at the campus and was shocked, confused, and angered, and it questioned campus ministry's role in all of this. These were the times when students began to live together, sometimes in communes. When we built new facilities at First Christian for students, we made sure to put in windows so we could keep an eye on their activities. Now they found their own places to do as they pleased. They began to experiment with marijuana and other drugs. They wore grubby clothes, let their hair grow, and used shocking language. Even the kids in our day care had learned the words that made adults gasp; and the students wrote them on the walls of the coffee house.

When a few went south to protest in the civil rights movement, no one got very upset, because it didn't touch our way of life. But when they protested the Vietnam war and began to spill out into the street and highways, disrupting traffic, breaking windows and getting arrested, members of the congregations and the town became angry. Our UMHE had offices downtown at that time, just across from the campus, which were used as a headquarters for the monitors who worked day and night to keep on top of the protests. Doctors who owned the building said their patients were upset by the presence of the questionable charactes and so we were evicted.

All of these factors contributed to questions about the nature of campus ministry and to declining support for it. Our state commission, the boards and campus ministers at our four campuses in Iowa argued and agonized and angered over how to deal with this crisis. Over a short period of years there were two staff reductions with selective, and rather arbitrary cutting the first time, and everyone cut the second time. I was fired both times, but applied for the openings and was rehired. We went from two and a half staff positions at our campus to one full-time position.

In the process of cutting finances, the denominations became involved in some reshaping of the ministry. Once again, local congregations were to be involved, as partners with campus ministers. The reorganization has been fairly positive and given some stability to the program. Denominations have tried to be more accountable to one another, to take more ownership, and funding has ever grown a little in recent years. But now with the farm crisis, church giving has fallen off, and the finances were once again threatened. Our center has some advantages in that many of our major programs are self-supporting, like the day care, and we do have a money-raising project by parking cars for football games.

We have, however, cut our budgets to the bare bones, so we do not know what the future holds for us. It seems that campus ministry is always living on the edge.

Growing Acceptance by the University

At the same time that our future is in jeopardy, we have growing acceptance by the University, which we have earned over a period of years and relationships. The Church may have been upset by our role in the Vietnam conflicts, but the University appreciated our efforts. In fact, when students began to protest again, over South Africa, the administration asked if we would be involved, not to take sides, but to monitor activities to try to prevent anyone from getting hurt. They asked one of the campus ministers to serve on a committee to bring recommendations to the administration regarding their South African investments.

There are many partnerships between campus ministry and university personnel in trying to serve students and others. We have close working relationships with the International Office of Education and Services, with the Special Support Services for minority students, with Orientation, with Counseling Services, and with others.

It seems to me that campus ministry has come a long way in the 31 years since I have been involved. Change has been a constant: times have changed, the Church has changed, the University has changed, students have changed, and campus ministry has changed. I would hope that there is another constant: that the Church continues to have a vital role in the life and mission of university communities.

CASE STUDY SIX: OUR UNFOLDING MINISTRY AT
TEXAS CHRISTIAN UNIVERSITY
Rev. John Butler, Campus Minister
Texas Christian University
Fort Worth, Texas

If there was need for a single descriptive characteristic of ministries in higher education in the last half of this century, there are many candidates. The one I would propose is that they are so separate from one another with widely different and intensely held identities, program, and operating styles. Funding and accountability structures, basic beliefs, the competitive market place of activities and ideas on campus, and the developmental tasks of young adults have each contributed to this phenomenon. These differences in both public and private higher education have frequently been shaped around the personality, skills, religious experience, and/or interests of the particular campus minister. Justification for these differences are usually made on the basis that they reflect the creativity and flexibility needed in the academic setting. And while there have been many creative and significant contributions from ministry in higher education, I am convinced that one of the substantial and as yet uncorrected weaknesses in this important ministry is the extent of separation that exists. This pattern has been easily reinforced in the larger church by a limited commitment to ecumenism and a strongly promotional approach to ministries in general.

When I began my task as University Minister in 1979 the denominational ministries at TCU were, like the rest of the country, very separated. The Methodists did their program and the Roman Catholics did theirs, and on and on and on. The staffs of these ministries met monthly for lunch to have a social time together, to report the activities of their respective ministries, and to plan a few programs requiring minimal cooperation. Being a Disciples campus minister on a Disciples-related school in a stereotypically Disciples style and content of ministry was not even on the list of priorities as I began my tenure in this ministry. I had been in "campus ministry" on both sides of the nation, in large schools and small, in local ministry and national staff. I had seen and learned from the best. I knew what had to be done, but I also knew that a new way around established weaknesses in this very old and important ministry was needed. I was convinced that new way was to become intensely and precisely ecumenical at every point and aspect of ministry.

Moreover, I was convinced that what had been the tradition of "my ministry" (what am I doing) had to become "our ministry" (what are we going to do).

We began by gathering the ministers (clergy and laity) of the historic churches working on the TCU campus on a weekly basis to begin the process of defining and performing a comprehensive, thoroughly ecumenical ministry. It would take some time, it would be difficult, we would have to repeat several steps as key issues and characters changed, but it was going to become a reality.

The first half of this primary goal is to actively encourage the full and yet precise expression of denominational ministries. We have intentionally helped one another tell and live the "story" of Christian meanings from a denominational perspective. We gather information and resources to enable a strong denominational identity and program. The several denominational ministries provide weekly fellowship, learning, service, and worship for all who would participate. Special occasions, retreats, statewide conferences, trips for fun and service give added meaning and opportunity for development for those in each of the denominational ministries. In every case, "membership" reflects a variety of denominational backgrounds. We encourage an exploration of faith and practice, making movement across the ministries easy and accepted. Some students become active in several denominational groups at the same time. We are very intentional about helping students see the importance of church heritage, knowing the polity and work of the churches, keeping each tradition in perspective within the full tradition, and doing what must be, for the present, denominational.

The second half of the primary goal for our ministry is to emphasize the hope and the reality of our oneness. Accomplishing this requires a precision and intensity about being ecumenical. We operate as one staff of ministers out of a single suite of offices in the student center. We design program, provide services, purchase and use resources, engage in the work of ministry on campus, and evaluate our work as a team of professionals. We challenge the students as well as faculty and staff to become as ecumenical in thinking and activity as is currently possible for them and the church. We provide current information about advances in ecumenism to campus constituencies. We do the same in the educational programs of local churches. We stay current ourselves with involvements in ecumenical organizations and with reflections on such developments as the Baptism, Eucharist and Ministry documents of the World Council of Churches, COCU, etc.

The basic foundation of both the denominational and ecumenical expressions of ministry is the historic church and its faith. We make extensive use of church tradition, resources, and current activity. And while it is often misunderstood at first, we make clear distinctions between the life of the church and the many non-church religious organizations that are active on this campus and in the larger society.

In 1981 we formed the Campus Christian Community (CCC) as our on-campus expression of ecumenism modeled after national and world councils of churches. Four task forces (worship, Christian education, social justice, and witness) form the backbone of the work of the CCC. Everyone active in the ministries of the denominations are automatically members of the CCC and open to participate in the work of the task forces. This work is guided by a council of representatives selected from each denominational ministry according to a formula based upon the religious affiliations self-reported by all students on campus. The Council meets weekly throughout the school year, and each task force does programming for CCC, for the denominations, and often in concert with the wide variety of campus organizations.

One of the important ingredients in our ministry is the ministry with and to minority students. This ministry occurs within its own heritage and identity on campus (We call it AGAPE, for the love and event that reconciles). The university provides a black clergy. The Presbyterian Church provides support for program budget. The United Methodist Church provides a clean and spacious place for Agape to meet. This ministry and all who share in it (both black and white) are full partners in the work of the church on campus.

The traditional components of ministry are a good way to see the process of building our ministry at TCU. Worship on many church-related colleges means at least Chapel, and TCU is no exception. Each week University Chapel is offered on a volunteer basis. After several years of experiments in worship, in 1979 we built our Chapel service around the COCU model. In 1985 we began using the model that has evolved from the BEM process of the World Council of Churches. Someone will occasionally ask about having a "Disciple" worship (including communion each week) as our model. Worship thus provides an opportunity for educating the community about what can and cannot be done in a worship setting that respects our diversity and reflects the degree of unity currently possible. Whether in the matter of inclusive language or music and other liturgical resources, we draw on the rich variety of traditions to shape our worship experiences on campus. Students and faculty, working with our Roman Catholic priest, prepare and provide a weekly Mass. Unlike many of the larger church-related universities, we do not have Sunday morning worship on campus. We encourage students to participate in the worship of the area churches on Sunday.

People on any campus have needs for which a pastoral response is sought. Pastoral counseling occurs around concerns as diverse as emotional stability, vocational choice, sexual identity, substance abuse, or academic performance for both students and faculty/staff. This is done completely without regard to denominational background of those seeking or providing the counseling (unless specifically requested). Several of the campus ministry team have graduate degrees in counseling and psychology. I meet weekly with the director of the TCU Counseling Center to explore issues and facilitate the quality of care we desire. Visits in the hospital and homes at times of crisis are done by all of us on the ministry team, though certain crises sometimes require the expression of a specific faith heritage. Individual support through decisions and stresses of life occur for students, faculty, and staff alike; and is provided by all of us (clergy and laity) who share in this ministry.

The educational component of ministry is as varied as the disciplines of the university. Guest speakers, films, discussions, debates, displays, and other media are as diverse as the places (residence halls, class rooms, student center, homes, and individual offices) and the issues (global concerns, equal access and opportunity, role of women, life and death issues, authority and doubt in faith, the practices and beliefs of the many expressions of Christianity, campus issues, etc.) through which Christian Education occurs. The denominational ministries, the Christian Education task force of the Campus Christian Community, the campus ministers, departments in the university, and other individuals each become shapers and providers of this important task. Annual mission goals of the CCC, of the several denominations, and of the university serve to both guide and evaluate our efforts.

Our response to social justice concerns are likewise varied in form and content. Our response to world hunger has evolved during the last four years to a campus wide, week long event (requiring year round planning and other preparations) for education and fund-raising. In these few years we have raised over $65,000 which is annually divided in equal shares among Church World Service, Catholic Relief, UNICEF, Oxfam America, Manna, and a selected local hunger relief agency. We have developed a similar campus wide response for clothing at the close of the school year, usually generating between 7 and 12 tons of clothing for use by people in need of emergency assistance (recently it has been the Kickapoo Indians of south Texas). University Ministries has provided key leadership and active participation in the continuing campus wide programs on Alcohol Awareness, Human Sexuality and Date Rape, Affirmative Action, and others. In addition, we have developed or assist others develop responses to global issues such as Central America, Nuclear War, South Africa, etc., that often best include combinations of campus and church responses. Currently we are exploring alternative strategies for responding to Aparthied in South Africa. Opportunities for voluntary service for those in need in our city (tutoring, making sandwiches, cleaning, etc.) are also provided on an individual and group basis.

We are constantly reminded of the need to provide public witness to the historic church and the faith it has preserved across the centuries. The average student arrives on campus prepared for the university experiences in many ways. The least prepared arena of knowledge and experience is consistently that of faith. Students and staff alike need a witness for a reasoned, practiced faith integrated into the complexities and diversities of the contemporary world. Students and staff need the witness of a vital ecumenism that is capable of affirming diversity, accepting personal doubt and the moral/spiritual failures of history, and of building the practical expressions of faith for the coming generations. Students and staff need a witness that assists them in making meaningful distinctions in the religious pluralism of our world and involves them in the decisions of an unfolding church.

The process of building a comprehensive and ecumenical ministry requires wisely using the resources of church and university, developing a team of professional clergy capable of working in this environment, and making the ministry a genuine "we," even when it seems we must for a time remain separated from one another, if not from God. I am hopeful that this process is visible to students and staff alike; and more importantly, assists in the process of faith development in the life of individuals as well as change in the life of the church in the not too distant future. The vision for ministry I began with, given to me by others in the church, shapes the programmatic details, serves as a principal tool in our annual evaluations, and in the final analysis, serves as the test of our long term effectiveness on this or any other campus.

Chapter **6**

1986 AND BEYOND: MINISTRY FOR THE COMING AGE

1986 and beyond: implications for future ministry

It is a brave person who ventures a wager on the precise future of higher education in America, let alone the future shape of the church's ministry in American higher education. Martin E. Marty, in describing the difficulty of future predictions once claimed: "Efforts to envision the cultural context of higher education beyond one generation are futile."[1] One may conceive of a generation as about eighteen years, about the length of time when those just born into the world will be approaching their college years. Even within such a relatively short span of time, some dramatic surprises and cultural shifts are bound to occur.

A quick look over our shoulder at the surprising events of the past eighteen years reminds us how difficult the task of predicting the future remains. Eighteen years ago, in the field of medicine, who would have predicted the outbreak of the fatal disease AIDS and its impact upon the culture? In business, the dramatic shortage of oil, followed by glut, and resultant price changes; wide fluctuations in interest rates; and consumer demand for personal computers and VCRs; none of these were perceived in the crystal ball of future projections. Even the giant car building industry in Detroit failed to predict the powerful impact of the imported Japanese automobile in a domestic market which they had taken for granted. One generation ago, who would have predicted that the President of the United States would be forced to resign?

Difficult though the task may be, we are challenged by the imperative to forge the church's mission and ministry in higher education for this coming new generation. Among American values, higher education remains a high priority, though the differing purposes of education are valued by a pluralism of constituents. Some are interested in higher education because they see it as essential for our nation's defense. The proposed "Star Wars" defensive scheme requires discoveries not yet attained by our scientists. Business depends upon the knowledge and creative processes which are fostered in the halls of higher education. Research in agriculture and fisheries has made an immense contribution to the growth of the worlds food supply. Individuals within our culture see education as a means to a profession, a vocation, a career. Others value education because, through learning, the highest potential for being truly human may be nurtured and sustained. Clark Kerr once said, "knowledge is now central to society. It is wanted, even demanded, by more people and more institutions than ever before. The university as producer, wholesaler, and retailer of knowledge, cannot escape service. Knowledge, today, is for everybody's sake."[2]

The contributions of higher education are enormous, and they benefit the entire human family as the reservoir of knowledge grows through the contributions of succeeding generations. The dedication to public service has brought the resources of higher education to bear upon finding solutions to societal and technical problems. By equipping individuals for creative and generative work in society it contributes to the public good. By teaching individuals to think critically and to pursue the truth, it ennobles and humanizes their lives.

Yet, knowledge itself is no panacea. Knowledge alone does not create virtue. We live in a world suffering through a crisis of meaning and purpose, and this nation is no exception. The crisis is felt when the world trembles at the threat of nuclear annihilation. It is felt in the hungry bellies of the starving, while others have surplus and surfeit. It is the nagging threat in the inheritance of polluted soil, water, and air that we are passing on to future generations. It is manifest in a crude and profane society which has lost confidence in the ideals of faith and duty and builds more and larger prisons to house its offenders. It is experienced by the countless individuals who feel lost in the landscape of pluralism, believing in nothing. As Ortega y Gasset claimed, we must rediscover the true relations between action and contemplation so that we may be guided by intelligence in the complex choices we must make in today's world. Ortega says:

> Few are the peoples who in these latter days still enjoy that tranquility which permits one to choose the truth, to abstract oneself in meditations. Almost all the world is in tumult, and when man is beside himself he loses his most essential attribute: the possibility of meditating or withdrawing into himself in order to come to terms with himself and define what it is he believes, what he truly esteems, and what he truly detests. In the world today a great thing is dying: it is truth. Why is it dying? For want of meditation. Without a certain margin of tranquility, truth succumbs. Without a strategic retreat into the self, without vigilant thought, human life is impossible.[3]

Will the university, left to itself, cultivate this search for truth in the young people who come in the search for knowledge? Can the church, through its ministries, contribute to the excellence of education by engaging students and faculty in processes of action and reflection which transcend departmental compartments and national borders? Harvey Cox has called for the creation of new structures through which the church can carry out its ministries. Cox claims that "the future witness of the church will be in the secular university..."[4]

One of the important witnesses which the church must find ways to bring to bear in its service within the secular university, is in the realm of values. Education's goal is to enable and empower individuals in qualifying their decisions and actions by knowledge and reflection. The dialectic of action and reflection is essential, for, as Whitehead has maintained, "education is the acquisition of the art of utilization of knowledge."[5] It is preparation for life. It is discovering the means to find meaning in an age of meaninglessness. It is affirming, as did Luthardt, that true faith is fully reconcilable with enlightened thought. Herein, is an arena for significant campus ministry:

> Faith is not merely an unenlightened feeling, nor religion merely a matter for the sentimental. Faith is the firm and joyful certainty of the heart which knows what it believes. Faith is not the opposite of knowledge, but the highest kind of knowledge, which is more worth knowing than any other. Those who believe and those who know, are not so opposed that the former belong to one, the latter to another party, or that they must be abandoning the world of faith who are advancing toward knowledge. A man does not cease to be a scholar because he becomes a believer.[6]

Where does the student test the soundness of his/her belief system in the midst of a college or university experience where former world views are shaken, old ideas and values are challenged, and the scientific method is applied to every arena of thought and life? Where can the dialectic between doubt and belief, which is so essential for spiritual growth, take place? Where will the elements of religious thought which have undergone the rigorous analysis of critical reflection be offered as a staple amidst the smorgasbord of "experiential" and "authoritarian" religious offerings which inevitably surround the typical college or university campus? Where can the future leaders of church and society be exposed to the best of our Christian tradition and become personally engaged with mature and committed leaders who will share the journey of faith with them? Where can the cries for social justice be heard and affirmed amidst the clamoring chorus which champions the cause of individualism and personal prosperity? I believe the church has created a unique opportunity to help the campus community in addressing these issues, and faces a special responsibility in living up to this challenge.

The magnitude of such a task is impressive! In the autumn quarter of 1985 there were 12,247,000 students enrolled in over 3,300 institutions of higher education in the United States. About 9.6 million attend public colleges and universities and approximately 2.7 million attend private and/or church-related institutions. Nearly one half, 45 percent of these students attend part time, 43 percent of the student population are 25 years of age or older, one out of every six is a member of a minority group and more than half of all undergraduates are women. This student population alone, to say nothing of faculty and administrators, is numerically formidable in contrast to the available leadership and financial resources which the church has committed to campus ministry.

Education for the future

The church must see the importance of education in the coming age. More and more students will claim the priority of education in preparing for their personal futures. In addition to the traditional function of undergraduate education as the transmitter of culture, the college degree has become a requirement for an increasing number of occupations. College education is now viewed as a passport to a richer, fuller life, and the key to economic progress. Research over the past few decades has substantiated the fact that

> . . . higher education contributes significantly to students' cognitive, emotional, and moral development, to their economic productivity and effectiveness as consumers, and to their family life, leisure-time activities, and health. College alumni who participate in follow-up surveys consistently cite the enduring benefits of higher education in making them aware of different cultures and ways of life, in promoting their understanding of science and technology, and in developing their interpersonal skills.[7]

The church must also recognize the vexing problems that exclude some students from reaping the benefits of education. Currently, one out of eight very capable high school graduates choose not to attend college. Among those electing to enter college, only half actually attain their goal of a bachelor's degree. More of those who do graduate today are majoring in narrow specialties and foregoing a liberal arts education in favor of occupational training. Such specialization leads to a fragmented education with limited and compartmentalized knowledge, losing the potential to foster the "shared values and knowledge that bind us together as a society."[8]

The Study Group on the Conditions of Excellence in American Higher Education suggested in their report, *Involvement in Learning* (1984), that we need new ways to measure the educational outcomes of our institutions of higher education. Furthermore, that the quality of undergraduate education could be vastly improved if

> . . . America's colleges and universities would apply existing knowledge about three critical conditions of excellence—1) student involvement, 2) high expectations, and 3) assessment and feedback.[9]

When students really become involved in the learning process, the intensity of motivation and effort increases and learning is enhanced. Campus ministry programs frequently engage students in reflecting about their current learning in the light of the Christian faith though discussion groups and Bible studies. Furthermore, the campus ministry center becomes a key meeting place for commuter college students, allowing them to become more "involved" through extracurricular activities which enhance the learning process.

Campus ministries play a key role in assisting students in sorting out their own "expectations" about what they want from college and what they are willing to put into it. The large public colleges and universities usually offer the potential for an excellent education, if one's courses and instructors can be carefully and thoughtfully chosen. Conversely, without some foresight and insight into the complex process of clarifying one's expectations and becoming sophisticated in achieving them, students may become isolated and wander through four-years' curriculum with at best a mediocre educational experience which is fragmented and far below their entering expectations.

Many of the innovative campus ministry programs involve students as peer ministers, traveling seminar participants, work-study partners, and interns. Through these projects, related to the learning goals of the students, opportunities for feedback and assessment occur in a collegial and non-threatening environment, synergistically enriching the learning experience.

These distinctive qualities of future education are more likely to lead to a "liberating" education; an education providing a base of knowledge and methods of learning which will enable students to continue as independent, "life-long learners."

I find a challenge for the church in its ministry to the campus. The church's agenda of advocacy for students finds one of its highest expressions by working in the institutions of higher education to advance and advocate for this kind of liberal or "liberating" education. The establishment of these principles is essential as we face the tasks of the future. The extent to which we are only poorly doing the task today is an indictment upon the institutions of our society, the church included, for the church has both a prophetic role and a service role in helping this to happen.

The church has a unique role in society because of its involvement with members literally from birth to death—from the cradle to the grave. Local congregations bear the responsibility, along with the family, for providing adequate and competent Christian education to children during their developing years. Students entering the secular universities, who have received good religious education, discover that their Christian world view serves them well in the exploration and search for new knowledge. Those who have received little, or poor religious education, may find that their belief system is more of a hindrance than a help. For example, Christian students need to learn early that Darwin's theory of evolution is not contrary to the Christian world view nor the belief system which affirms a creator God. Without this insight, they find their faith threatened in their first natural science class in college. Christian students need to have an adequate understanding of the Bible including how and when it was written and what kind of literature it contains. Otherwise, in their first "English Bible as Literature" class they are "blown away" by the introduction of higher and lower criticism, the discovery of inconsistencies in the Gospels, or the identification of myths in the Bible. Many campus ministers can attest to helping students avoid "throwing the baby out with the bath water," around such issues as the integration of new knowledge with their Christian faith. Local congregations must help prepare their student members for higher education by providing them with an adequate religious education before they arrive on campus.

For the past few years this nation has agonized over the "crisis of public education." Objective data from college admission scores indicate that today's schools are failing to adequately teach the basic skills so important for future success in higher education, and for survival in modern society. There is still a significant "drop-out" rate in high school age young people. Too few students in public school graduate with skills in dealing with questions of ethics and values. The problem of illiteracy is becoming an embarrassment to this society. When the church addresses such issues in public education today—this should be seen as a precursor ministry to higher education.

It was thought when television became widely available in the homes of America that it would be a potent educational tool, and it continues to have that potential—but this potential has never been adequately utilized. In fact, much of the "teaching" from television today is of negative value:

> During the past three decades, television has provided America with a distorted image of itself, alternating the idealized and the sordid. It has minimized the contribution of women, minorities, the aged, and the handicapped to society. It has exalted violence and enshrined commercial values. . . . Instead of educating the young, television has sold them products.[10]

When the church addresses these issues through the Federal Communications Commission, such actions should be conceived as a part of the church's ministry to higher education.

When the goal of world peace is so important, and so fragile, this country needs to develop within its young people a sense of the world as a global community. The challenge to altruistic service, combined with opening the doors for young people to make a practical contribution through the Peace Corps and Volunteer Services to America are examples of a positive contribution which our government has offered. What better way to work toward such a goal than by providing opportunities for learning and service in other countries where the people, the culture, and the language may be seen, felt, heard, and spoken every day. There students may cultivate a sense of empathetic awareness for the needs and problems of others and gain a better perspective of the cultural and political context in which these problems arise. To a limited extent, campus ministries have taken work-study groups to Mexico, El Salvador, Nicaragua, South Africa, to name but a few. Such new opportunities could be magnified on behalf of the church, with greater financial resources to fund such efforts.

Still other opportunities for service and learning could be developed within the borders of this country wherein students would learn a great deal about domestic problems within the cultural and political climate of the United States. The opportunity for action and reflection would facilitate such learning. Internships should be developed in which the colleges and universities cooperate with institutions of government and the private sector to provide such opportunities. The church should play an increasing role in facilitating internships at home and abroad for college students as a priority for its mission in higher education.

Service learning is now generally accepted as a desireable mode for the education of students. This concept has been steadily gaining acceptance, and as recently as the 1985 Convention, the American Association of Higher Education cited "service-learning" as a top priority emphasis for institutions of higher education. This concept is not new to campus ministry, and the Dallas Community College Ministry provides an example of service learning in Rev. Betsy Turecky's PRAXIS Project, engaging 500 students and 45 faculty in an educational opportunity outside the classroom. Students in this program were required to spend a minimum of ten hours in community service after an orientation and training session conducted by the host agency. In addition students then participated in two, hour-long reflection sessions, often facilitated by the campus minister or ministry volunteer. Finally, each student met the course instructor's requirement for appropriate reporting, usually an oral report or a reflection paper.[11] Such a project provides the "action-reflection" style of learning which is so important in meeting the developmental needs of young adults. It also provides an opportunity for the church to work in partnership with the institutions of higher education.

The challenging agenda of higher education

Nor does the task end with the educational experience of the student, in experiencing a liberating education, as important as that is in itself. The fact is, higher education as an enterprise, is being challenged. There are powerful monetary temptations to shape the direction of scientific research toward the military goals of the Pentagon. In some cases, powerful business interests set the agenda for the college curriculum. Institutions will soon be entering an era of increased competition for students. The consensus of just what constitutes a liberal arts education has dissolved in the face of competing claims. The budgets of state supported higher education have gone through a serious reduction and on many campuses, faculty and staff have not received a pay increase for two years or longer. On private colleges, faculty are too often paid at the lowest salary level and expected to produce at the highest performance level. Too many faculty are bored and dissatisfied with their work, disillusioned by the apparent apathy of students and the lack of support from state legislatures. The church must be in dialogue with the leaders in higher education in order to work together toward solutions. In addition, such conditions serve to remind us that students are not the only parties on the campus who need the pastoral concern of the campus minister.

Students seem bent on obtaining credentials and qualifications to compete in the job market, and too little interested or concerned with the kind of education which liberates them for critical awareness or ideas. When this is the case, students often graduate without the capacity to reflect critically upon their own ideas, and those of others. They move on, but without the empowerment, which accompanies a deeper understanding of the self and the major forces shaping modern life. Perhaps, most importantly, they may miss the moral core of education, the assumption of responsibility for enlightened action in the world—the commitment to apply what they know for the good of others—for society—not simply for the self. Such an education is liberating, and as Zelda F. Gamson claims, "This latter emphasis implies that the proper education is not what has already been defined as liberal education but is whatever is liberating in a particular context for a particular student body at a particular moment in time."[12]

A reexamination of the nature and purpose of campus ministry: (Should the Church Go to Campus?)

The contributions of higher education are distributed widely throughout society, benefiting individuals, institutions, and society as a whole. The church is enriched by the fruits of higher education. If we begin with the premise that "all Truth is from God," it follows that in the discovery and teaching of knowledge, higher education is congruent with the purposes of God. The church is the beneficiary of higher education when its leaders and scholars are equipped to better understand and respond to the problems and issues of the modern world, or in the application of scholarly methods which enhance our understanding of the Bible and the developing history of the faith community.

Can the church, in turn, make a contribution to higher education? To put it even more bluntly, does the church have any business on the campus? This is a question which is increasingly being asked by laypersons in the churches, and it is good that we should ask, for this is a theological question which deserves answering.

There are several assertions of faith which are central to the argument as to whether or not the church should be involved in higher education, and which have a bearing on how the church should be involved.

Theological presuppositions underlying ministry in higher education

To begin, the "people of God" have a unique world view, holding as Christians do, the notion that the kingdom of God claims one's ultimate loyalty amidst a pluralism of claims and kingdoms. Christians live with both the reality of the kingdom of God and the hope for its ultimate reign. From this view, the world is God's creation, and the processes, persons, and institutions of higher education are a part of God's creation. Thus, the church does not take God to the campus, God is already there.

The church goes to college to announce the presence of God and to celebrate the mighty acts of God, to proclaim the gospel. Such ministry affirms the goodness of God's creation. In the context of the college campus, this proclamation means that God loves the world, not just the church, not just Christians, not just the people of this nation—but all the created order is loved by God. God's creation continues in the processes of human learning, the discovery of new truth, and the application of new ideas. The church needs to be there as partners in the dialogue, the world of higher education is an appropriate context for ministry.

Just as obedience to the Lordship of Christ calls individual Christians and communities to repentance and renewal, so the claims of Christ are like a plumbline in the midst of educational institutions, demanding faithfulness to love and justice in the service of humanity. The human world continues the creative activity of God through participating in the development of the mind and encouraging opportunities for learning and growth which engage these critical faculties in planning and shaping a better future. Such a future engenders the highest respect and regard for persons, assisting them in the development of their highest potential.

The Christian community gathers around word and sacrament to celebrate God's activity in the modern world, to refresh and renew commitment to the disciplines of the kingdom of God. Within the communities of higher education, Christians rely on the support of the faith community in seeking their vision of Christian vocation. The principalities and powers of this world constantly threaten to divert us from the work to which we are called, by compromise, expedience, or self-aggrandizement. The people of God who join in the ministry of the church on the campus encourage the life of a self-conscious community which regularly opens itself in reflection and confession to the leading of the Spirit of God toward wholeness and integration, toward loving service to others.

In Jesus Christ we encounter God's "Word made Flesh." Through Christ, the people of God encounter God's love and justice incarnate, and learn of our duty and obligation toward our brothers and sisters. Hearers and believers of the Word are instructed to go into all the world to share the "good news" by word and by deed. This includes the world of higher education where the gifts of knowledge, insight, and wisdom have the power to dispel darkness, suffering, isolation, and want. Such gifts should be shared with all.

On the campus, the church's ministry is directed to persons who compose the community of higher education, and to the issues which emerge in the processes of this enterprise. Ministry must always find its focus on persons. It is clear by now that such ministry will include, but not be limited to students, and will encompass the faculty and administration as well. It is also clear that to be faithful to the gospel, such a ministry must confront the structures of the university which oppress individuals or groups and frustrate the just governance of the institution. Furthermore, the ministry of the church will look and listen with sensitivity to the issues surrounding the learning process and call the university to fulfill its highest purpose and mission in the world. Such a prophetic ministry should be carried out with the deep humility which regards the failures of the church, alongside the university, and seeks to ask the right questions, without pretending to hold all the right answers.

Finally, the church must be open to sharing its life with the university, for it has much to gain, as well as to offer. Theology itself needs the gifts of higher education in developing a rational method of bringing consistency and coherency to the theological dialogues of today. The life of the church is dependent upon the competent exercise of scholarship in achieving its highest goals.

From these premises, the church has a responsibility to serve the world, of which higher education is very much a part. If the church is to truly be the church, it will be involved. It will bring its message of love and justice into every arena of human experience. It will work cooperatively with higher education in seeking to develop a society in which every individual may achieve his/her full potential. The church will support the ideals of higher education in educating the whole person. The church will encourage education which liberates individuals from ignorance and prejudice, which fosters the integration of values, and encourages a sense of responsibility for the well being of the general culture that transcends narrow individualism. In humility, and remembering its own shortcomings, the church will confront those uses of knowledge which serve injustice or threaten the dignity and worth of human individuals or human community. The church will foster the pursuit of wisdom in higher education, and consider herself an ally in penetrating the mysteries of the cosmos which grant us a fuller revelation of God's handiwork. The church will be a valuable partner in advancing the noblest aims of higher education in service of the human family. In a pluralistic society, the church will walk that tight rope between relativism and dogmatism in the clear assertion of the eternal values found in the Gospel which enlightens life and lifts it above the profane and beyond the narrow interests of the self.

Many of the college and university faculty and staff are members of local congregations. The church has a unique concern for these persons as they seek to fulfill their professional responsibilities. The church community must find ways to affirm the faculty member devoted to being a good teacher, the secretary who keeps the department running smoothly, and the gardener who contributes to the beauty of the campus. The church must be in dialogue with the mathematician or nuclear physicist who has just turned down a lucrative contract for a "star wars project" from a commitment to the just and humane use of knowledge.

The church is involved in higher education through its student members. The majority of those more than 12 million students enrolled autumn quarter, 1985 are members of a local congregation, or from families who belong to the church. These young people will be among the leaders of the corporations and institutions of American culture. Many of them will provide leadership within the church. The church has a responsibility to minister to its students during the course of their academic pilgrimage.

In 1893 when the Disciples of Christ began the first Bible Chair in this country, they had made a decision that the church had a responsibility to be involved in higher education. I believe that mandate for intentional and purposive ministry in higher education has not changed, even though the forms of expression are changing. The issues of wholeness, integration, and justice continue to challenge our best efforts in the educational arena. From a theological perspective, there is a clear argument that the church should be involved in a ministry to higher education. The question remains, how should the church be involved? What should be the shape and content of its ministry and mission? These are questions of mission priorities and functional strategies which must be addressed by the church at every level. They are important questions, and they will occupy the remainder of this chapter.

In 1985, the Disciples of Christ identified 60 ordained ministers in higher education, serving either as campus ministers in private/church-related colleges, or on state supported campuses, either community college, state college, or state universities. Each was requested to participate in a survey seeking information about their perceptions of campus ministry. From this number (60), 27 actually returned the survey instrument. These responses provide interesting insights concerning the future directions of campus ministry from those currently involved in carrying out such ministries.

There was unanimous agreement from all responding Disciples campus ministers that the church's ministry on the campus should be continued in the future. The majority of these indicated a high sense of job satisfaction in their current ministry. The rationale which was offered in support and justification of campus ministry can be summarized according to the ways in which campus ministry: 1) contributes to the needs of persons on campus such as faculty, administration and staff; 2) contributes to the developmental needs of students; 3) contributes to the formation of societal leaders with a global vision; 4) contributes to the integration of faith and values in education; 5) addresses issues of justice in higher education and society; 6) contributes to the life of the church through the development of competent leadership.[13] [14]

When asked about the primary mission of the church on the campus in the next two decades, Disciples ministers responded: 1) to foster and support ethical responsibility for excellence in education; 2) to nurture and support students in the search for wisdom as citizens of a global village, who will be life-long learners, prepared for leadership in the church and society, working for peace and justice; 3) to further develop our ecumenical partnerships in ministry; 4) to carry out a ministry of pastoral care, priestly function, and prophetic action on the campus.[15]

Campus ministers identified similar priorities in defining additional activities projected into the next two decades, adding 1) participation in the governance of the university; and 2) working toward enlightened participation in a global community.[16]

The same survey instrument was sent to campus ministers from a variety of other denominations, serving on campuses supported by state or regional United Ministries in Higher Education Commissions. The responses were generally quite similar to those of the Disciples campus ministers, however, particular attention was given to 1) problems of funding and student apathy as major frustrations in ministry; 2) the need for seminary courses to assist in the preparation of future campus ministers; 3) the desirability of involving the local churches in campus ministry; 4) a strong emphasis on the need for ecumenical cooperation; 5) the need to develop lay "program associates" to augment the work of the professional campus ministers; 6) respect for the unique and individual style of ministers who tailor a ministry based upon their talents and the specific needs of a particular campus; 7) the importance of providing a competent presentation of the gospel and its ethical implications; 8) the need for greater understanding, acceptance, and support from the denominations.[17]

A survey instrument was also sent to all 34 Disciples regional ministers, of which 26 were returned. From the 26 regions which responded, a total of $257,690.00 was given through the budgets of the regional offices in the previous year, either directly to the local campus ministry boards, or to the state commissions which in turn distributed monies to the local campuses.[18]

When asked about their expectations from campus ministry programs the regional ministers emphasized the following: 1) to provide a ministry to students, faculty, and the institutions of higher education; 2) to provide a Disciples presence; 3) to work ecumenically through our covenants; 4) to initiate contact with students from the local churches seeking their involvement in worship, study, social service around issues of peace and justice; 5) to assist the university in educating students for service in society; 6) to represent the faith message in the academic community; 7) to speak to the issues of the day which impinge on the university; 8) to build better connections with the local churches and the region.[19]

Current criticism of campus ministry from the regional ministers include the following: 1) it reaches too few of the students; 2) a more holistic program is desired which goes beyond a few of the dominant social issues; 3) much work needs to be done in "up-dating" the understanding of laypersons about the nature of campus ministry; 4) campus ministers need to communicate with the church about campus ministry, and promote it in congregations and through the structures of the region.[20]

Current strengths of campus ministry noted by the regional ministers included: 1) the growing focus upon establishing the worshipping community; 2) we have developed good facilities, staffed by committed campus ministers in strategic locations; 3) campus ministers have innovated new and exciting approaches in college ministry which are affirmed by the church; 4) strong programs with faculty and staff; 5) there is good comprehensive planning for all campuses within the region; 6) the ecumenical dimension and approach to serving the campus is valued as well as its efficiency through the pooling of resources and personnel; 7) we have an excellent corp of campus ministers working under stressful conditions; 8) a strength is seen in the ownership of the local campus ministry boards involving good people and good administration; 9) a strength in the good relations between campus ministry and the local churches in the region.[21]

The regional ministers suggested changes for the future including: 1) campus ministry needs a better image and greater visibility; 2) more funding is needed for campus ministries; 3) more congregations need to be involved as partners in ministry; 4) campus ministry needs to develop clarity of purpose and mission and communicate this to the faith community.[22]

Assessing the issues—implications for the church's ministry on campus

The church's ministry on campus proceeds from a theological conviction that God calls us to our ministry in the world, and the institutions of learning are a vital aspect of that world. Planning for the church's ministry in higher education must also proceed from an awareness of contextual changes in the society, in education, and in religion. The shape of ministry will be influenced by these changes, and the failure to take these contextual changes into account will certainly inhibit the effectiveness of the ministry and undermine the confidence of the funding sources as well as the constituency whom we would serve.

The church's ministry on campus will be a person-centered ministry. Although there will be a great deal of diversity from campus to campus, such a ministry will take into consideration the developmental needs of the persons involved in higher education; the diverse tasks related to the roles of students, faculty and staff; and it will be sensitive to the particular needs of special disadvantaged populations.

The church's ministry on campus will be oriented to the issues within higher education, concerned for its excellence, confronting those forces which detract from free inquiry and the pursuit of truth, and encouraging those processes which lead to a liberating education for all.

The church's ministry on campus will find expression through the life and work of denominations. Ideally, the mission to higher education will be owned and expressed by the denomination at every manifestation: national, regional, and local. Those engaged in ministry within higher education will likewise be reciprocal partners and participants in the various levels of the church, listening and speaking in the informing dialogue.

The church's ministry on campus will seek and support every effort to bear witness to the oneness of God and God's kingdom, to the common elements of our faith which draw us together in a united mission to the world. For the Disciples of Christ, especially, the commitment to restore the "oneness" of the church continues to be an organizing principle.

The church's ministry on campus will address the issues of justice in higher education and in society. In doing so, the ministry will involve students during one of the most formative stages of their life, encouraging their faith development and understanding of the implications of the gospel today. Such ministry is a vital contribution of the church to the future leaders of both church and society through encouraging the faith development of the future leaders of church and society.

Future challenges for the Christian Church (Disciples of Christ) in ministry within higher education

We turn now to consider the unique opportunity and challenge for the Christian Church (Disciples of Christ) in forging a ministry within and for higher education in the last years of the twentieth century.

Considerations for local congregations

The local congregation is a vital partner and ally in ministry in higher education. Originally, many of the Disciples churches were strategically located near the edge of a college or university campus with the specific expectation that they would truly be a "university church." Considerable work needs to be done to renew, or develop, our understanding of what it means to be a *university church* today. Such a concept must take seriously the consideration that the university or college is included within the boundaries of the parish. The special needs and issues of the campus should inform the concept of the congregation's mission in its particular community, whether it be a community college or a large state university. A natural link with the campus is through the faculty, staff, and students who participate in the local congregation. Hopefully, however, the sense of mission will go far beyond service to its own members, and involve the congregation in outreach to the educational institution to explore ways in which the church might best serve the persons, structures and issues on the campus.

Some local congregations are of sufficient size and strength to provide a vigorous ministry within the campus community. For example, a full-time associate minister could be employed to help the congregation fulfill its mission involving the campus and the church would open its facilities and create programs serving the campus needs. Such a congregation would also take seriously the Disciples' historic nonsectarian position in formulating working relationships with others to serve the campus. It should also be a vital partner with any UME ecumenical organization which might be serving the campus.

Other congregations, due to constraints of size, leadership, and funding would need to work primarily in partnership with other local congregations of various denominations, and with the ecumenical campus ministry program. This usually entails the provision of lay delegates to serve on the local board of the campus ministry centers, the allocation of financial support, the participation of laypersons in campus ministry, and reciprocally, the engagement of university faculty in local church programs.

The following paradigm of the "average congregation" clarifies some of the practical considerations in the need for such a partnership:

HOW MANY STUDENTS?

If a hypothetical average congregation of 300 members had a population distribution such that it was an exact microcosm of the United States population, there would be:

−27 members of traditional college age, of whom

−13 would be in college.

−4 of the 13 would be residential college students, and

−9 would be commuter students.

(Five of these commuters would be part-time students, and there would also be three older congregational members involved in continuing education at a college or university.)

If the young students *not* away at college continued to live in the community and attended church with the same average frequency as others in their age bracket, there might be two college students and four other young adults present on an average Sunday.[23]

Smaller congregations have faced exactly such a situation regarding the numbers of participating students and have often given up any attempt at ministry to college students, to say nothing of the larger issues of the campus community. The challenge to such congregations is to form partnerships with other local congregations, or ecumenical programs, to provide ministry to the campus.

Considerations pertaining to the regions

Currently, the major source of funding (about 80 percent) for Disciples campus ministry in the public sector comes through the 35 regions. In recent years there has been a gradual but steady decrease in both the number of strength of congregations in many regions. Although many regional budgets have increased in dollar amounts, the purchasing power of those dollars has been critically eroded by inflation, while new demands upon the budget arise every year from good and worthy causes. In some regions, the contribution to ministries in higher education is a significant percentage of the region's budget for outreach within the region. Yet, it is rather shocking to realize that, among the Disciples, there is scarcely a region which contributes enough annual dollars to underwrite the salary of one campus minister in that region, let alone support staff and program.

In 1985, the 26 regions responding to a survey for this study indicated that $257,690.00 was allocated for support of ministry in higher education. Of course, many regions have made prior investment in capital for campus ministry buildings, and although it does not appear on the balance sheet, this investment is a form of ongoing support. It takes only the simplest arithmetic to calculate that at a hypothetical salary level of $25,000 per year, the regions which reported are giving enough to support about ten full-time campus ministries salaries. Yet in the 35 regions we have more than sixty Disciples ministers serving in campus ministry today. (this figure includes college chaplains also) The fact of the matter is, nearly all of our Disciples campus ministers receive a significant proportion of salary and program support from other denominations with whom we are in partnership.

The survey of regional ministers referred to above (see Appendices) reveals that in some instances there has been an erosion in the covenant between the Disciples regions and the campus ministry centers within those regions. I believe that this is due in part to an unforeseen and unfortunate consequence which arose following the decision to form state commissions to assist in the governance of campus ministry. In the 1950s most regions had direct contact and representation on each local campus ministry board within that region. Annual appeals for financial support came directly to the regional office and periodic progress reports were offered as a means of responsible accountability.

By the late 1960s and early 1970s many regions saw wisdom in forming state or regional UMHE commissions in which the governance of campus ministry was vested. At first there was a clear sense of covenant between the denominational judicatories, the regional board, and the UMHE commission. In the new arrangement, the Disciples and all other denominations in partnership in campus ministry gave their usual budget allocation to the commission, rather than directly to the local boards as they had done before. Often the regional minister or an associate regional minister was one of the denominational representatives on the commission. The work of campus ministry was clearly the work of the region. The campus minister was known by the region. Additional dollars to campus ministry meant the campus minister could get a raise in salary, whereas a cut in dollars toward campus ministry would surely result in a cut in program or a salary reduction. The connection, or covenant, was both personal and vital.

With the passing of time a curious phenomenon occurred. The personnel who had created the state commissions and forged the covenants moved on with staffing changes and retirements. Members of the original commissions likewise changed as their rotating terms of service expired. With increasing frequency, regional ministers and associate regional ministers no longer attended the UMHE commission meetings, but sent lay-delegates to represent the region. Many regional ministers and regional boards began to look at the campus ministry programs as no longer programs of the region, but as participants in the state commission's program. The state commission came to be seen as another ecumenical agency, worthy and deserving of support, like other agencies such as the state council of churches, rather than a very special program agency which had been created by the denominations to serve a particular function on their behalf.

In Genesis we find the story of Isaac redigging the wells which had first been dug by his father Abraham to provide water for the flocks of sheep tended by an earlier generation:

> Isaac dug again the wells made by the servants of his father Abraham and sealed by the Philistines after Abraham's death, and he gave them the same names as his father had given them.
>
> Isaac's servants dug in the valley and found a well of spring-water. (Genesis 26:18-19)[25]

The state UMHE commissions were formed during a period of creativity when the denominational partners had a strong and clear vision about a future in campus ministry emphasizing cooperation and mutual support. These commissions have served the denominations well and have provided a region-wide strategy for planning and implementing campus ministries.

Like Isaac, who redug the wells of his forbearers which the Philistines had filled with the desert sands, so they no longer provided life giving waters for the shepherds and their flocks, so today, we must redig the wells which have dried-up through neglect. We must renew our covenants, and reclaim our investment in campus ministry.

The process of renewing these covenants is a major task for the years immediately before us, yet one with considerable promise for all concerned parties. Ministries in higher education will benefit from the sense that their work is "owned" by the region and that the promises of money and the provision of lay representatives in boards which establish policy and program are taken seriously. The regions will benefit from this engagement with the world of higher education.

Specific elements of covenant renewal will include, but not be limited to the following: 1) regions will need to renew, or build into their governing structure, a committee which is responsible for campus ministry in the region. Through this committee the vision of ministry, the hopes and concerns of the regional church can be channeled to both the state or regional commission on United Ministries in Higher Education (UMHE), and directly to the local boards at the campus ministry centers. It is imperative that this committee is accountable in reporting to the regional board so that this vital connection can be maintained without "drying up." This committee would ordinarily provide from its membership representation from the denomination at the meetings of the state UMHE commission, bringing the theology of campus ministry, the concerns and issues of the Disciples into the considerations of the Commission's work. Reciprocally, these representatives would report back to the region the needs, concerns, and changes for this ministry. Furthermore, this committee, along with the regional minister, would be responsible for the appointment, or ratification, of Disciples delegates who serve on the local boards of campus ministries within the region.

A second element of renewal: 2) this committee should be responsible for oversight and negotiation of the region's appropriate contribution to the budgetary support of ministries in higher education within the region. In the past, there have been disastrous consequences when monies have been suddenly and arbitrarily shifted away from campus ministry in order to fund new programs or cover budget deficits, without adequate consideration and consultation with our participating ecumenical partners. Such cases have not only resulted in a financial crisis for campus ministries, but have created considerable tension in our ecumenical partnerships. The campus budgets are finely tuned and carefully pruned in these days of scarcity. Like a pie, with a slice provided from each supporting denomination, if one denomination removes a slice or reduces its size, the whole may be placed in jeopardy.

A third element of renewal: 3) this committee should assume responsibility for communication and education about the church's ministry in higher education for the region as a whole. This would involve coordinated mailings from the regional office, an invitation for ministers in higher education to present some aspect of their work at each regional assembly, and the encouragement for the observance of a reinstituted "Higher Education Sunday" in the local churches. It is clear that at least for some regions, the flow of information about campus ministry, its mission, its successes and needs has become like a dry well. This flow of information and dialogue must be replenished.

The partnership between the region and the work of the campus ministry is so important that this challenge for renewal should claim the attention and high priority of regional ministers and boards, as well as campus ministers and local boards, and Disciples representatives involved in the state UMHE commissions.

Considerations at the general level

Today, as in the earliest days of the movement, Disciples polity places a high value on congregational autonomy. This allows a great deal of diversity between the theology and practice of Disciples congregations across the country. Furthermore, the strong emphasis on the role of reason in faith, combined with the strong belief in the priesthood of all believers encourages diversity and pluralism among the members of this denomination. These factors suggest that it is unreasonable to believe that a central policy of governance for ministries in higher education involving Disciples can be supplied from the general manifestation. Nor is there significant monetary incentive to move in that direction since only a small percentage of funding for campus ministry comes from the national level, and most of this is in the form of small program grants administered for special projects and programs. Currently, about $9,000 to $10,000 is available annually for this purpose through Phase I Campus Ministry Program Grants through the Division of Higher Education.

Nonetheless, Disciples involved in college and university life remain open to authentic leadership from the general manifestation of the church which offers sound theologial reflection pertaining to ministry in the changing context of contemporary higher education. The Division of Higher Education is now in a solid position to provide such leadership. In future years, the Division should be an ongoing vital source of communication to other manifestations of the church in the ongoing and essential task of providing information ranging from theology to strategy in undergirding this important ministry of the church. The Division can play a significant role in providing a larger vision to the 750,000 participating members in over 4,300 congregations in the United States and Canada. With clear respect for local autonomy, this educational and edifying role can support the courageous pioneering that is occurring in some areas, and stimulate reflection which may help us all in overcoming our provincialism, sectarianism, and individualism.

The Division of Higher Education has already begun to work toward such a goal, and this book on campus ministry, its companion volumes on church-related colleges and theological education is a major step forward. The Division has given innovative leadership in the area of capital development, seeking endowment funds for campus ministry in order to enlarge the Phase I Campus Ministry Program Grants and to provide sufficient funds so that the Phase II Grants intended to support campus ministers in special studies or continuing education may be actualized.

The Division should play an enabling role in strengthening the partnerships between campus ministries and the regions. This objective can be enhanced by regular communication with the regions which keeps them informed of the holistic vision for campus ministry which is affirmed by the Division, and by sharing with the regions the evolving developments and commitments in our ecumenical partnerships. On the other hand, the Division can play a strong role as interpreter to state commissions, local boards, and Disciples campus ministers of the issues and concerns which are heard from such a "listening post" with the regions.

Ecumenical Considerations

As the challenges and opportunities for future involvement in ministry in higher education have been described at the local, regional, and general manifestations, one of the presuppositions has been that the Disciples will continue to work ecumenically on the campus. Such an important presupposition merits further examination.

The future of the Disciples in ministry in higher education lies with its ecumenical partnerships. This hypothesis is substantiated by Disciples theology and reinforced by practical necessity, and should be considered in just that order.

The *raison d'etre* for the Disciples Movement was found in the sincere desire of the founders to bring unity to all Christians. It was the belief of these early leaders that the key to Christian unity lay in an appeal to the restoration of the belief and practice of the church as it was described in the New Testament. Since its beginnings coincided with the opening of the Western frontier, this movement went westward with the covered wagons. The first half century witnessed the dispersion of Disciples congregations along the common path of population movements toward the West Coast, carrying into every corner of this nation a fervent appeal to unity. The second half century gave rise to growing involvement in the work of foreign missions, where this same organizing principle was in operation. It was as recently as the mid-1960s that members of this "brotherhood" admitted they had in fact become a "denomination." Much of our energy has been absorbed since then by issues of restructure and problems of finance and becoming a truly responsible denomination. The time is at hand to move ahead with the church's work.

Hopefully, we will be led by a Disciples theology which has not lost sight of the goal of Christian unity as we work toward the New Age. Ideally, we will seek to discern the Spirit of God moving in our midst and respond with appropriate reform and change. The practical realities reveal in an overwhelming fashion the impossibility and impracticality of addressing the issues of ministry in higher education in isolation, as a single denomination. Remember, there are over twelve million students, in over forty-three hundred institutions. Disciples presently have more than sixty campus ministers enjoying only marginal financial support scattered among these many colleges and universities.

How should Disciples recruit campus ministers for the future? Disciples must seek out the brightest and most talented for the challenging work of campus ministry. Seminaries must develop both course work and practicums and internships to assist these in preparation for competent witness and ministry on the campus. Disciples theology and ecumenical commitment imply that future recruitment of ministers to work in the context of higher education, must call and equip those who can learn to work in an ecumenical partnership. It implies that the essential mission in this ministry is the living out of the Incarnation in the arena of higher education. Such theology implies that in the coming age, new communities will be gathered around the worship and service of God whose Spirit is at work in the university. It suggests that Christians will be empowered by this Spirit in working to improve a society which remains imperfect; toppling the idols of scientism, nationalism, sectarianism, and individualism.

One model currently in existence for the training of campus ministers is that instituted by Rev. John Butler, campus minister at Texas Christian University. John Butler is a seasoned veteran in ecumenical campus ministry, and in collaboration with Brite Divinity School, has for several years brought seminarians to the Texas Christian campus as campus ministry interns. His commitments to ecumenicity and the example of denominational cooperation which he has helped to implement in TCU's campus ministry program provides an excellent role model for the future.

The principles of ecumenical partnerships will shape the future of campus ministry in all of its manifestations. Ministers of local congregations serving the campus must find avenues of cooperation with other congregations. Chaplains on private and religious college campuses must work with those of other denominations in serving the campus community. Campus ministers at state supported campuses must blend their talents and resources in a unified effort with other denominational partners in ministry for the most sound and effective approach to the persons and issues of today's campus.

Now, more than ever before, regional strategies are essential in providing a comprehensive and consistent plan for campus ministry within states and regions. Regional strategy can only be done rationally through intentional and committed denominational partnerships. Furthermore, good Christian stewardship requires the pooling of our financial resources, the shared use of buildings, equipment, and support staff for ministry.

The commitment of Disciples to ecumenical ministry at the general manifestation through the Division of Higher Education's involvement in United Ministries in Education must continue, for it permits participation in those programs which we can do together, but which none could attempt alone. The very successes of our ecumenical partnerships in campus ministry will serve as a model and help provide guidance for the consideration of other avenues of ecumenical cooperation or unity within the denomination. The realities of budget and staff force us at the practical level in the continuation of a lean network of interdependent national staff persons whose only hope of providing leadership at the nationwide level lies in committed ecumenical cooperation. Our hope for the future is through the exploration of new avenues of cooperative ministry on the college campus.

Epilogue

Mandates for Ministry in the Coming Age

Nearly one hundred years ago the Disciples of Christ pioneered a bold new venture in ministry at the secular, tax-supported, state universities and colleges. It began with the vision of faithful church women who saw the importance of the church following its young people to the campus to provide care and continuity for the Biblical literacy and religious development of their students.

This new ministry of the church was spawned in controversy. Some felt it would compete with the established mission priorities. Others felt it would detract from Disciples church-related colleges. Still others felt it was too expensive for the numbers which might be reached. Yet, in time it became clear to all that the vast majority of Disciples students were being educated on state supported campuses and the imperative of defining the church mission there was evident.

The original mission was to provide college level courses in the Bible and in religion in a nonsectarian fashion, through the Bible Chair movement. However, from the beginning, Bible Chair instructors were preachers, counselors, evangelists, recruiters for full-time ministry, fund-raisers, and public relations experts. In time, these additional activities of the instructors transcended in importance the traditional role of teaching the Bible. Two important contributions had been made by the Bible Chair movement at that time: first, the way had been opened for colleges to form departments of religion, and second, the movement was the precursor for what today we call campus ministry.

The arena of higher education has gone through some radical changes and college courses are not contained by the traditional private college or state university campus boundaries. Today's campus has expanded into the community and course work is offered in churches, libraries, community colleges and in industry. Even more expansion is predicted for the future with opportunities for course work to be made available through technological links between computers and campuses.

Campus ministry has gone through its own metamorphosis with the changing times. The focus of its mission has grown wider with the passing of each generation: from student work, to campus ministry, to ministry with and to the persons, issues and structures of higher education. The resulting evolution of purpose and objectives has led to misunderstanding and confusion for some and others have gone so far as to disown campus ministry. On the other hand, many have encouraged and supported the changes which have occurred.

Campus ministers are in an unusual place. Although college chaplains are an integral part of the institution which employs them, campus ministers on the state supported campus have no formal legitimacy. They are neither student, staff, nor faculty, yet they work full-time on campus, addressing themselves to the needs of the campus community and working for healing, wholeness and integration. They are ministers, yet they have no congregation which reports to the *Year Book* nor bears any of the usual marks of a congregation. Their work is not self-supporting, nor do they generate revenues for the church—rather, they are supported by the outreach giving of the church. As professionals, they respond to diverse and sometimes competing expectations: to work with students—but with faculty as well; to involve all Disciples students on the campus—but the unchurched as well; to provide a gathered community of the faithful for worship and faith development—but to be available to the searching, the wandering, and the confused; to provide competent pastoral counseling—but to engage in an issue-oriented ministry; to be experimental, experiential, existential, and ecumenical. The church has placed campus ministers on campuses across the country, and in some cases have forgotten why they are there.

It is time to reclaim the vision of those far-sighted church women, and forge a clear direction for the future mission of campus ministry. It is time to re-dig the wells of nonsectarianism and to renew the covenants with our partners in Christian mission. It is time to dream new dreams and to follow new visions which will lead us into untried avenues of service as new opportunities surprise us around the bend. It is time to appreciate the rich diversity which exists in campus ministry and to encourage the creation of a new future. It is time to support campus ministry as an integral mission of the church.

As we look to the future, we will not discover "one model" for campus ministry, for the contexts in which ministry occurs are so different from campus to campus, and the talents and particular contributions of campus ministers and ministry boards vary widely. Nonetheless, the experiences and successes of the past few decades in campus ministry demonstrate the richness and creativity of such diversity. There are, however, some lamp-posts which can illumine our path for the future and provide some general guidance. Guided by this attitude toward change and reform, our ministry in higher education for the future age must take into account the following:

—Religious illiteracy is rampant among the current generation of young people. Ministry in higher education must play a key role in providing opportunities for experiential faith development.

—Campus ministry must recover the art of competent Bible study. There is a significant interest in the Bible among college students and much of what passes for Biblical studies today is in the hands of para-church groups where it is not done well.

—Christian community, rather than denominational fellowship, is the key to ministry in the coming age, as those engaged in experiences of learning, action-reflection, and doing theology also learn to worship and serve together.

—Ecumenical partnerships, which carry out the mandate of the unity of the church are especially important in higher education, they are essential for the future, and such ministries will be precursors to other manifestations of the church in their work toward cooperation and union.

—Experiential education in values is too frequently missing in current higher education, but opportunities for such may be stimulated by the ministry throughout the curriculum, and at times may be directly provided in praxis groups and action-reflection theology groups through campus ministry.

—Celebration of the mighty acts of God will lead to opportunities for Christian worship within communities of the people of God gathered on the campus where persons can share the life of faith in response to the claims of the gospel. The locus of worship in some cases will be in the local congregation, in others it may be in the campus ministry center.

—Perception of life as a global citizen in an essential ingredient in a liberating education today, and ministry in higher education has unique opportunities to provide leadership in creating such learning experiences within the campus community through its ability to transcend departmental compartmentalization.

—Issues of peace and justice as well as other major value issues will follow logically from the implication of one's self-understanding as a global citizen. Ministry in higher education for the coming age will promote such values campus-wide, not simply within the gathered community. Ministry should be inclusive of international students and promote intercultural student exchange.

—The campus as the parish is a concept for the future, wherein the persons assembled as participants in higher education and the issues of higher education become the subjects of ministry. This is not to be confused with the current tendency of Roman Catholics who develop "student parishes" which are largely indistinguishable from any other Catholic parish.

—Fostering a liberating education will be a convergence point for the church and the university in the future age in which the pressure to obtain credentials and career training is paramount.

—Life-long learning will be a key concept for the future and the challenge to campus ministry is to create new avenues of service appropriate to the needs of the "on-going" learner.

—New partnerships between campus ministry and the local congregation must be formed to adequately respond to the needs and issues of the campus community and to assist the congregation in its mission to the campus.

—New problems call for new strategies. Some regions which face reduced funding due to the economy must consider moving from the concept of a resident campus minister on every campus to a regionalized strategy in which a professional campus minister will provide oversight and support to local boards and congregations which provide for the ministry in their community.

—Peer ministries should be developed which recapture the practice of students ministering to one another, using the resources of the campus ministry for training and apprenticeship.

Finally, it is the hope of the author that this little volume which undertakes a study of the Disciples in campus ministry has served to shed some light on the history of this ministry as well as some hopeful direction for its continued unfolding.

References

1. Parsonage, Robert Rue, Editor: *Church Related Higher Education*, Valley Forge: Judson Press, 1978. Martin E. Marty, "Future Church-Culture Relations and their Impact on Church-Related Higher Education—the student nexus" p. 303.
2. Sandin, Robert T., *The Search For Excellence*, Macon: Mercer University Press, 1982. p. 193.
3. Sandin, *Ibid.* p. 222.
4. Cox, Harvey, *The Secular City*, New York: The Macmillan Co. 1965. p. 194.
5. Sandin, *Op. cit.* p. 68.
6. Sandin, *Op. cit.* p. 41.
7. *Involvement in Learning* (Realizing the Potential of American Higher Education) Final Report of the Study Group on the Conditions of Excellence in American Higher Education. Sponsored by the National Institute of Education, Washington, D.C., October, 1984. p. 6.
8. *Ibid.* pp. 9-10.
9. *Ibid.* p. 17.
10. Levine, Arthur, *When Dreams and Heroes Died*. San Francisco: Jossey-Bass Publishers, 1980. p. 135.
11. Turecky, Betsy, *Church and Campus Calling*, Dallas: UME, 1985 "Service Learning: Service Through the Class Room, Betsy Turecky pp. 130-135.
12. Gamson, Zelda F., and Associates, *Liberating Education*, San Francisco: Jossey-Bass Publishers, 1984. p. 218.
13. *Table 1*, Appendix, Disciples of Christ: Campus Ministers.
14. *Table 2*, Appendix, Disciples of Christ: Campus Ministers.
15. *Table 3*, Appendix, Disciples of Christ: Campus Ministers.
16. *Table 4*, Appendix, Disciples of Christ: Campus Ministers.
17. *Table 8*, Appendix, Ecumenical Campus Ministers.
18. *Table 9*, Regional Ministers: Disciples of Christ.
19. *Ibid.*
20. *Ibid.*
21. *Ibid.*
22. *Ibid.*
23. Gribbon, R. T., *Students, Churches, and Higher Education* (Congregational Ministry in a Learning Society) Valley Forge: Judson Press, 1981. p. 67.
24. *The New Jerusalem Bible*. New York: Doubleday and Co. Inc. 1966. p. 44.

Appendix

TABLE 1. CAMPUS MINISTERS: DISCIPLES OF CHRIST

—60 Disciples campus ministers were sent the survey
—27 Returned the survey:
   — 9 Responses from private or church-related campuses
   —18 Responses from state-funded campuses

Funding

—11 Programs report funding increase over 10 years on state campuses.
— 3 Programs report funding decrease over 10 year period.
— 4 Programs did not report on this item.
— 7 Programs report funding increase over 10 years on private campuses.
— 2 Programs did not report on this item.

Job Satisfaction

Job satisfaction was reported on a scale with 0 lowest 10 highest

Ministers on State Campus:
  4 ranked it 5
  1 ranked it 7
  4 ranked it 8
  4 ranked it 9
  4 ranked it 10
  1 did not rank this item.

Ministers on Private Campus:
  1 ranked it 4
  4 ranked it 8
  1 ranked it 9
  2 ranked it 10
  1 did not rank this item.

Question: Should campus ministry continue?

Should the church's ministry in higher education be continued in the next two decades?

 9-from private colleges responded—Yes
18-from state supported campuses responded—Yes

TABLE 2. CAMPUS MINISTERS: DISCIPLES OF CHRIST

RATIONALE JUSTIFYING RESOURCES FOR MINISTRY IN HIGHER EDUCATION:

A. CONTRIBUTES TO THE DEVELOPMENTAL NEEDS OF STUDENTS:

—at this stage of life, many students avoid local church, but are responsive to campus ministry
—a pivotal time in young lives
—the church should be there
—faith development is critical in these formative years

B. CONTRIBUTES TO THE FORMATION OF SOCIETAL LEADERS:

—a positive contribution to world-wide leaders of the future
—students will become major policy makers
—need our values

C. CONTRIBUTES TO THE INTEGRATION OF FAITH, VALUES & ETHICS IN EDUCATION:

—provides integration of ethics in education

165

—provides the values of the church amidst competing values
—provides spiritual guidance during a rebellious period
—campus ministry is providing care for the souls of campus folk

D. ADDRESSES ISSUES OF JUSTICE IN HIGHER EDUCATION AND SOCIETY:

—addresses ethical issues in higher education
—asks the questions of how the church relates to society
—our denomination has a commitment to learning
—issues of peace and justice need to be integrated in education
—church needs to be present where society is shaped

E. CONTRIBUTES TO THE LIFE OF THE CHURCH:

—maintains ties to the church community throughout adulthood
—need to develop leaders for future church and community
—a powerful role in leadership development for historic church
—ministers to the financial base of tomorrow's church
—campus ministry is a form of mission and evangelism
—campus ministry provides innovative models of ministry for local churches
—these students are the future of our church and society
—helps keep the church in touch with the real world
—campus ministry directs some folk into ministry: professional and lay
—last year two students chose a Christian vocation through campus minister

F. CONTRIBUTES TO THE NEEDS OF PEOPLE ON CAMPUS: FACULTY, etc.

—because of the faculty, the church should be on campus
—issues arise in research which need the leaven of the gospel
—teaching is an important function, church needs to be there
—essential part of the church's mission
—to be in the academy relating to the needs of staff, faculty, and students

---

The comments of the campus ministers are organized under the six major headings which were representative of the content of the sample comments which are listed above.

TABLE 3. CAMPUS MINISTERS: DISCIPLES OF CHRIST

Question: WHAT IS THE PRIMARY MISSION OF THE CHURCH'S MINISTRY IN HIGHER EDUCATION DURING THE NEXT TWO DECADES?

HIGHER EDUCATION IN GENERAL:

—to foster ethical responsibility for excellence in education
—to critique the role of the university in the culture
—help higher education resolve its conflicts: seek its direction

TOWARD ENLIGHTENED PARTICIPATION IN THE GLOBAL VILLAGE:

—to assist students in seeing the world as a whole, a human family
—to nurture and support students in their search for wisdom
—to encouarge students as responsible citizens of global village

—educating students for community service and life long learning
—support students in seeing the modern world through the eyes of faith: raising issues of peace & justice on the campus
—to assist in leadership development
—to work toward a more humane and peaceful world through education

TOWARD ECUMENICAL MINISTRY TO THE CAMPUS

—encourage ecumenicity: respect for the traditions of the faith
—redefine the direction of ministry for the UME denominations
—not just Disciples students, but an ecumenical focus of ministry
—ministry to the whole campus, focus on ethics in professional schools
—serve as bridge between church & university: our common goals
—to establish new patterns of ministry for a sophisticated and secular culture

A MINISTRY OF PASTORAL CARE; PRIESTLY FUNCTION; PROPHETIC ACTION

—pastoral care for students, & vocational counseling
—assist students in faith development and Christian growth
—to offer worship, counseling, and a gospel of hope
—prophetic: to proclaim the Good News, evangelism
—to encourage faith development & seeking Church vocations
—serve non-traditional students, who often have a broader vision
—to provide ministry to faculty, staff & students: campus community
—to challenge constituents with the demands of the gospel message
—to demonstrate inter-relationship between faith and knowledge, as well as between church and society

TABLE 4. CAMPUS MINISTERS: DISCIPLES OF CHRIST

Question: WHAT ARE SOME OF THE CHIEF ACTIVITIES OF A CAMPUS MINISTER IN IMPLEMENTING THE CHURCH'S MISSION IN HIGHER EDUCATION IN THE NEXT TWO DECADES?

PARTICIPATION IN THE GOVERNANCE OF THE UNIVERSITY

—work on university committees, especially planning & evaluation
—participate in all campus activities
—support and affirm the administrators & faculty
—develop relationships with university administrators, be available
—raise questions about the purposes and values of higher education

TOWARD ENLIGHTENED PARTICIPATION IN THE GLOBAL VILLAGE

—plan activities which encourage a global world view for students
—develop a ministry to international students on campus
—raise the issues of peace and justice as essentials of our faith
—organize study-action groups on global issues for action-reflection
—organize peace-study groups on campus

TOWARD ECUMENICAL MINISTRY TO THE CAMPUS COMMUNITY

—develop ecumenical ministry on the campus
—build a "council of churches" on the campus
—develop ecumenical worship services
—form allies with other campus religious groups, local churches to achieve the goals of campus ministry

168   CAMPUS MINISTRY IN THE COMING AGE

A MINISTRY OF PASTORAL CARE; PRIESTLY FUNCTION; PROPHETIC ACTION

—help facilitate moral and faith development
—provide worship, pastoral care, outreach & social action
—develop a community of students for an intentional spiritual life
—develop the intellectual sophistication of religious ideas
—develop faithful responses to the developmental needs of students including: pastoral care, teaching values, quest for identity
—develop personal relations with faculty and administrative staff
—counseling, teaching, worship, supportive student programming
—develop a Christian community for action-reflection
—help students understand their own denomination
—teaching, preaching the gospel, provide opportunities for community service where the faith is "lived out."
—gather the community for worship & fellowship & Christian learning
—help students with life/work planning, vocational assistance

TABLE 5. KEY FUTURE TRENDS IDENTIFIED IN A FUTURES SURVEY FOR THE CAMPUS CHRISTIAN MINISTRY AT THE UNIVERSITY OF WASHINGTON, SEATTLE, WASHINGTON, 1985

SOCIETAL TRENDS:

1. GLOBAL

—continuing war/peace struggle
—expanding weapons technology
—growth of Third World Countries—economically & politically
—international economic interdependence
—continuing struggle for power between major world powers
—conflict between religious and political idealogies

2. ECONOMIC

—unemployment and underemployment
—dual career families
—growing discrepancy in incomes of the rich and poor
—cutbacks and abuses in government aid
—loss of economic opportunity for youth
—crisis in the tax system
—feminization of poverty

3. TECHNICAL

—growth in the uses of computers and robots
—growth in world-wide communication and information
—genetic manipulation in agriculture and medicine
—encountering the limits of physical resources
—expanding pollution of the environment

4. PERSONAL

—loss of relationship in family and society
—emotional starvation of children and older adults
—continuing emergence of women and minorities
—growth of fundamentalism in all aspects of life

TABLE 6. FUTURES SURVEY, CAMPUS CHRISTIAN MINISTRY AT THE UNIVERSITY OF WASHINGTON IN SEATTLE, 1985

EDUCATIONAL TRENDS:

1. GOVERNANCE

—increase in the costs of education
—access to education for low income, minorities, women
—de-emphasis on faculty tenure
—decreasing resources for higher education
—trend toward private education & business sponsored education

2. QUALITY

—shift from liberal arts education toward occupational training
—less personal contact between faculty and students
—use of computers for independent learning
—loss of quality faculty through disillusionment
—increase in global studies and intercultural issues
—need for inclusion of values and ethics in all education

3. VOCATIONAL

—growing scarcity of jobs for liberal arts background
—pressure for medicine, law, engineering & business
—continuing need for retraining: multicareer experience
—increasing role in education of: business, military, industry
—increasing number of low paying jobs/decrease in high pay

TABLE 7. FUTURES SURVEY: CAMPUS CHRISTIAN MINISTRY AT THE UNIVERSITY OF WASHINGTON IN SEATTLE, 1985

RELIGIOUS TRENDS

1. INSTITUTIONAL

—increase in minorities and women in leadership roles
—increase in lay involvement
—growth in neo-denominationalism
—decline in dollars in mainline denominations
—push for the church to provide goods and services
—need to respond to the needs of the baby boom
—clergy seek specialization
—older average age of members in mainline denominations
—decline of membership in mainline denominations

2. FAITH ISSUES

—dialogue between diverse religious groups
—polarization between spiritual growth and social action
—growing impact of liberation theology & feministy theology
—growth in privatized religion and authoritarian religion
—revitalization of faith in non-western cultures
—growth of fundamentalism: splintering Christian groups
—interest in "experiential" religion

3. SOCIAL JUSTICE ISSUES

—increased involvement of the church in social issues

—influence of fundamentalist groups on society & policy
—medical-ethical issues: abortion, scarcity of resources
—"base" communities working for social justice
—continuing activism of the peace movement
—concern for the underserved, the underprivileged, vulnerable
—issues involving alternative life-styles

TABLE 8. SURVEY: ECUMENICAL CAMPUS MINISTERS

100 survey instruments were sent to campus ministers of other denominations who participate in U.M.E.

54 responses were returned from 38 full-time and 16 part-time

FUNDING: The majority of respondents indicated that adequate funding is a problem; even when dollars have increased, income has not kept pace with inflation and the rising cost of living.

CHIEF SOURCES OF SATISFACTION: a summary of varied responses:

counseling
working in faith development with students
celebrating worship
developing visiting theologican series
working in an ecumenical team
working with faculty in relating faith to the teaching disciplines
teaching relevant courses in the Experimental College
leading Bible studies for various campus groups
freedom to initiate new and innovative programs
working with a student community
the issue oriented campus program
involving local congregations as partners in ministry
theologizing in an academic community

53 out of 54 INDICATED CAMPUS MINISTRY OUGHT TO BE CONTINUED

RATIONALE JUSTIFYING THE FUTURE SUPPORT FOR CAMPUS MINISTRY INCLUDED:

the student generation is the future leadership of the church
the church must challenge the student generation to serve society
we cannot abandon our students to the right-wing groups and cults
the church has an obligation to foster faith development
to provide pastoral care to students during a critical phase
to support faculty and administration in doing their tasks
to confront the issues in higher education on behalf of the church
to develop in future leaders the religious, value & ethical dimension
the church needs to be involved in the most influential institution (higher education) which is shaping society's future
for the reasons reported in the Danforth Study
to continue the church's presence during a stage of important decisions
the spiritual dimension must be given priority during education years

PRIMARY MISSION OF THE CHURCH'S MINISTRY ON CAMPUS IN NEXT DECADES

to develop a religious consciousness in the student generation
recruit able leadership for the Christian ministry

to assist students in faith development during their academic progress
to listen and learn from higher education—God is already there
to model a theocentric life in the milieu of higher education
to equip the faculty for ministry on the campus

PRIMARY MISSION OF THE CHURCH'S MINISTRY ON CAMPUS IN NEXT DECADES

to be the prophetic presence on campus
to witness to the centrality of God in community and individual life
to witness and work for peace and justice
to be the faith community on campus addressing the issues
to help students grow in faith, in understanding of the world and themselves in
    relationship to God
to provide pastoral care for the campus community
to keep the ethical questions before the university
to be present and visible on campus
to offer sound theological and Biblical studies
to help bring into being the "kingdom of God"
to contribute to the "humanization" of the university
to maintain a creative relationship between college & congregations
sustain a lively community of faith on the campus
to interpret what it means to love God in a complex society
to bring a pastoral, priestly, and prophetic ministry to campus

THE CHIEF ACTIVITIES OF CAMPUS MINISTERS IN THE FUTURE SHOULD BE:

educational: teaching the Bible and assisting faith development
pastoral: counseling and providing pastoral care
issue oriented: helping students confront the issues of our day such as peace,
    justice, hunger, equality, ethics
community: to lead and gather the worshipping community
service: to introduce students to active "servanthood"
bridging: local congregations with the college or university
to perform the traditional modes of ministry for the campus
support systems: attend to the systems which enable ministry
develop constituency groups of faculty, students to address issues
the Danforth model applies here, even more than before
all campus ministers should develop their special gifts & talents and have the
    freedom to create their own unique ministry

ECUMENICAL COOPERATION AND TEAMWORK BEST DESCRIBES FUTURE CAMPUS MINISTRY

The overwhelming majority of respondents indicated that an ecumenically based campus ministry was the model for the future. Reasons given in support of this ranged from:

common sense
to witness to the oneness of the church
the best stewardship of personnel and resources
because denominational differences aren't important on the campus
to avoid sectarianism and a self-serving institutionalism
because it's the only way we can afford to provide this ministry

TABLE 9. SURVEY OF REGIONAL MINISTERS IN
THE CHRISTIAN CHURCH (DISCIPLES OF CHRIST)

26   Returns were received from regional ministers

7   regions send monines directly to the campus ministries in the region

$20,000
  8,500
  8,000
  3,600
  2,600
  1,000
    200   For a total of $42,700.00

13   regions send monies to the state commission which distributes:

$34,000
 33,040
 30,000
 28,750
 28,000
 18,500
 15,000
 10,600
  8,000
  6,400
  1,200
  1,100
    400   For a total of $214,990.00

5   regions reported giving no monies to campus ministry

1   region did not report on this item

TOTAL: $257,690.00 REPORTED BY THE REGIONS IN SUPPORT OF CAM-
PUS MINISTRY

Regional ministers reported conceptualized ecumenical campus ministries supported
by Disciples funds from the region as:

    a. An integral part of the mission & ministry of the region   *18*
    b. An agency outside the regional program deserving of support   *4*
    c. Other: "It's archaic"   *1*
    d. No answer   *3*

OF THE 8 CONCEPTUALIZING CAMPUS MINISTRY AS "OTHER" THAN
AN INTEGRAL PART OF THE REGIONAL PROGRAM, THE FOLLOWING
REPRESENTATIVE COMMENTS:

EXPECTATIONS FROM CAMPUS MINISTRY PROGRAM:

Focus on the Christian community through 1) worship, 2) education and 3) mission
    to the campus community, with the congregations
To be prophetic—to work with congregations
To provide worship, growth in the faith, evangelism, counseling
To develop a regular worshipping community which communicates the gospel
    through witness in action, and service to others
Desire the involvement of campus ministers in the "whole church"
Represent the Disciples of Christ on the campus, and minister to all

CRITIQUE OF PRESENT CAMPUS MINISTRY

Needed, a better image, greater visibility
Lacking, a connection with the congregations
Missing—a comprehensive view of campus ministry for the entire region
Shortage of funds—lack of expertise in development—to much expected of the campus ministers with too little support
The congregations need to become involved in doing campus ministry
We need more direct Disciples involvement and Disciples support
This institution should be totally rethought—become related to local congregations
Need to develop responsible connectedness, clarity of purpose & mission global mission perspectives as a focus for the faith community

CURRENT STRENGTHS OF CAMPUS MINISTRY IN YOUR REGION

Individual services, worship and education opportunities, and some witness to social
    issues and campus concerns
We have committed and sincere campus ministers—a few good buildings
The church is represented on the campus

OF THESE 8 REGIONAL MINISTERS

3   thought campus ministry should remain about the same
5   desired changes as indicated in the above critiques

OF THE 18 CONCEPTUALIZING CAMPUS MINISTRY AS AN INTEGRAL PART OF REGIONAL PROGRAM THE FOLLOWING REPRESENTATIVE COMMENTS ARE MADE:

EXPECTATIONS FROM CAMPUS MINISTRY PROGRAM:

Ministry to students, faculty, and the institution of higher education
Ecumenical dimension
Provide a Disciples of Christ presence for our church's students
Provide worship, study, fellowship and counseling for all church-related students
Build bridges of understanding between campus & local congregations
Solicit names of students from local congregations, make personal contact within
    first month of the quarter, provide faith-sharing experiences for students, with a
    balance of social justice issues
To provide a Christian presence on campus, teach Christian ethics, and provide
    counseling from a Christian perspective
Assist university in educating students for service in society
Speak to the issues of the day which impinge on university
Provide better "feedback" and reporting to the regional church
Enlist local pastors and congregations in effective campus ministry
Strengthen ties to the local congregation
Campus ministry needs a complete overhaul and reorganization
Campus ministry represents the faith message for the academic community
Better visibility, stronger partnership with the region

CRITIQUE OF PRESENT CAMPUS MINISTRY

Make campus ministry the presence of the church on campus
It reaches too few of the students
Update the understanding of the local church members about campus ministry
Expand the creative imagination of our campus ministers
Needed: a more holistic agenda, "peace, women, minority" issues dominate
Desired: much more promotion and communication with region & congregations

Less time in committee work—more time directly involved in campus life
Take a more active role in reaching out and contacting students

CURRENT STRENGTHS OF CAMPUS MINISTRY IN YOUR REGION

Growing focus on the worshipping community, and on better counseling
The ecumenical dimension and approach to serving the campus
Exciting and innovative new approaches which we affirm
Good facilities, good location, committed campus ministers
A program strengthened by pooling finances of supporting groups
An excellent corp of campus ministers who work under stressful conditions
Comprehensive planning for all the campuses in our region
Great strength is the ownership of the local boards
Good relationships between campus ministries and local churches & our region
Some excellent programs designed for the campus community
Strength in reaching faculty and staff—weakness in reaching students
Good people involved, good administration in implementing ministry

OF THESE 18 REGIONAL MINISTERS

1   thought campus ministry should be phased out
5   thought campus ministry should remain about the same in the future
12   desired changes in campus ministry as indicated in above critique

TABLE 10. A LISTING OF DISCIPLES BIBLE CHAIRS

A. Disciples Bible Chairs begun by the Christian Woman's Board of Missions:

1. University of Michigan	1893
Ann Arbor, Michigan	
2. University of Virginia	1897
Charlottesville, Virginia	
3. University of Georgia	1897
Athens, Georgia	
4. University of Kansas	1901
Lawrence, Kansas	
5. University of Texas	1905
Austin, Texas	
6. Tri-State College	1908
Angola, Indiana	

B. Bible Chairs of the Disciples, not sponsored by the Christian Woman's Board of Missions:

1. University of Missouri	1896
Columbia, Missouri	
2. University of Indiana	1910
Bloomington, Indiana	

C. Modified types of Bible Chairs

1. Eugene Divinity School	1895
Eugene, Oregon	
2. Washington State College	1908
Pullman, Washington	
3. University of California	1898
Berkeley, California	
4. University of Nebraska	1946
Lincoln, Nebraska	

OPERATING STRUCTURE FOR
UNITED MINISTRIES IN EDUCATION

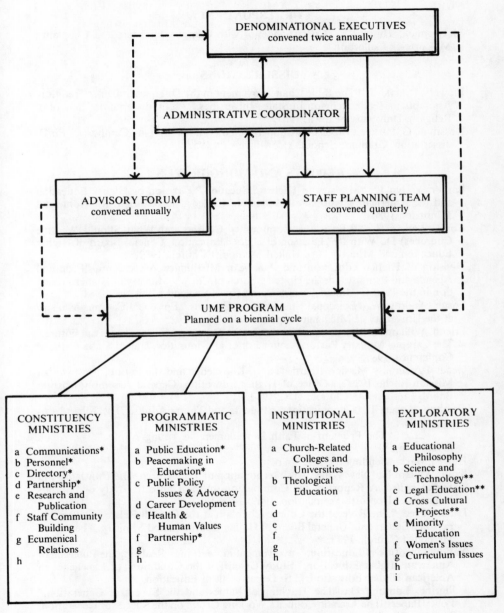

DENOMINATIONAL EXECUTIVES
convened twice annually

ADMINISTRATIVE COORDINATOR

ADVISORY FORUM
convened annually

STAFF PLANNING TEAM
convened quarterly

UME PROGRAM
Planned on a biennial cycle

CONSTITUENCY MINISTRIES

a Communications*
b Personnel*
c Directory*
d Partnership*
e Research and
   Publication
f Staff Community
   Building
g Ecumenical
   Relations
h

PROGRAMMATIC MINISTRIES

a Public Education*
b Peacemaking in
   Education*
c Public Policy
   Issues & Advocacy
d Career Development
e Health &
   Human Values
f Partnership*
g
h

INSTITUTIONAL MINISTRIES

a Church-Related
   Colleges and
   Universities
b Theological
   Education
c
d
e
f
g
h

EXPLORATORY MINISTRIES

a Educational
   Philosophy
b Science and
   Technology**
c Legal Education**
d Cross Cultural
   Projects**
e Minority
   Education
f Women's Issues
g Curriculum Issues
h
i

* Programs and Services in the 1983 Plan of Ministry
** In the 1983 Partnership Program

BIBLIOGRAPHY

CORRESPONDENCE

McCormick, Thomas R., Correspondence with Campus Ministers and Chaplains; McCormick Collection.

DISSERTATIONS

Flowers, Ronald B., "The Bible Chair Movement in the Disciples of Christ Tradition: Attempts to Teach Religion in State Universities." Ph.D. dissertation, School of Religion, University of Iowa, 1967.

Rossman, G. Parker, "Protestant Cooperation on State University Campuses." Ph.D. dissertation, Graduate School, Yale University, 1953.

REPORTS AND MONOGRAPHS

Barker, Verlyn L., "Ministry in Higher Education." Division of Higher Education and the American Missionary Association, United Church Board for Homeland Ministries, 1984.

Conn, Robert H., "Who is the Community College and What Should We (the Churches) Do With It?" Division of Higher Education, General Board of Higher Education and Ministry, The United Methodist Church, 1982.

Division of Higher Education and American Missionary Association, "Proposed Agenda and Promises for the United Church of Christ's Ministry in Higher Education in the 1980's." United Church Board for Homeland Ministries, 1981.

Foster, Andrew W., "Episcopal Chaplains on Campus." Episcopal Campus Ministry at the University of Michigan (unpublished), 1984.

Friend, William B., "Empowered by the Spirit: Campus Ministry Faces the Future." The Campus Ministry Pastoral Letter Editorial Committee, United States Catholic Conference, 1985.

General Assembly Mission Board, "Faith, Knowledge and the Future, Presbyterian Mission in the 1980's." Office of Higher Education, General Assembly Mission Board, Presbyterian Church, U.S., 1982.

Gribbon, Robert T., "Congregations, Students and Young Adults." The Alban Institute, 1978.

──────── , "The Problem of Faith Development in Young Adults." The Alban Institute, n.d.

Harris, Mark, "Tending the Fire." n.d.

Kolb, William L., "New Wine: An Interpretation of *The Church, The University and Social Policy*, A Report of the Commission on the Danforth Study of Campus Ministries." Danforth Foundation, 1969.

Lamar, Fred, "The Role of the College Chaplain at the Church-Related College: A Personal Statement." General Board of Higher Education and Ministry, The United Methodist Church, 1983.

National Institute of Education, "Involvement in Learning: Realizing the Potential of American Higher Education." Study Group on the Conditions of Excellence in American Higher Education, U.S. Department of Education, 1984.

Pelligrino, Edmund D., "The Teaching of Values and the Successor Generation." Policy Papers, The Atlantic Council's Working Group on the Successor Generation, The Atlantic Council of the United States, 1983.

Riddell, Glenn, "Religious Emphases at Eureka College," n.d.

Schroeder, Phil, "The Mission of the Church in Higher Education: A Paper of the Center for the Study of Campus Ministry." CSCM Yearbook, 1976.
_____ , and Witt, Elmer, "Theologizing on Academic Turfs: A Paper of the Center for the Study of Campus Ministry." CSCM Yearbook, 1978.
Shockley, Donald G., "Ten Theological Theses for Campus Ministry." Division of Higher Education, General Board of Higher Education and Ministry, The United Methodist Church, 1985.
The United Church of Canada, "Campus Ministry: Information for Chaplains and Campus Ministry Committees." Division of Ministry Personnel and Education, The United Church of Canada, 1985.
United Ministries in Education, "Report of the Policy and Planning Committee on the Question of Restructure to the Policy Board of UME." United Ministries in Education, 1983.
United States Office of Education, "Higher Education in American Democracy: Report of the President's Commission on Higher Education," Volume VI. U.S. Government Printing Office, 1957.

PERIODICALS

Chapman Bulletin. Orange, CA.
The Disciples Divinity House Bulletin. Chicago, IL.
*Footnotes**, 1979-1986. St. Louis, MO.
Seattle Times. Seattle, WA.
The Student Work Bulletin, 1937-1951. Indianapolis, IN.

DIRECTORIES AND YEARBOOKS

Directory of the Division of Higher Education, Christian Church (Disciples of Christ). 1978-86.
Year Book and Directory of the Christian Church (Disciples of Christ), 1916-1986.

ARTICLES

Campbell, Alexander, "Bacon College," *Millennial Harbinger*, August 1937.
Campbell, Minnie M., "The State Universities as well as our Colleges Need the Bible," *Missionary Tidings*, April 1894.
Colyer, C. P., "The Possibilities of Bible Work," *Missionary Tidings*, July 1901.
Conn, Robert H., "Campus Ministry: A Mandate for Wholeness," *Occasional Papers*, No. 51, October 10, 1983.
Heiges, Donald R., "The Church's Ministry on Campus," *The Student Work Bulletin*, September 1958.
"History of the Bible Chair Movement," *Missionary Tidings*, January 1894.
"Indiana School of Religion Celebrates 25th Anniversary," *Christian Evangelist*, October 21, 1935.
"The Inter-Varsity Christian Fellowship," *The Student Work Bulletin*, March 1952.
Jewett, F. L. "Religious Activities in State Universities," *Missionary Tidings*, November 1910.
_____ , "The Texas Bible Chair Report for 1910-11," *Missionary Tidings*, November 1911.
McCaw, John E., "The Student's Claim on the Church," *World Call*, May 1946.
"Report of the Permanent Committee Appointed to Make Arrangements for the Endowment of an English Bible Chair at Ann Arbor, Michigan," *Missionary Tidings*, December 1892.

Rossman, Parker, "Joint Commission on Campus Christian Life Pilot Projects for 5 Years Experiments," *The Student Work Bulletin*, February 1959.

Rowe, Jonathan, "How SATs Are Reshaping U.S. Schools," The *Christian Science Monitor*, December 6, 1985.

Shockley, Donald G., "Campus Ministry: A Contrarian Investment," *Christian Century*, October, 1985.

Todd, Joseph C., "Indiana Preachers," *Christian Evangelist*, September 14, 1911.

Young, C. A., "Bible Teaching at the University of Virginia," *Christian Evangelist*, December 14, 1899.

_____ , "The Work of the Bible Chairs," *Missionary Tidings*, December 1895.

BOOKS

Austin, C. Grey, *A Century of Religion at the University of Michigan*. University of Michigan Press, 1957.

Baldridge, J. Victor; Roberts, J. W.; and Weiner, T. A., *The Campus and the Microcomputer Revolution*. Macmillan, 1984.

Bolin, Gene, *Christian Witness on Campus*. Broadman Press, 1968.

Brubacher, John S., *On the Philosophy of Higher Education*. Jossey-Bass, 1982.

Catelon, John E., *A Protestant Approach to the Campus Ministry*. Westminster Press, 1964.

Chickering, Arthur W., *Education and Identity*. Jossey-Bass, 1969.

Cox, Harvey, *The Secular City*. Macmillan, 1965.

Earnshaw, George L., ed., *The Campus Ministry*. Judson Press, 1964.

Eurich, Alvin C., *Campus 1980*. Delacorte Press, 1968.

Forrest, W. M., *Sowing the Seed of the Kingdom*, Christian Woman's Board of Missions, 1900.

Fosdick, Harry Emerson, *The Living of These Days*. Harper and Brothers, 1956.

Galpin, C. J., and Edwards, R. H., eds. *Church Work in State Universities*. 1910.

Gamson, Zelda F., and Associates, *Liberating Education*. Jossey-Bass, 1984.

Garrison, W. E., and DeGroot, A. T., *The Disciples of Christ: A History*. The Bethany Press, 1958.

Gribbon, Robert T., *Students, Churches, and Higher Education: Congregational Ministry in a Learning Society*. Judson Press, 1981.

Hallmann, William E., ed., *The Challenge of the Community College to the Church*. United Ministries in Education, 1980.

_____ , ed., *So There's A Community College in Your Town*, Revised Edition. United Ministries in Higher Education, 1976.

Healey, Robert M., *Jefferson on Religious in Public Education*. Yale University Press, 1962.

Henry, David D., *Challenges Past, Challenges Present*. Jossey-Bass, 1975.

Horn, Henry E., *Lutherans in Campus Ministry*. National Lutheran Campus Ministry, 1969.

Larson, Bob, *Larson's Book of Cults*. Tyndale House Publishers, Inc., 1982.

Levine, Arthur, *When Dreams and Heroes Died*. Jossey-Bass, 1980.

Meyers, Eleanor, ed., *Getting Educated about Education*. Education for Change Project, U.S. Committee, WSCF, 1980.

Neinast, Helen R., and Turecky, Betsy Alden, eds., *Church and Campus Calling*. United Ministries in Education, 1985.

The New Jerusalem Bible, Doubleday and Co., Inc., 1966.

Parsonage, Robert Rue, ed., *Church-Related Higher Education*. Judson Press, 1978.
_____ , ed., *Invitation to Dialogue: The Theology of College Chaplaincy and Campus Ministry*. Education in the Society Unit, National Council of Churches of Christ, 1986.

Quebedeaux, Richard, *I Found It!: The Story of Bill Bright and Campus Crusade*. Harper and Row, 1979.

Rankin, Robert, ed., *The Recovery of Spirit in Higher Education*. Seabury Press, 1980.

The Report of the President's Commission on Campus Unrest. Arno Press, 1970.

Riesman, David, *On Higher Education*. Jossey-Bass, 1980.

Sandin, Robert T., *The Search for Excellence*. Mercer University Press, 1982.

Shedd, Clarence P., *The Church Follows Its Students*. Yale University Press, 1938.
_____ , *Two Centuries of Student Christian Movement*. Association Press, 1934.

Simmons, J. I., and Winogard, Barry, *It's Happening*. Marc-Laird Publications, 1966.

Smith, H. Sheton; Handy, Robert T.; and Leotscher, Lefferts A., *American Christianity: An Historical Interpretation with Representative Documents*, 2 Volumes. Charles Scribner's Sons, 1960.

Smith, Seymour A., *Religious Cooperation in State Universities*. University of Michigan Press, 1957.

Sparks, Jack, *The Mindbenders: A Look at Current Cults*. Thomas Nelson, Inc., 1977.

Statello, Daniel E., and Shinto, William M., *Nuts And Bolts, Planning for Ministry in Higher Education*. United Ministries in Higher Education, n.d.

Stephens, Michael D., and Roderick, Gordon W., eds., *Universities For A Changing World*. John Wiley and Sons, 1975.

Underwood, Kenneth, *The Church, The University, and Social Policy: The Danforth Study of Campus Ministries*, 2 Volumes. Wesleyan University Press, 1969.

Viser, Festus J., ed., *The University in Transition*. Memphis State University Press, 1971.

Westerhoff, John H., ed., *The Church's Ministry in Higher Education*. United Ministries in Higher Education, 1978.

INDEX

180

DATE DUE